THE BOURGEOIS CENTURY

The Evolution of Western Society

GENERAL EDITOR
PETER BROOKS, Ph.D.
Lecturer in History, University of Kent at Canterbury

OTHER PUBLISHED TITLES IN THIS SERIES

THE BOURGEOIS CENTURY

A History of Europe 1780—1870

K. R. PERRY

MACMILLAN

© K. R. Perry 1972

First published 1972
Published by
MACMILLAN EDUCATION LIMITED
Basingstoke and London
Companies and representatives
throughout the world.

SBN 333 05390 7

To My Parents and to those Gentlemen of MHEc., to whom I
promised this dedication a long time ago.

Printed in Great Britain by
ROBERT MACLEHOSE AND CO LTD
The University Press, Glasgow

Contents

PART TWO:
THE REVOLT OF THE INDIVIDUAL

PART THREE:
UNEASY EQUILIBRIUM 1815—48

17 DIPLOMACY 1830–48   198

18 REVOLUTIONARY MOVEMENTS   207

PART FOUR:
THE DISINTEGRATION OF VIENNESE EUROPE

19 THE 1848 REVOLUTIONS   215

20 ECONOMIC AND SOCIAL DEVELOPMENT
    1848–70   240

21 NEW DEPARTURES IN GOVERNMENT   256

22 DIPLOMATIC REVOLUTION:
    CRIMEAN WAR AND ITALIAN UNIFICATION   269

23 EMPIRES RISE AND FALL 1860–70   284
    France: Liberal Empire   284
    Austria: Decline and Defeat   291
    Prussia: Prelude to Empire   292
    Victories and Defeats   300
    Russia: Reform in isolation   302
    Defeat of France   305

    APPENDIX A
    The Historiography of the French Revolution   321

    APPENDIX B
    The Revolutionary Calendar   323

    BRIEF LIVES   324

    BIBLIOGRAPHY   344

    INDEX   350

List of Plates

List of Maps

General Editor's Introduction

For some time students have found difficulty in getting to grips with more advanced historical study because many textbooks have proved daunting in size and style. Faced with so much factual content and detailed narrative readers have often been denied the balanced yet scholarly judgements that both enliven the past and communicate its signifcance.

In an attempt to combat this trend, *The Evolution of Western Society* consists of a series of volumes specifically designed for those seeking an introduction to relatively advanced work. Written in readable prose, while avoiding gimmicks, these lively studies present a more topical approach to history by expounding a given period in terms of main-point analysis. In a dozen volumes, a team of university lecturers and schoolmasters, who are both authorities in their specialist fields and experienced teachers, will give their readers a wide coverage of British and European history from the decline of the Roman Empire to the conflicts of the contemporary world. Each book contains adequate narrative for those obliged to satisfy the demands of public examinations, but every effort has been made to focus interest upon analysis rather than description, and to convey the spirit of each period by means of selected source quotation and visual material. Full bibliographies are included to guide further reading, and, in addition to charts, diagrams and maps, all volumes contain a section devoted to brief lives of important figures. Whether artists or churchman, statesmen, or military leaders, scientists or philosophers. Above all, each book is an exercise in three-dimensional history, and presents the reader with the findings of modern scholarship in a comprehensive comprehensible and stimulating form.

Peter Brooks, 1972

Acknowledgements

It is impossible adequately to cover a period of this importance in so few pages and I therefore apologise to those readers who find this book inadequate on any particular topic. The virtues of the book, if virtues there are, are due entirely to the help and patient encouragement of many people. Above all I wish to acknowledge the superhuman patience of Dr. P.N. Brooks who has had to sift through my illiterate drafts more times than I imagine he would wish to remember. His good advice has been of inestimable benefit to me.

I wish also to record my thanks to my admirable typist Mrs A. H. Mead, to Mr J. S. Jones for his help in reading the typescript and in undertaking some of the more tedious labours, and to various past and present Paulines for their comments, help and encouragement.

Austrian National Library, 1a; Bibliothèque Nationale, 2a, 3, 4b, 5a; Ivor Guest, 6c; Musée Carnavalet, 2b; Musée Conde, 4a; Musée du Louvre, 6b; Punch 5b; Radio Times Hulton Picture Library, 1b, 7a, 8a, 8b; Rheinisches Bildarchiv, Cologne, 7b; Städelsches Kunstinstitut, Frankfurt, 6a.

Part One :
The Old Regime

CHAPTER ONE

Europe in 1780

No century has seen greater changes than that which succeeded the last years of the *Ancien Régime*. Europe passed through three revolutions, those of 1789, 1830 and 1848, two at least of which were to be of lasting and widespread importance. Of more profound importance perhaps, were the slower but more extensive, economic and social changes which led to the political revolutions. The spread of industrialisation, particularly in the Western countries, and improved techniques in agriculture were forces which slowly made the old social systems, based on landed influence and the vestiges of feudal society, anachronistic, administratively insufficient and increasingly weak. All countries during the ninety years after 1780, had in some way to adjust to the rise of the new industrial, commercial or professional middle class. It is the rise and decline of this class which is probably the most significant factor in European history between 1780 and 1870.

Such generalisations are, of course, fraught with danger. The social, economic and political conditions varied widely from country to country in 1870 as they had in 1780. In Germany the middle class, though economically powerful, seemed prepared to submit to the political preponderance of the Junker class which German unity had perpetuated. It is a commonplace that in Russia the middle class remained economically, socially and therefore politically weak, as the failure of the February revolution of 1917 only too eloquently demonstrated. Despite these exceptions, the middle class throughout Europe was making its presence felt and the victories of the class in one country encouraged the struggle of the embryo class elsewhere. British society in this period was transformed; so was that of Germany, Belgium, France, even Italy. But the social structure of Russia, Poland, East Prussia, the Austrian territories, particularly Hungary, and other Eastern territories would with modifications have been recognised by a time traveller in 1780.

Europe in 1780 was still the Europe of the great dynasties: the Hapsburgs, Bourbons and Hohenzollerns are apparently safe on their thrones. Under them is a society, aristocratic, semi-feudal, hierarchic and, on the surface, static. The peasants though poor, probably poorer than they had been in 1680 in many places, were too busy as well as too conservative to be troublesome, while the middle class seemed derisively small in most places, or too engrossed in the unaristocratic pursuit of making money to demand the share in power which its corporate intelligence and economic power warranted.

The dynastic power, externally confident, continued to plot its territorial gains at the expense of weaker neighbours and continued to try to govern millions of people by personal rule tempered only by inefficiency and the obstruction of sectional interests. Europe seemed socially and politically secure. Nationalism was not as yet a force to be reckoned with and it was still possible to rule a polyglot Empire, like that of the Hapsburgs, in the name of a dynasty. The Hungarian 'nationalism' which faced Joseph II's reforms was the struggle of a dominant class to preserve its privileges rather than any more modern concept. The Bohemian nobility only discovered the Czech language when their privileges came under scrutiny.

The very idea of a nation was as yet merely embryonic, although it partly grew from the work of the despots. Frederick the Great's Prussia absorbed the Slavs of Poland because Polish land would be of immense economic value to the kingdom of which he was 'first servant'. Joseph II was willing to trade Belgians for Bavarians without thought for the population. Geographical and economic necessity, with armed might, still dictated the boundaries of Europe.

Europe was itself only the vaguest of ideas to most of its inhabitants. What was Europe, what was Hungary, Poland, Prussia or any other country to the peasant who had to scratch a living, or to the serf whose horizon was set by the distance he was allowed to travel without permission? Even his master's horizons were in general local. Only the rich could travel, and most nobles were relatively poor, scorning the city, loathing the towns and able to concentrate only on their own rights and jurisdictions. At most, for the majority, the greatest area they cared about was that governed by the local Estate, if the monarch had allowed them to keep one.

Yet beneath the surface Europe was undergoing change; monarchs forced their subjects to look beyond immediate surroundings, writers spread the Enlightenment, merchants opened up new trade routes. Parts of Europe would remain for years, despite the work of 'absolute' monarchs, locked in their backswood fastnesses while others were already becoming recognisably 'modern'.

Europe then was not a unity with a single mind, and outlook. It was as diverse as the terrain which it covered and which moulded its people. The poor soils of Sicily, Andalusia, East Prussia, Holland, Northern Russia and parts of Poland imposed their own character on the people just as the good soils of England and France, the Netherlands and Scandinavia conditioned their people. Trade routes, rivers, seas and, where available, roads equally determined the outlook of a people living by them, or impossible distances from them.

The year 1780 was threshold of a whole new social, economic and political world, but it was also as deeply embedded in a world as local and diverse as the medieval age it so frequently resembled.

Nobility

In 1780, before the industrial revolution had made its mark on European life, landed wealth was still, despite the growth of commerce and even industry in England, France and elsewhere, the most important form of wealth, carrying with it fiscal and political privileges and a virtual monopoly of high office in army and state. The nobility paid no taxes or less than their countrymen, often possessed representative assemblies, and filled all important posts at the centre of power and in local government as well as holding nearly all commissioned posts in the army.

This power and privilege was not everywhere supreme or deserved, nor was it everywhere unchallenged. The 'revolutionary' Hapsburg Emperor Joseph II made a considerable assault on the privileges of the aristocracy in all his lands but was forced at the end of the reign to beat a hasty retreat which left the aristocracy almost as strong as before.

Prussia, and to a lesser extent Russia, had been more successful in moulding a nobility of actual benefit to the state. In Prussia the Junker class had been transformed during the eighteenth century into a service nobility. Although it had lost local political privileges, it had nevertheless been invested with all important administrative functions. Above all, its position as a privileged class, supported and upheld by the Hohenzollern monarchy, had been consolidated.

Whereas in Russia compulsory service had been abolished in 1762, those nobles who chose to enter the service of the Crown at court, in the bureaucracy or army were given extra privileges.

Although in neither country was the nobility servile it could prove troublesome and disobedient. Yet on balance in both Russia and Prussia it was at least working for its living and proving a benefit to the state, and this was in marked contrast to the aristocracies of Spain, Portugal and Italy.

There was generally among the European aristocracies a movement aimed at increasing, or protecting, their privileges against the monarchies. This movement reached a peak at the beginning of the period. The Russian aristocracy, whether performing state service or not, increased its powers at the expense of the state and the serfs during the reign of Catherine the Great (1762–1796). By the end of her reign it was fast losing its character as a service nobility. The Hapsburg aristocracies successfully resisted attack while the Prussian Junkers themselves could on occasion resist even Frederick the Great, as when they ignored his decree abolishing serfdom in Pomerania. Even in France where a developing middle class, large, prosperous and well-educated, flaunted its new wealth, the aristocracy in 1780 was in the process of protecting its privileges by reserving positions in administration, army and church solely for itself.

The powers of the nobility throughout Europe, like its privileges and duties varied enormously. The Polish aristocracy, even after the first Partition, might excite the envy of others. Though hardly united, this noble oligarchy possessed, in theory at least, the right of electing its King, and any nobleman could, by wielding the *liberum veto* in the Diet prevent the passage of law displeasing to him. The results of these powers can be seen in the disappearance of Poland as a country in 1795, but the Hungarian aristocracy too had a privileged position in the Hapsburg Empire, possessing considerable independent powers of local self-government in the flourishing Estates, and possessing in the Diet the power of electing the King of Hungary.

It was in the Eastern and Central areas of Europe above all that the aristocracy seemed to exhibit those traits most characteristic of the class. Here, where a middle class hardly existed, where towns were alien, industry and trade rudimentary because of a lack of raw materials or communications, and where serfdom was still in force, the nobility and gentry had complete control of their localities and offered most resistance to change or the arm of the central government. Even in the West such conditions were to be found mostly where economic backwardness prevailed as in the kingdom of the two Sicilies. Even in prosperous England, however, the landowners dominated the counties as Justices of the Peace.

There was throughout Europe a recognisable community of interest embracing all the aristocracies. But it is misleading to refer to the aristocracy as though it was a uniform concept. The English landowner, and to a large extent the French, leased his land on more or less advantageous terms. But in Hungary, Poland, East Germany and Russia the land was worked by serfs whose owners possessed great economic and jurisdictional rights over them. The greatest divide however was wealth. In England historians are used to the difference implied by the terms aristocracy and gentry. In Europe this variation of wealth and social position existed to a much more marked degree.

A noble was not necessarily wealthy. A survey of the Russian nobility in 1777 shows that a third of all serf owners owned less than ten serfs, while a really rich noble like a Sheremetev might own one or two hundred thousand. For the less wealthy there was in Russia the chance of advancement through state service, but, as one of Catherine the Great's ministers once pointed out, some young nobles were prevented from coming to apply for work because they could not afford the necessary clothes and boots. The poorer nobility had only their privileges to mark them out from their serfs and were thus insistent on keeping them. Joseph II's reforms in Hungary were resisted with such passion because it was only by a harsh application of a serf economy that the gentry could survive as a class, but there were also a few immensely rich and powerful families like the Esterhazys. The Polish nobility was divided into the great noble families like the Czartoryskis, and the poor *Szlacta* who often acted as their retainers in inter-noble feuds or in the wars of the Confederations. In Prussia the army and state service were the life blood of many Junker families who were by no means wealthy. The disparity of wealth was not only a feature of the East, though it was mainly a feature of poor agricultural districts; France had her *'hoberaux'*, Spain her poor *'hidalgos'* and England had that submerged gentry which was never elected to parliament, and which lived as an equal with the parson.

In these situations it was usually the poorer nobles who were the most vociferous in demanding the support or extension of their privileges, while their richer neighbours might be able to afford change more easily. Thus in France the richer aristocrats might have the capital to enclose and might prefer a free economy whilst those without capital insisted on the protection granted them by privilege.

The aristocracy was not merely divided by differences of wealth which could and did lead to division of interest, but there were also different types of nobility. In France where there were approximately 250,000 in the *noblesse* less than two per cent were of the genuine and ancient *noblesse d'épée*. Beyond them were the far more extensive ranks of the *noblesse de robe* which included the members of the parlements, holders of hereditary offices, tax farmers, intendants and other officials. Even within the *noblesse d'épée*, the *noblesse de cour*, those wealthy and grand families whose padded presence shielded the King from reality and unpleasant opinion, formed a separate group. Under the threat of royal reform these groups had coalesced but the members of the separate orders of nobility well understood the precedence due to them.

In Russia where, despite the abolition of compulsory service in 1762, the service nobility was officially seen as the most important, there remained a very real gap between the families who had achieved noble status through service and those noble families which had existed before the reforms of Peter the Great. As in France birth and ancestry, not a useful occupation, gave one social pre-eminence. Only the Prussians seem to have secured a situation where birth and service to the state went completely hand in hand. Spain where twenty per cent of the population were of the *noblesse* had, despite Bourbon reforms, a largely functionless aristocracy. In the Austrian lands neither an efficient bureaucracy nor an obedient hard working aristocracy was achieved. Nearly all reforming monarchs suffered from the fact that it proved impossible to run a country effectively, in the absence of a large middle class, without the aristocracy. But the aristocracy was not prepared to be the agent of an absolutist monarchy and either endeavoured to preserve its privilege purely on a basis of birth and not social usefulness or would only serve the Monarch if he in turn secured those very privileges which he needed to destroy. The clash between the needs of a reforming Monarchy and aristocratic privilege is the most important theme of the 1780s.

This class with its legal, fiscal, social and political privileges, however much these might vary from country to country, was the most important element in the society of a Europe which was still rural. Only in the West where the Atlantic seaboard promoted trade and industry was that nobility yet being seriously challenged by any more important economic element.

Church

From time immemorial the younger sons of the nobility had made the church their career; and it is perhaps particularly fitting that the aristocracy at the beginning of the period should have continued to follow the pattern since both corporations were under attack from the monarchs of the time and from 'enlightened' opinion generally. In France, this process reached a peak immediately before the revolution when practically all posts in the top-heavy hierarchy were filled by aristocrats who did not, as the history of Talleyrand shows, have to be either righteous or faithful.

It was the aristocratic nature of the hierarchy, and its insistence on maintaining its privileges rather than on spreading the Gospel, that brought the Roman Catholic Church into such disrepute. The criticism did not come only from outside the church. There were of course church reformers but the most vociferous critics were perhaps the lower clergy, underpaid, overworked and sharing the prejudices as well as the lives of the peasants. The lower clergy gave support to many of Joseph II's church reforms in Austria and to those of Leopold in Tuscany. In France they had been *Jansenists* and *Richéristes* and still looked to an increase in their influence as an approach to reformation. In 1780 Louis XVI had had to forbid the *curés* from demanding greater representation. The lower clergy saw the wealth of the church and they saw also the spiritual decay of the church and its declining influence.

Above all the church seemed to lack drive and purpose. It had no philosophy with which to counteract the enthusiasm of the Enlightenment. Monasteries, which in the Romantic enthusiasm of the nineteenth century were to find defenders, seemed to intelligent men wasteful, often immoral and always useless institutions. The whole drift of eighteenth century thought militated against the life of contemplation. Joseph II had many supporters when he came to close down all monasteries which performed no 'useful' function, not least because the money from their suppression augmented parochial stipends.

In France, despite the fact that a certain number of decayed houses had been swept away, monasteries were little regarded. Too many religious houses served too few monks and took up too much valuable rural and urban land without performing any useful function. When there were too few parish priests and teachers in catholic Europe it seemed unreasonable to leave untapped the spiritual, intellectual and real wealth locked up in over-ornate monastic houses, and in the Empire suppression was indeed followed by a real attempt to increase the number of parish priests and give them adequate education.

The position of the parish priest throughout the Catholic lands was a source of constant criticism. He was rarely an immoral or even lazy person, but often forced by economic circumstances into minor pluralism which mirrored the excesses of his superiors. He was frequently ill-educated, as superstitious as those he served and, despite the tithe, poor. In France tithes had long been alienated to the upkeep of abbeys and cathedral chapters reserved for nobles. The *curé's* annual stipend amounted to no more than one hundred livres. There was no incentive to enter the priesthood, and even after Joseph's reforms in Austria only half the parishes had priests. In few Catholic countries would an intelligent man become a parish priest because the money, prestige, and prospects of advancement were so low. The superstition of the church, so derided by the Enlightenment, tended to be self-perpetuating.

The plight of the monasteries perhaps symbolises that of the church in general at the end of the eighteenth century. It was not particularly immoral but it was unenthusiastic and stagnating.

This is perhaps hardly surprising when 'reason' was the watchword of all 'enlightened' men. Reason meant war on superstition, tradition and privilege, three qualities the church possessed in abundance. Few were the churchmen who had the heart to deny the peasant his prized superstitions. Among the aristocrats and urban middle classes scepticism was smart and widespread. There, the Masonic societies, anti-clerical in origin, enjoyed a vogue. Even where the reformer was sincerely religious he tended to be an anti-clerical and, as in the nature of Roman Catholic doctrine, the priest remained central to the life of the church, church and doctrine suffered attack together.

Nevertheless the Enlightenment did stir the clergy themselves to try to reform their church; the followers of the German bishop Febronius and his book 'Concerning the Condition of the Church and the Legitimate Powers of the Pope' began to look to a future of decentralised reformed churches with only tenuous spiritual links with the Papacy, rejecting dogmatism and healing the breach between Catholic and Protestant. For the rulers of dynastic states the powers of the Papacy, though much reduced remained peculiarly irksome, and besides reforming the churches within their dominions rulers sought to regulate their relations with the Papacy in a manner that would not compromise their own Absolutism. The slights offered to the Papacy in the eighteenth century, and the succession of powerless, weak and not over-zealous Popes had compromised the dignity of the Roman Catholic Church, seriously damaging its prestige and making it unable to resist demands for the abolition of the Jesuit order.

Despite such qualifications the church remained immensely powerful. Its hold on the peasantry was very strong, and there was little division of interest between the peasant and his *curé*. In France the Church was in a semi-autonomous position, regulating its own taxes in its own assemblies. It owned ten per cent of French land and in other countries, particularly Spain, its share of the nation's wealth was even greater. Despite the onslaught of men like Pombal in Portugal, Charles III in Spain and Joseph of Austria and Leopold of Tuscany, it retained considerable powers. In France it controlled education, propaganda, censorship, nearly all charitable works and a considerable part of the Civil Law. The danger for the church was that it did not possess the loyalty of the politically important classes while being associated with those classes in the minds of the under-privileged.

It was not only the Roman Catholic Church however which felt beleaguered by the twin forces of Enlightenment and Scepticism. Catherine the Great continued the harrassment of the church in Russia, secularising its lands, diverting its income to state-run charitable institutions in a way which remarkably resembles Joseph II's attempt to transform the

Church into a department of state. The churches might justifiably feel that the position of the church described in
Rousseau's *Social Contract* was rather too rapidly approaching.

Protestant churches too saw the results of this desire of the
Despots to see the church as a useful adjunct to the Absolutist state by performing charitable works, by inculcating
the habits of morality and, particularly in Prussia and
Austria, by preaching the necessity and good of obedience to
the sovereign.

The whole position of the Church as supreme arbiter of
opinion was likewise under discussion. Its machinery of
censorship and exclusive educational rights were everywhere
in 1780 under close scrutiny. This attack on ecclesiastical
exclusiveness heralded a general onslaught on the entrenched
privileges of the *Ancien Régime* and the increased attention
paid to religious minorities was an augury of individual
freedom which the French Revolution introduced. In the
Sweden of Gustavus III the Lutheran Church lost its exclusive position; in Prussia Frederick the Great welcomed men of
all religions and gave work to Jesuits, for sound economic as
well as Enlightened reasons. Joseph II of Austria would
tolerate men of all christian religions and to a lesser extent
Jews also, while both Catherine and Frederick posed as
defenders of religious minorities in Poland. Such activities
loosened the foundations of religious exclusiveness, whatever
the motives impelling the Despots' actions. In 1788 the last
Assembly of the French clergy before the revolution, while
continuing to require the exclusion of Protestants from
public office could almost zealously accept that they were
fellow Christians.

Peasantry

In a society so predominantly rural the peasants inevitably
constituted the largest class. Yet like all other social groups in
1780 this was by no means an homogeneous unit. It was not
simply the difference between free and servile peasants.
Within these two categories there were degrees of servitude or
freedom. Status depended also on the way a peasant held his
land and on whether his plot was adequate to give his family

at least a subsistence standard of life.

The distinction between free peasant and serf was largely geographical and the Elbe serves as a fairly convenient dividing line separating the predominantly serf populations of the East from the free or semi-free populations of the West. In Great Britain, the Iberian Peninsula, Italy and, except for a few areas, France legal serfdom did not exist, while in South Germany it was relatively mild. However in certain parts of Denmark, Holstein particularly, it flourished. Nor must it be assumed that the peasant of the West was necessarily better off. In the opinion of some historians the Russian peasant might eat more nourishing food than his English, or certainly Scottish, counterpart while it would be foolish to assume that the serf in East Prussia, enjoying some royal protection, was worse off than the Irish peasant or the near savage of the Kingdom of the Two Sicilies.

In Eastern European countries, however, serfdom could be of the most oppressive kind, particularly where the nature of the soil and lack of communications made even the serf owner relatively poor as in large areas of Hungary, East Prussia, Poland and Russia (though in Northern Russia labour services were unknown). What made serfdom more oppressive in the areas east of the Elbe was that it was of comparatively recent date and therefore vigorous.

In Russia, serfdom grew in the seventeenth century and was severely intensified during the eighteenth because in the vastness of the Russian landscape it was easier to pin down the scattered and small population if the landlords could be used as the local administrative units controlling the peasants. By putting the landlord in charge of conscription and the poll tax, Peter the Great had increased the lord's control over his serfs. The serf was detached from the land and attached to a person. During the century, and perhaps most of all in the reign of Catherine the Great, the power of the landlord over his serfs had increased. He could exile his serfs to Siberia, transfer them from one estate to another and even in some cases make free men into serfs. The Tsars themselves extended serfdom by grants of land to favourites and by expanding the boundaries of the State of Poland, Lithuania, the Ukraine and Crimea. In 1780 about one half of the total male population were serfs.

While numbers of serfs increased their position declined, and the will or power of the sovereign to intervene seemed lacking. Serfs were sold at auction despite prohibitions and sometimes at the wall of the Winter Palace itself. The punitive powers of the landlords could make life utterly miserable, and although the death penalty was not wielded by the landlord, if the peasant died undergoing the eighteen cudgel blows allowed as punishment then nothing could be done as he had no legal rights and was even forbidden to petition the Tsar. Naturally not all owners were evil but it is doubtful whether the total of six, punished during Catherine's reign, was more than the tip of a monstrous iceberg.

Not all peasants in Russia were serfs; State peasants formed a population which stood legally midway between freedom and serfdom but they were more likely to see their position worsen than improve. If the land they farmed was given to a court favourite they immediately became serfs while they also ran the risk of being assigned permanently, or for varying periods, to work in mines or factories in the Urals. Here they worked with the serfs of the factories in appalling conditions such as those that led to the Pugachev revolt.

In North-East Germany too, serfdom had developed in the seventeenth century. Here it was a result of the demand for agricultural produce and the post-war labour shortage. Like his Russian counterpart the North German serf had to perform labour services or pay cash in lieu and was unable to move, work or even marry without consent. As in Russia, his landlord had been given an increasing number of judicial administrative and military duties to perform which subjected the serf to even more landlord jurisdiction. At least in Prussia, unlike Poland, Russia and Hungary, some attempt was made to alleviate the lot of the serfs who formed the backbone of Prussia's army. But no king in Frederick the Great's position could afford to alienate his nobility to the extent of forcing them to obey decrees which they found irksome, especially when the royal agents were themselves Junkers.

The Austrian monarchy had by 1780 made several attempts to limit labour services demanded in their Bohemian and Moravian provinces but it was not until their culmination in the great measures of Joseph II that any attempt was made to extend these reforms to Hungary. There the economic situation of the gentry and the peculiar position of Hungary in its relations with the Hapsburg monarchy had made the Emperors wary. The failure of the Hapsburgs to solve the problem of the declining position of the serfs, because of aristocratic disobedience, determined Joseph II to make a final assault on serfdom when he became sole ruler in 1780.

Until the day of release the only relief open to the serf lay in revolt. Catherine the Great's reign had seen as many as fifty revolts in a single year, culminating in Pugachev's rising (1773—5). At the beginning of this period those provinces of Russia on the Baltic shores were experiencing unrest while in the Hapsburg provinces Bohemia had only recently been quietened and in 1784 Transylvania would erupt. A significant point is that nearly all these revolts were triggered off by rumours of an approaching end to serfdom.

But it was in the West that the most important of the peasant revolts came; in France in 1789. What is said about the French peasant could equally apply to his Rhenish counterpart for their social and economic situations were so similar.

In general, and compared to his Eastern brothers, the French peasant was free and relatively well off. The number of serfs was small and they were concentrated in the East. Even there they were not exposed to the arbitrary jurisdiction of a nobleman but had the King's justice. Four-fifths of France's population depended on agriculture for a livelihood and the peasants owned nearly a third of the land, a greater proportion than owned by church (one-tenth), nobility (one-quarter) or bourgeoisie (one-fifth). In England few peasants owned land, most being landless labourers, but even in France the proportion of property owners varied greatly. Ownership did not however imply wealth. Most plots were too small to support a family and so great was the desire of the peasant for land that the practice of dividing inheritances continued at a time when the rural population of France like that of Europe in general was increasing.

A peasant might be a leaseholder as well as a property owner or, more usually, he might be a leaseholder only. He might be completely landless. The most numerous type of leaseholder was the *métayer*, or sharecropper, who, in return for being provided with farm, equipment and livestock would give a proportion, usually a half, of the harvest yield to the landlord.

Free though the peasant might be he was still often subject to certain feudal privileges of the local aristocrat and landlord who possessed hunting rights, judicial privileges, owned tolls, and exacted feudal payments.

The peasant in France was increasingly irritated by these payments especially in the 1780s as he was also threatened by agricultural capitalism and enclosure, feudal reaction and agricultural depression. He was above all land hungry and these tensions were to grow in the 1780s until they burst into violence in the summer of 1789.

Depressed or unfree though the European peasant might have been, he nonetheless still managed to enjoy a vigorous community life centred on the village. Even in Russia there were reports of the *mir* or village community organising the buying of 'serfs' on behalf of the serfs of the village, usually so that the rest could devote more time to their handicrafts business. In France and Germany too, community feeling was strong. Here as elsewhere traditional farming methods lay behind the continuance of a community spirit. The need to allocate the strips in the open field system was as common on both sides of the Elbe as the attendant disadvantages of the system at the time of increasing population. Direct taxation imposed on the community also had to be allocated and perhaps common property and common rights administered.

The vigour of the communal life was partly kept alive by the conservative character of the peasant, a quality which was to be of immense service to the church and the nobility in the upheavals following the French Revolution. Traditional methods of cultivation were the norm in most areas of Europe though there were regional variations even within one country, often according to the crop grown. It was in the Netherlands, England, parts of Scotland and a few areas of

France that new techniques were able to be applied and the change from a subsistence to a market economy with special-isation and enclosure achieved. Much of Europe however was far from this state. Southern Italy and Sicily, much of Southern Spain, Poland and parts of Russia were particularly backward in their methods often as a result of poor soils and poor communications which killed incentive.

In most of Europe where progress was not so great as in England or backwardness so desperate as Sicily, agriculture generally stagnated. The legal position of the serf, the poverty of the peasant, his overriding desire for some land to farm and the rising population on the land militated against experiment by the peasant himself, by the landlord who had easier ways of making money in his feudal privileges, and by the state which feared the social consequences of new tech-niques involving enclosure.

It was a hard life for the peasant. A third of the harvests were failures, starvation was too commonplace to be noticed. As ever, however, it is unwise to generalise. In any country some areas enjoyed worse conditions than others. Brittany was backward because it had poor soil; Normandy was prosperous and could afford enclosures. Similar contrasts are noticeable in Germany, Spain and Russia where, in the North, slash and burn tillage contrasted with the relatively prosperous but still, by English standards, backward wheat-lands of the Crimea or the Ukraine.

The outlook of the peasant varied with his condition. The French peasant owner did not have the same outlook as the *métayer* or landless peasant, nor the serf as the free peasant. The Russian serf who employed serfs under him and who might in a few rare cases be a millionaire did not have the same outlook as the serf who merely worked the land. Local customs, and good or bad communications added their own flavour to those differences which divided the peasant from his brother inside or outside his own country. These differ-ences were as important for the future history of Europe as the bonds which united them; conservatism, religion, attachment to the land and hostility to the landlords.

The Middle Class

The middle class was even less homogeneous than the peasantry and indeed in some areas practically non-existent. The bourgeoisie, that class dependent for its livelihood on commerce, the professions or the income from loans to government (*rentes*), was strongest in the west of Europe, in those areas where the peasant was free, and where a money economy, trade and capital flourished. It was strong numerically in England, France, the Netherlands and in cities of Northern Italy and Western Germany. Elsewhere its economic and numerical importance was minimal. Poland, Russia, Prussia, the Hapsburg territories and Spain and Southern Italy lacked a financially and commercially strong middle class.

In Russia less than two per cent of the urban population engaged in any trade which was more than very local. This was hardly surprising when roads were non-existent and when rivers froze in winter, flooded in spring and dried-up in the summer. Russian towns were tiny and when Catherine the Great had introduced her provincial government reforms in 1775, 250 villages had been raised to the rank of city. In 1780 out of an estimated Russian population of 28,000,000, probably only 180,000 lived in towns. Similar conditions prevailed in Poland and Hungary where aristocratic hostility towards the towns as centres of the governmental efforts at centralisation, was fanned by the fact that the town population was mainly composed of aliens. Here as in Russia the lack of merchant enterprise was compensated for, and perpetuated by rural industries. These were owned by landowners who had the advantages of cheap or free raw materials and the labour dues of their serfs. In Russia too some serfs built up large industrial empires for themselves.

In such Eastern territories where despots held sway, state paternalism hindered the growth of an independent, financially strong, middle class. While both Joseph II and Frederick the Great strove to increase the numbers of industrial units in their territories, being good Mercantilists, both of them distrusted the middle class and showed hostility to capitalist production and techniques. Joseph II, for example, forbade the introduction of spinning machines for reasons of social stability, and Frederick the Great prevented enclosure of peasant lands. So while Joseph encouraged the bourgeoisie by sweeping away guild restrictions and by ennobling certain of its members, and while Frederick worked through entrepreneurs like Spitzberger and Daum, they both discouraged capitalism, the one force which above all would have increased the influence and wealth of the bourgeoisie.

The bourgeoisie was not only a commercial but also an official class. Here too, however, in most territories this class was unimportant. An official class could only grow under the impetus of a growth in the size of the commercial class or through the agency of a Napoleon. In Prussia the chief administrative posts, like senior military posts, went to the Junker class. In Hungary where Joseph attempted reforms, much administrative power was in the hands of local Estates, and in the other Hapsburg territories the local officers of the central government were aristocrats. In Russia the local government reforms of Catherine the Great concentrated even more local power into the hands of the aristocracy and gentry. This was hardly the fault of the monarchies; they had no choice when the bourgeoisie was so small. Only in centres of government, in Vienna, and to a lesser extent in Berlin or St Petersburg could any real bourgeois official class exist.

Great Britain, France and the Netherlands were the only countries where a middle class existed which was at all self-sufficient. In Great Britain and the Netherlands this class had some political influence even if, in Great Britain, society and politics were still dominated by the aristocracy. In France, however, despite increased economic power its influence was waning.

The French bourgeoisie of merchants, rentiers, professional men and even industrialists possessed wealth and intellect but no political power. As the century advanced moreover, it lost those avenues to preferment available through service in administration and the armed services. By 1789 all Intendants, the most important local agents of the Crown, were noble and the *noblesse de robe,* the nobility of the officials was becoming closed. *Fermiers Généraux* — independent tax farmers — had become also a closed caste. At the beginning of the period it also lost the advantages which it had been able to gain by entry into the nobility. In 1781 commissioned entry to the armed services was restricted to those with four generations of nobility.

The French business classes, though powerful, suffered from the loss of the colonies and were constantly humiliated by the pretensions of the aristocracy and the prevalence of vested interests supported by the biased and reactionary *Parlements*. It was no wonder that the bourgeoisie felt that the only way to defeat the exclusiveness of the aristocracy, which the Crown seemed either unable or unwilling to weaken, was to demand representative government.

Even the French bourgeoisie, however united though it was against the common enemy, was as divided within itself as the other classes in that country. While a proportion of the urban middle class might wish to see the ending of the gild system, and the freeing of trade within the country and in relations with other countries, another section saw its salvations in the protection of its privileges by the continuance of the system. The interests of the *Fermiers Généraux,* the wealthy farmers or indirect taxes, were not those of the tax reformers. What united the bourgeoisie was not so much economic interest as a dislike of the aristocracy, and a desire to see their social status recognised. Yet social status meant all things to all men.

Such resentments were not peculiar to France. They are visible in the Reform movements in England and in the Netherlands where such tensions gave the revolutionary and nationalist aspiration of France a useful lever in the 1790's. As yet the rest of Europe was spared such upheavals simply because the middle class was so small, but it would be true to assert that throughout Europe the social and political organisation of the states hindered the free growth of the middle classes.

But if the bourgeoisie was hampered by such difficulties it yet possessed great opportunities. Its wealth could not long be ignored by either the aristocracy, which was already showing itself covertly willing to marry its sons into the great financier families, or by government whose swelling debts made it impolitic to ignore such people's demands. But the

B

bourgeoisie also possessed education, and in an increasingly complex society, in which there was an ever growing need for specialised functionaries, its importance could only be augmented.

In America there was already an example of what could be; in Europe an educated class possessed a literature to feed and political and social philosophies to define its ideas and prejudices. The *Ancien Régime* would ignore the bourgeoisie at its peril.

CHAPTER TWO

Dynastic Rivalries

'The first duty of a ruler is to maintain himself; the second is to expand.' *Frederick the Great*

Between the feudal Empire of the middle ages and the modern nation state there had to be a transition period when the peoples of a geographical, ethnic or political area were organised, moulded and made more aware of themselves as a unit. By 1870 this process had been largely completed in Europe; by 1970 a similar process had been carried out in the under-developed parts of the world. Just as in the Afro-Asian world this has largely been the work of foreign powers, ruling as absolutists, so in Europe the process had to be accomplished by absolute powers — the powers of dynasties, Hohenzollerns, Bourbons, Romanovs and Hapsburgs. Their work therefore, was necessary and, on the whole, progressive. But as the colonial powers were forced to give way to the power of emergent nationalism, and found that absolutism without popular support was not omnipotent so eighteenth century absolutists were to find that their power was not limitless. The powers of the monarchs had developed to answer the needs of new situations: the breakdown of the old solid order because of inflationary economic changes, the collapse of the old imperial power and the rise of new states like Russia. The old decentralised organisation of society and army was incapable of meeting such pressures. The rulers therefore drew into their hands the reins of government, attempting to establish a firm dynastic control over the economy, society, and military organisation, in order to prevent the destruction of the state by more powerful neighbours.

Such centralisation involved an increase in the power of the monarch at the expense of the established classes, chiefly the nobility and the church. Economic, administrative and judicial centralisation would gravely affect the privileges of these classes at a time when it was financially inexpedient for them to face such pressure. Hence the eighteenth century saw a struggle between centralist monarchy, and aristocratic or privileged bodies. This struggle was to continue until the French Revolution gave both monarch and aristocrat a common enemy.

The decade 1780–1790 was crucial in this struggle between absolutism and particularism – a period in which the historian can discern distinct differences in the way the battle was fought throughout Europe. These dissimilarities are largely the result of variations in the organisation of society in Eastern and Western Europe. Thus the weapons in the struggle between Romanov and *dvorianstvo* were unlike those employed by Bourbon and *noblesse* and the outcome too was dissimilar. The lessons to be drawn about the weaknesses of absolutism, however, remain the same.

This decade saw the final flowering of eighteenth century absolutism at its most impressive. Joseph II of Austria, Frederick the Great of Prussia and Catherine the Great of Russia are usually dignified with the sobriquet 'Enlightened Despot'. This term will bear closer examination.

'Enlightened despotism' is one of the great red herrings of eighteenth century history and like most controversial terms was coined outside the century it was supposed to explain. We might join Professor Hartung in preferring the phrase 'Enlightened Absolutism', since despotism has an unfortunate pejorative tone.

No eighteenth century monarch could be an absolutist. Absolute control over the people of a country can only be wielded through the agency of an ideology which can mould the attitudes of a people. The only comparable ideology in the eighteenth century to modern fascism or communism was catholicism, and since most catholic monarchs were in revolt against papal powers, this was not a possible weapon. Catholicism implies obedience to the Pope and no one can have two absolute masters. It was for this reason that absolutists, from Louis XIV to Napoleon, opposed the powers of the Pope. Absolutism also requires huge machinery of administration, a bureaucracy utterly obedient and able to oversee the lives and activities of all citizens. None of the states had, or could have had, at that time, the educational techniques or institutions to supply such a bureaucracy even if there had been a class able to supply enough potential pupils. No country, except perhaps France, had such a class, the middle class, in anything like sufficient numbers to supply a business, professional and bureaucratic élite. Monarchs for their local government had to rely therefore on the traditional rulers of the provinces, the nobility and gentry, the very people whose privileges were most threatened by an absolutist's reforms. All that the monarch could do was to hope to educate or persuade the nobility to be unquestioning servants of the dynasty — an almost impossible task in which only the Hohenzollerns partly succeeded. Add to these difficulties of communication, and it is clear that absolutism was not a possibility.

Impossibility of achievement, however, by no means implies lack of intention, and it is necessary to discover whether in fact the absolutists intended to be 'enlightened'. This is something which can only be decided by a detailed assessment of their reigns, but some generalisations are useful.

The term in question is too often lavished unsparingly on monarchs who are merely 'Benevolent Despots' — rulers who wish to use their great power for the benefit of state and people. Most monarchs in the eighteenth century at least attempted to do this so we are in danger of *embarras de richesse* unless we limit the term and give it definite meaning. We must restrict ourselves therefore to the period of the Enlightenment. The enlightened absolutist must have been familiar with the writings of the men of the enlightenment; Montesquieu, Voltaire, Diderot, Rousseau, Beccaria, D'Alembert and others. Unless the absolutist can be shown to have had contact with the ideas of such people he or she cannot be honoured as an enlightened despot.

Catherine the Great corresponded avidly with Voltaire, the darling of all eighteenth century progressives, and invited

Grimm, a leading Encyclopédiste, to come to Russia, while her 'Instructions' to the Assembly at the beginning of her reign show clearly that she was well versed in Beccaria and Montesquieu. Frederick the Great had entertained Voltaire at Potsdam while Joseph II, admitted to having read Voltaire's works when he refused to visit the sage of Ferney. These three absolutists were, then, conversant with the works of the masters of the enlightenment.

But it is possible that Voltaire was merely Frederick's tame court philosopher and that Diderot fulfilled a similar function at St Petersburg. Even if the two monarchs were genuinely flattered by the attentions of their philosophers and vice versa and even if both were intellectually stimulated by new ideas it is true that no philosopher was ever happy at court. Working knowledge of the ideas of the enlightenment does not mean that the absolutists applied them. World figures rarely like to be accused of being out of touch with modern ideas any more than one likes to admit that one has not suffered from the same interesting diseases as ones friends. The philosophers were the public relations officers of the eighteenth century. As Frederick the Great wrote to his nephew, explaining the attention he had paid to d'Alembert:

> . . . this philosopher is listened to in Paris as an oracle. . .he does nothing but speak of my talents. . . Moreover I like to be praised. . .Voltaire is not of such a character so I drove him away.

An enlightened despot who is enlightened only out of office hours cannot with justice be said to deserve the title. An enlightened absolutist must systematically strive to put into operation the ideas of the Enlightenment. This involves reform of the legal system on more efficient and humanitarian principles, religious toleration, the removal of the privileges of certain classes and the servile status of others, a free economic policy based on physiocratic principles, the removal of censorship and many other similar measures.

These are noble enough principles but unfortunately European monarchs had other pressing problems. They had constantly to face the threat of war, necessitating large armies and great expenditure; they had strong aristocracies on whom they relied for many administrative and military functions; they had undernourished industries in need of care and protection. Behind them lay centuries of decisions, practical and empirical answers to immediate problems. Even absolutist rule involves the art of the possible. They ruled by compromise, gaining or losing ground according to the exigencies of the moment. They did not ignore improvement — Frederick the Great did reform his legal system — but no ruler started with *tabula rasa* on which he could draw what he desired, and it is therefore doubtful whether any monarch of a great territory could rule according to the principles of the enlightenment, except where he knew it would offend no-one who mattered. It was the small territories and those not threatened by outside forces which could experiment in idealism. Baden and Weimar were small states threatened by no-one; Prussia, Russia, Austria and France were countries afraid of each other, having conflicting territorial needs, depending on armies which needed the leadership of those very classes threatened by enlightened ideas. Enlightened absolutism was a luxury which few could afford. Leopold of Tuscany was an enlightened despot, weakening the political and economic power of the church, taxing the nobility, planning a representative assembly. Leopold of Austria continued his brother's capitulation to particularism and reversed many of his brother's enlightened measures. It was the same man but in a different situation. Only perhaps in one sense was there anything different about the enlightened despots in general. They had dropped the idea that their right to rule came direct from God. They preferred to base their right on the fact that their kind of rule was the most efficient possible. Even Frederick the Great who said 'they say what they like and I do what I like' worked on an assumption that he might be called to account for his rule. Catherine too sounded a note of practicality in her 'Instructions'.

The forms of government, therefore, which best attains this end (the Supreme Good) and at the same time sets less bounds than others to natural Liberty, is that which

coincides with the Views and Purposes of rational
Creatures, and answers the End, upon which we ought to
fix a steadfast Eye in the Regulations of Civil Polity.

Practicality was the keynote. It was a sign that government
was growing up, but if absolutism failed it had no sanction on
which to fall back.

It was fear of one's neighbour which most inhibited experiment in government and it was war which seemed the most
characteristic feature of absolutist policy and fulfilled many
of the aspirations of their more powerful subjects.

Men are called 'Great' not because they are virtuous but
because they are victorious. So Catherine of Russia and
Frederick of Prussia are dignified by the title but Joseph of
Austria is not. Contemporaries looked on military success as
the most tangible evidence of greatness. Modern historians,
too, have tended to concentrate a great deal on the military
aspects of the rule of the despots, but with a disapproving
eye. The monarchs are frowned upon for going to war too
easily, for dismembering other states with impunity and
without concern for their inhabitants. The impression is given
of a diplomatic jungle in which might signifies right.

In the last analysis might does usually signify right in
international affairs, but the monarchs rarely ran into warlike
situations happily and usually tried to avoid conflict. In the
absence of international peace-keeping machinery war might
be avoided at the expense of an innocent party; but at least it
was avoided. Of course the rulers of Europe had an advantage
over statesmen of today in their aggressive policies: they
were, on the whole, their own masters. But while in a world
where many states have constitutional regimes and where
public opinion counts, there is an advantage in being an
absolutist, in a world where all rulers have the same advantages there is no benefit. On the contrary such a situation
tends to make rulers more suspicious, but also far more wary
of precipitate action.

Monarchs rarely went to war for frivolous reasons; that is a
prerogative of the twentieth century. They usually went to
war for some territorial or economic advantage to their state.
Thus, in 1740, Frederick the Great had invaded Silesia

because without it his state could have made no economic, and therefore political and international, progress. Since monarchs were not able to separate the interests of their states from their own, such actions were seen as natural and justified. The historian may now view them as unsatisfactory excuses for war, but in the eighteenth century this was not the case. For it should more often be realised that the eighteenth century was not yet much troubled by nationalism and it did not often greatly upset the area involved in a war if it acquired different rulers, provided the social arrangements of the area were not unnecessarily disturbed. The only calculations of importance were whether an acquisition was of advantage to the state which desired it and whether the state had the means of procuring it. Nineteenth and twentieth century standards of international morality hardly apply.

Other forces made wars likely, and in the context of the eighteenth century, justified. The economic doctrine of mercantilism is fiercely protectionist since it is based upon the assumption that the world has limited amounts of specie at its disposal. Thus one state can prosper only at the expense of another and states must not only protect and encourage their own industries, but must seek to acquire economic advantages over others and prevent others from acquiring such advantages over themselves. Not only, therefore, did the absolutists vigorously encourage their own industries, but they sought to acquire ports, the control of rivers and trade outlets, and to increase their populations and industrial and agricultural output by encouraging immigration or by acquiring other territory. This is noticeably the case in the Partition of Poland.

Thus economic considerations were added to strategic and other less tangible considerations to make international rivalry particularly fierce in the years preceding the French revolution. All these considerations must now be examined in some detail, and some attempt made to discover how the absolute monarchs coped with their conflicting aims and interests.

Russia

In 1780 Russia was unquestionably the most powerful state

in Eastern Europe, and, probably, the whole continent. The vast expanse of Russia's territory, from the Baltic to the Black Sea, gave her that power. Russian expansion had always been in two directions; towards the Baltic coast and towards the Turkish Empire and Constantinople. To turn in both directions at once was impossible since this would involve fighting on too many fronts and would attract the jealousy of Austria and Prussia which had no interest in seeing Russian expansion go unchecked in both directions. It would also attract the opposition of France which had long had close relations with the Porte. Russia usually therefore attempted to neutralise one end of the axis while engaged at the other end. In the 1780s Catherine was turning back to Turkey.

Russian expansion into the Turkish Empire had important advantages. Ownership of the Rivers Bug and Dnieper gave Russia control over considerable trade coming from the interior of Poland and Europe to the Black Sea. Expansion beyond the Dniester would increase that control, and fuller expansion, taking in Moldavia and Wallachia, would bring her to the Danube. On the Eastern shores of the Black Sea Russia was expanding into the rich lands of the Caucasus. The treaty of Kuchuk Kainardji (1774) had given Russia a useful lever with which to prise open a way into the declining Ottoman Empire by giving Russia rights of protection over Orthodox Christians there.

Austria

Austria would obviously be seriously affected by any Russian moves as she had interests of her own. Ever since the loss of Silesia, Austria had been trying to find outlets for her products. With the failure to make effective use of the Austrian Netherlands and Prussian Control of the Vistula, Oder and Elbe this problem was to become more serious. Austria was in danger of becoming landlocked and required control of the River Danube. Hence Austria had an interest in seeing the decline of the Turkish Empire but not, of course, at the cost of great Russian expansion towards the Danube. If the Hapsburgs were to expand territorially, as must be the case if Austria was to match Russia and not be overtaken by

Prussia, they had to expand eastwards, unless Joseph could succeed in expanding towards the Bavarian Rhine. Austria was at the point of having to choose whether to be an eastward or westward looking power. Joseph had, therefore, some interest, with Russia, in seeking to hasten the decline of the Ottoman Empire, but none in seeing the further Partition of Poland whose first partition in 1772 she had failed to prevent. Poland could be a useful buffer between Austria and the German lands on the one side and Russian expansionism on the other, and Austria could not want Prussia to control trade routes to the Baltic ports totally. Austria did not wish to be caught in a Russian clamp but did need to expand for economic and strategic reasons. The borders of Hungary were still undefined and earlier in the century (1719) Austria had acquired Belgrade which she had since lost. Dynastic pride was thus also involved.

Prussia

Prussia had by 1780 already achieved much. The scattered provinces had, to a large extent, been welded into a whole and the Hohenzollerns had succeeded in joining East Prussia to the main part of Prussia by the acquisition of West Prussia in 1772 which had given them control of traffic on the river Vistula. But they still did not control the free port of Danzig on the mouth of the Vistula and had no port which was comparably useful or successful. This was therefore a clear wish of the Hohenzollern Kings and their diplomatists.

By great efforts Prussia had become a major power, but of the three Eastern powers she was perhaps the most vulnerable. The main expansionist urge was eastwards into Polish territory, but Russia was pressing on the same area from the opposite direction. By 1780 it perhaps suited them both to leave the buffer between them. But Prussia, unlike Russia, and to a much less extent Austria, did not also have major interests in the East. Thus Prussia tended to be of use to Russia only intermittently and was in danger of being treated carelessly. This was dangerous when Austro-Prussian relations remained, for historical reasons, unfriendly. Prussian chances of expansion depended on Russian goodwill even more than Austrian chances.

The three powers all had expansionist needs but these were by no means easily compatible. Prussia would fear Russian successes in the Near East which the Austro-Russian entente might bring. Austria would also be alarmed by many Russian successes here, but would ally with Russia to share in the spoils. Austria would oppose Russo-Prussian expansionism in Northern Europe at the expense of Poland. For no power, but Russia, involved in such calculation was there security. No power could afford to sit still, but only Russia was in a position to move. Russia thus largely dictated events in this area.

France and Spain

To the south and west lay France and Spain, the former being in all men's estimations the major European power. Her financial and human resources gave her immense strength which in 1780 was being employed against Britain, her 'national enemy'. France's main interests lay in colonial expansion overseas, in checking Austrian expansion towards the Rhine and Austro-Russian success in the Near East. In 1780 France was paradoxically allied with Austria as a result of the disastrous Seven Years' War; Marie Antoinette was Joseph II's sister. Such an alliance was false since both distrusted each other's motives on the Rhine. It was not to French advantage to see the dismemberment of Poland which had been a useful ally in Northern Europe, curbing the expansionist efforts of the Northern powers. For the moment, however, France was absorbed in her perennial war with Britain; this time in helping the American colonists to drive the British from North America and hoping to recoup some of the economic losses resulting from the Seven Years' War. The naval and commercial rivalry of England and France was to be a permanent feature of the international scene until 1815 and its ghost, though not its substance, was to linger even longer. Spain, attached to France by the Family Compact, had her own reasons for distrusting Britain and, like France, had colonial interests which produced constant causes of dissension. Gibraltar and Minorca in Europe and the West Indies in America would be useful jewels in the Spanish Crown from a strategic and economic point of view. Spain joined France in the War of American Independence, and in 1783 emerged with Minorca and East Florida, but without Gibraltar, which was to remain a potent reason for war with Britain for a very long time.

In the early nineteenth century the great British foreign minister Castlereagh declared that he wished to operate a new order in European diplomacy — openness, honesty, sincere desire to reach just settlements were to be a sharp contrast to the apparent perfidy, deceit and naked aggression that seemed to characterise the diplomacy of the absolutists. This is unfair, for rarely can any group of rulers have been faced by more difficult problems than the spreading influence of the French revolution and the sharp rivalries engendered by the weakness of the Ottoman Empire and the suicidal rivalries within Poland. The years between the accession of Joseph II to sole rule and the completion of the Third Partition of Poland are the last years in which traditional rivalries were settled by absolutist diplomacy and deserve close attention.

Turkey, Poland and international rivalries 1780–95
The Polish and Turkish questions cannot easily be separated. Russia was concerned with both, and Russian expansion could not be allowed to go unchecked by the rest of Europe, and in particular by her Austrian and Prussian neighbours. Thus Prussia might put pressure on Russia in Northern Europe if it appeared that Russia was making too many gains in the south. To the north lay Poland, a nation which has for at least two centuries been the territory which has had to suffer from the expansion of her Russian and Prussian neighbours. Already in 1772 she had served as a convenient victim to sacrifice on the altar of Russo-Prussian friendship. Part of her territory had been partitioned between Russia, Prussia and Austria as a convenient way of preventing a war resulting from Russian successes in Turkey. It was obvious that in a similar crisis such decision could be taken again and as we have seen the powers were in 1780 by no means territorially satisfied.

Poland was hardly in a position to resist powerful

neighbours unless she could persuade one of them to help her. In 1772 she had lost one third of her territory and half her population without succeeding in reforming those faults in ·her constitution which made her so very vulnerable. Not only was Poland agriculturally and industrially backward, but she also had strong territorial magnates who, with their gentry retainers, very often acted independently of the weak Crown. Their chief weapon was the *liberum veto* which enabled any member of the Polish Diet (Seym) to veto a measure to which he, or his protector, took exception. Since Peter the Great's time Russia had guaranteed the continuance of this weak system to ensure that Poland remained a willing client state. Rousseau, hardly an advocate of strong government, put his finger on the uniqueness of the Polish situation:

> In Poland the progressive weakening of legislation has proceeded in a unique way; it has, in effect, lost all its vitality without ever having been subjected by the executive power.

Although, as the Confederation of Bar had shown, there was a reforming, or anti-Russian, section to the nobility, divisions in this class always enabled appeals to be made to outside powers. Religious as well as political divisions added to the confusion and weakness, which were accentuated by the economic disadvantages of Prussian control of Vistula trade, and the imposed trade treaty of 1775.

By 1780 the alliance between Catherine and Frederick was cooling. Frederick, unlike Joseph of Austria, could be of no use in an expansionist war against Turkey. Joseph was very ambitious and besides the territorial and economic advantages he could see in a war against Turkey there was a distinct advantage to Austria in breaking the alliance of Prussia and Russia which had played so large a part in Austria's decline and which had forced her to rely on the detested alliance with France.

As early as 1780 Catherine received Joseph in state, though it is doubtful whether he was told of the romantic hopes she harboured of creating a new Empire although

Britain's Ambassador, Sir James Harris, knew about it in 1779.

> Prince Potemkin himself pays little regard to the politics on the West of Russia; his mind is continually occupied with the idea of raising an Empire in the East; he has so far infected the Empress with these sentiments that she has been chimerical enough to christen the new-born Grand-Duke, Constantine.

When in 1782 Austria heard officially of the plan Joseph saw advantages and disadvantages. There were advantages certainly in acquiring the Dalmatian coast and Serbia but a Russian-ruled Kingdom in Moldavia and Wallachia and a new Russian Empire at Constantinople were rather more than he could willingly grant. Besides he was well aware of the failings of his armies.

Thus nothing was done, though negotiations fitfully continued. Russia meanwhile annexed the 'independent' Crimea and extended her influence in Georgia. Such manoeuvres were feared not only by Turkey but also by Prussia which began first under Frederick the Great and then under Frederick-William II, to cast an apparent fatherly eye of approval on the reforming forces in Poland, so as to put pressure on Russia in the event of Russian successes in a war.

Joseph of Austria, too, was alarmed by the preparations Russia was obviously making for war, particularly in building battleships at Sebastopol. Forced to choose between staying out of war and possibly seeing Russia make huge gains, and entering the war when his army was ill-prepared and his internal reforms at a critical stage, he made the latter choice, when Turkey, fearing invasion, declared war on Russia in 1787.

Austro-Russian successes hardly lived up to expectations. Russia lost her fleet, and though she took the strategic fort of Oczakov on the Dniester in June 1788 and reached beyond the Dniester to the Danube, progress was slower than expected, and Austrian participation hardly brought the added strength needed since Joseph could not find the number of troops he had promised. Nor was that all, since

Sweden invaded Russia in 1788 (making peace finally in 1790).

More pressure in the north came from Prussia and Poland. Prussia, afraid of the effects of the Austro-Russian alliance and always vulnerable to attack on two fronts, moved towards friendship with Poland, offering her King, Stanislas Poniatowski, an alliance in 1787, and encouraging the Poles to throw off Russian tutelage and reform their administration when the Diet met in October 1788. Stanislas was too wary of Catherine to accept the first offer, but the Poles were nevertheless grateful for Prussia's support. Unfortunately however, Prussian support was in the nature of a temporary panic measure and should Russia turn her attention northwards again Prussia would quickly break her links with Poland and agree to any advantageous Russian proposals, to compensate Prussia for Russian gains in the Near East.

Poland herself was eager to take advantage of Russian preoccupations. A group of Polish nobility, predominantly from the lesser *szlacta,* who had been inadvertently encouraged by the constitution imposed by Russia in 1775, took advantage of the Diet of 1788 to initiate reforms aimed at making Poland stronger, more centralised and more self-sufficient. Sadly, many nobles, particularly the great nobles and their client gentry, were opposed to such measures and though they, for the moment, chose to be quiet, they were maturing their plans with secret help and money from Catherine.

The Four Year Diet which began in 1788 initiated many reforms, culminating in the Constitution of 1791. They abolished the *liberum veto,* set up a hereditary monarchy which on Stanislas's death was to devolve on the Saxon line, created a bicameral legislature, a cabinet and attempted to end the distinctions which bedevilled most countries' attempts at economic progress east of the Elbe. There was, however, no attempt to diminish the privileges of the nobility: in fact the new constitution guaranteed them.

Sadly the new reforms were already pointless and doomed. Prussia had never intended Poland to be so strong, since she had hoped to acquire Danzig and Thorn. Thus Frederick-William was horrified by the Diet's resolve to create an army of one hundred thousand. When Prussia allied with Poland in 1790 it was not to create a permanently strong nation but to put pressure on Russia and Austria and to extract rewards from Poland in return for Prussian aid in recovering Galicia from Austria. Although Prussia had gone so far as to ally with Turkey in 1790 both of these alliances were merely expedients.

The ground was cut from under Poland's feet in 1790. Joseph II of Austria had died with his country in revolt from Budapest to Brussels and without having made anything like the territorial gains he had hoped for. His successor, Leopold, in an attempt to calm his country and avoid bankruptcy was anxious to extricate Austria from the war with Turkey. Prussia was only too willing to help separate Russia and Austria, and at Reichenbach the Hohenzollerns and Habsburgs were reconciled for the first time in fifty years, and Austria escaped from the disastrous war. Thus a major reason for support of Poland was gone and the ensuing constitution of 1791 mortally offended Frederick-William.

Also in 1791 came another blow to Poland's aspirations; the Anglo-Prussian Alliance collapsed. Pitt the Younger opposed Russian ownership of the fort of Oczakov because it gave her control of the trade carried on that river from Poland. That trade was important for Britain since it included timber and naval stores. Unfortunately the British parliament thought that Oczakov was too far away to fight over, and refused to endorse Pitt's ultimatum to Russia. Thus Prussia saw the collapse of a major ally against Russian expansion, and was well aware that, when Russia had finished her war with Turkey, she would turn to Poland for revenge. Frederick-William thought it wise to begin to conciliate Russia, in the realisation that only through Russia could he now get Danzig and Thorn, since Poland would be unprepared to give it to him and he could not take it without the risk of war with Russia.

One last factor propelled the powers towards a peaceful solution: the increasing violence of the French revolution and the chauvinism of its demagogic pronouncements. The absolutists were not yet attuned to discerning the difference between the essentially conservative nature of the Polish

constitution based on the three Estates and the more revolutionary national, liberal constitution of France. They were a
little alarmed.

In July 1791, Austria and Prussia guaranteed the new
constitution of Poland. This might seem a strange step in
view of what had gone before, but until 1792 Russia was still
at war and Prussia needed the support of Austria, which, as
we have already seen, wished to preserve a Polish buffer state
against Russian expansion.

The flexibility of Frederick-William's principles was amply
demonstrated in 1792 when Russia finally made peace with
Turkey in a treaty extending her frontier to the Dnieper and
giving her Oczakov. By this time Austria and Prussia were at
war with France much to Russia's pleasure. The convention
of Targowitz, April/May 1792, between Catherine and the
reactionary forces in Poland, convinced Prussia of the need to
abandon Poland finally, protesting that Prussia had agreed
merely to guarantee 'a' Polish constitution rather than the
existing one. Frederick-William signed a secret Partition
Treaty with Russia, unknown to Austria. Prussian troops
moved quickly into Thorn and Posen. In September 1793 the
Polish Diet, surrounded by troops, ceded these areas to
Prussia, and Lithuania and Ruthenia to Russia. Catherine was
quite well aware that Prussia must be compensated for
Russia's own rather poor gains in Turkey since she could
never be happy with a permanently resentful Prussia to her
west. Thus again Poland was used to keep the peace between
the Eastern powers while satisfying as far as possible their
individual economic and territorial requirements.

Austria alone had allowed herself to be caught out in the
Second Partition. Militarily the weakest of the three powers,
and threatened most by the revolutionary armies, she had
failed to guarantee her interest in preserving a strong Poland.
After the second partition Poland was too weak to serve
Austria's purpose and Leopold's successor Francis I was
determined not to be caught out again. When, in despair at
the fate of Poland, a rebellion led by the patriot Kosciuszko
broke out in 1793 the three Eastern powers each invaded
Poland, even, in Austria and Prussia's case, at the expense of
the war with France. In 1795 Poland ceased to exist. Russia

had increased her population by nearly six million people, and Prussia and Austria each by something under half of that figure. Prussia and Russia now faced each other directly. There was no longer any Poland to be sacrificed to prevent war. The rivalry of Slav and German peoples would have to be solved in some other way in the future.

The cynicism of the powers involved may seem shocking, but principles have rarely guided foreign affairs with success. Prussia above all, faced with a jealous Austria and a pressing Russia, had to follow a foreign policy of self-protective machiavellianism to survive. Monarchs sought, where possible, peaceful solutions to situations which threatened war and on the whole recognised that great powers had to be compensated and sources of friction avoided. Great powers had the right to be considered even if the smaller powers did not. The Eastern question between 1780 and 1795 is perhaps most interesting as the last example of diplomacy before liberalism and nationalism complicated the affairs of Europe. Already in the west the new world was causing the Eastern powers to look over their shoulders, but the Partitions of Poland are essentially examples of dynastic diplomacy at work. It could hardly be said that it was any more cynical than the new methods being forged in France.

CHAPTER THREE

The Absolutists
of Eastern Europe

Good God, even their souls are to be put in uniform
Mirabeau

In 1780 Frederick the Great had only six weary years to reign. Undoubtedly one of the great monarchs of the eighteenth century he is also perhaps entitled to honour as an 'Enlightened Absolutist'. Most recent biographies have attempted to see through Voltaire's spite and Mirabeau's scorn to the real monarch. He was a cultured man; he had entertained Voltaire at court and he and Catherine the Great flattered each other on their progressive views. He used French as his natural tongue and wrote well in the language. He played the flute idiosyncratically but not, apparently, badly and wrote rather bad music. Certainly he was in revolt against the cold and boorish temper of his father, but perhaps more significant than Frederick's taste for things French was the more martial aspect of his daily life. His personal frugality and his habit of wearing military uniform all day, spoke more of the spirit of his hard and moderately poor Junkers than of the perfumed luxury of a French court which could afford excesses. Throughout his life Frederick honoured both the Great Elector and his own father at whose hands he had suffered so much, but whose thrift, hard work, and military enthusiasms he followed.

Frederick had inherited a country which, despite his father's brave work, was not a unity, was vulnerable to attack, lacked anything but the most rudimentary industry and possessed no commercial links with other territories. In 1741 Prussia wrested from Austria the territory of Silesia which, with its linen industry, provided in 1780 seventy per cent of Prussia's exports. He had acquired, by the first Partition of Poland, the territory of West Prussia, which joined East Prussia to the main part of his dominions and gave him control of the important Vistula trade route. He had acquired the Baltic port of Emden, though this was never an entirely successful alternative to Danzig. His Mercantilist-inspired aid to manufacturers had established a healthy metals industry, using the capital of the state and the expertise of entrepreneurs, and he had given similar aid, less successfully, to silk, porcelain and wool industries. Trade in her territories was facilitated by canals joining the Elbe and Oder while population increase was encouraged by immigration and land reclamation schemes on the lower Oder. Despite a loss of half a million people in the Seven Years War twenty-three years of peace from 1763 to 1786, immigration, new acquisition of territory and growing confidence, had doubled the population of two and three quarter millions between 1763 and 1786. Above all, the army had doubled in size.

The achievement of Frederick was thus immense, but the price heavy. Like the rest of Europe, Prussia was affected by a conflict between centralising monarchy and provincial, privileged nobility. Frederick's predecessors, the Great Elector and Frederick-William I, had to a large extent solved the problem. They forged the army into an instrument of centralisation, making it the avenue to all preferment in all branches of dynastic service, both central and provincial. The major role in both army, and administration, they assigned to the Junker class of the Eastern provinces whose own relative poverty made them willing to accept state service on such advantageous terms. Thus they solved the problem of creating an obedient bureaucracy and of governing the provinces, not by beginning to create a bureaucratic class but by transforming the army into a bureaucratic training ground. The *Landrat* and *Steuerrat* was thus a Junker involved with military discipline performing a bureaucratic task. The Prussian monarch, henceforth, was not merely King but First Junker of Prussia. The life of Prussia acquired a militarist flavour.

The development of a military caste system reached its final fruition in Frederick the Great's reign. By the end of his father's reign Prussia had reached the utmost bounds of its possible power and organisational efficiency, given the resources at its disposal. Frederick had thus sought a way out of the impasse by acquiring rich new provinces. Such a policy created in Austria and Russia immediate and potential enemies, and forced Prussia henceforth to rely utterly on the efficiency of its army, especially when the nation, even in 1786, was the weakest and least defensible of the three major Eastern powers. Unlike those of France, Prussian resources were not limitless, and Prussia could not be both a military power and loosely organised. Prussia put all her reliance on the army. Thus the alliance between the monarchy and the Junker aristocracy was firmly and permanently cemented, to be broken only in 1918 in the defeat of both.

The Junker aristocracy became a service nobility, serving the state and seeing its privileged position preserved by the dynasty which could not afford to offend it. The continuing vulnerable position of Prussia meant that no monarch could afford to break the bonds. Thus the work of Frederick the Great in strengthening and preserving his state had grave disadvantages. The caste system imposed a rigid social framework in the country which pervaded all life. The middle class assumed a lowly position, was discouraged from challenging the Junkers' wealth, and forbidden to acquire land. The importance of the Junkers meant that Frederick had been unable to free the serfs of Magdeburg and was never able to apply the land tax throughout his territories. The needs of the army led Frederick to forbid landlords to eject serfs from their land and he made serf tenure hereditary with unfortunate results for agricultural progress. A vast treasure was seen as a necessity in case of sudden war, so industry existed on mercantilist lines discouraging capitalism and industrial expansion. As it was the army of 200,000 consumed eighty per cent of state revenue. State monopolies also led to price inflation and most of the industries Frederick created under artificial circumstances collapsed. He forbade the introduction of spinning machines into Silesia because he feared the growth of capitalism, and the weakening of that class from which he drew his conscripts. He feared the independent person, particularly the capitalist. The military nature of his régime required people to fit into neat categories and to be easily controllable. The middle class man and particularly the entrepreneur was not trustworthy since he was neither officer nor private. Over-regulation and excessive bureaucratic control were hallmarks of the Hohenzollern régime. It became the most slavish country in Europe. Enlightenment was to be found at Potsdam only in religious toleration and in the legal reforms of Cocceji. Elsewhere 'Policy is in the interest of the state, within and without'. Enlightenment was for those areas where it offended least, and although intellectually Frederick saw the evil effects of serfdom and on occasion went out of his way to aid individuals he never forgot that he was 'First Junker'.

Absolutism certainly existed. Like his father, Frederick worked long hours, rising every morning at five. Incapable of delegating, he had taken control of all ministries and took all decisions, against which no appeal was allowed.

> Now a system can only emanate from a single brain; it must be the sovereign's. Idleness, pleasure seeking, and imbecility are the causes that keep princes from the noble task of securing the happiness of their people.

Unfortunately his successor spent more time in filling and rocking cradles than in securing the efficient functioning of a system of government which required undivided attention.

The Hohenzollern absolutism was probably the most successful in solving the problem of the aristocracy, but this brought with it great disadvantages accentuated by other factors, chiefly that of Prussia's geographical position which perpetuated and strengthened a system of government allying a military privileged class to an absolutist monarchy. While such a regime existed, and while the bourgeois class remained so weak, it was unlikely that the effects of the French Revolution would be felt in Prussia. The Prussian monarchy solved the problem of the struggle between absolutism and particularism and vested interests by leaving both largely untouched and by providing the army to absorb the energies of both.

When Frederick the Great came to his throne his

predecessor had firmly established the principle of a service nobility; when Catherine the Great came to the throne, in 1762, her predecessor, Peter III by ending the obligation of service had, in theory, destroyed the principle. Although there is no evidence that Catherine had intended to curb the power of nobility at the beginning of her reign, or to help the peasantry, the opposition of the *dvorianstvo* in the Assembly of 1766 and the weakness of the townspeople soon convinced her that such ideals were not worth the loss of a throne. Like other absolutists, Catherine realised she lacked the resources or manpower to create a bureaucracy, and was obliged to rely on the goodwill of the nobility for the government of the country. Thus in Russia as in Prussia the autocrat and the aristocrat entered into partnership, but contrary to the Prussian case the aristocrat was visibly the senior partner. When Catherine's successor, Paul, attempted to curb the privileges of the nobility he was murdered and Catherine herself, like so many of her predecessors, was on the throne of Holy Russia only by virtue of palace revolt and two convenient murders rather than by right of succession. Not the least reason why Catherine decided against a bureaucratic organisation for her state was the sheer size of Russia which precluded efficient government and demanded decentralisation. Finally the great social revolt of the serfs and industrial workers of the Urals in the Pugachev rebellion had convinced her of where her safety lay.

Thus Catherine allied herself with the wealthier court nobility and the gentry to govern her vast territory and, as might be expected, was obliged to make concessions to this class in return for their loyalty. Already Catherine had created a Nobles Bank to provide almost unlimited credit to meet the appalling indebtedness of her nobility, so that their social status might be preserved from the results of their financial ineptitude. In 1775, she had begun a process designed to give the *dvorianstvo* control of provincial administration and law by increasing the power of the provincial governors, doubling the number of provinces and by introducing a measure of *dvorianstvo* election into the choosing of the subordinate officials in the new courts, though the chief officials continued to be appointed by the government and there was no control over officials by the gentry.

In 1785 however she went even further by setting up provincial assemblies of nobles to be called together every three years to hear the governor and to choose a provincial marshal, though the latter choice was limited since the governor supplied the names. More important, however, the assemblies could present their needs and requests and they could appoint representatives to take their complaints to the Empress or the central government.

These are signs of a monarchical capitulation to the *dvorianstvo*: in reality the surrender was not so great. The 'powers' of the new assemblies were minimal and they still did not appoint the most important officials. The governor, though a nobleman, was close enough to the sovereign to feel a sense of awe and dared not disobey. Besides these facts, no noble who did not perform, or had not performed, service to the state, could vote for, or sit in, the new assemblies and those whose annual income was less than one hundred roubles were debarred. Thus Catherine's bureaucratic leanings did not entirely give way to *dvorianstvo* importunity. It was as though she withdrew the bureaucracy to the centre and did not try to over-extend its competence or stretch its manpower too far. The service requirement preserved the control of the wealthier *dvorianstvo* and prevented the rise of the poorest *'hobereaux'* who, as was once pointed out to Catherine, were often too poor to buy the clothes and boots to get them to the imperial recruiting centres.

Her desire to satisfy the demands of the nobility can also be seen in her attitude to the serfs. In her 'Instructions' (1767) she had shown concern for the serfs and her dislike of the institution. In 1783, to pacify the Cossack landowners she introduced serfdom into little Russia where it did not exist previously and extended the poll tax, the prime depressive influence on free peasants, to the Baltic provinces. During her reign 800,000 state peasants of semi-free status were transferred to her favourites and to serfdom. The rights of landlords over their serfs steadily increased during the period until in the 1780s it reached the point where serfs were forbidden to petition the Tsarina against the malpractices of their owners. The plight of the serfs is vividly described in Radischev's *A Journey from St Petersburg to Moscow*.

A few steps from the road I saw a peasant ploughing a field. . .It was now Sunday. The ploughing peasant, of course belonged to a landed proprieter who would not let him pay a commutation tax. . .

Radischev asked the peasant why he was working on Sunday:

In a week sir, there are six days, and we go six times a week to work in the master's fields; in the evening, if the weather is good, we haul to the master's house the hay that is left in the woods. . .God grant that it rains this evening.
   No matter how hard you work for the master, no one will thank you for it. The master will not pay our head tax; but, though he doesn't pay it, he doesn't demand one sheep, one hen, or any linen or butter the less.

In later sections Radischev describes the break up of a serf family because of the master's bankruptcy.

The lad of twenty-five. . .the companion and intimate of his master. Savagery and vengeance are in his eyes. . .You will become the property of another.

Although in 1771 Catherine forbade the sale of serfs without the land they worked her orders were not obeyed and serfs in Alexander I's reign were being sold near the walls of the Winter Palace.
   Even if it is accepted that from a purely administrative point of view serfs are a better proposition than free peasants, Catherine's abandonment of them is hardly excusable, unless it is realised that the mutual dependence of *dvorianstvo* and autocrat precluded anything being done to end the continuing decline of the serfs' position.
   The impossiblity of being an autocrat in the situation in which Catherine found herself is emphasised by the fact that

at the beginning of her reign the Financial College was millions of roubles in arrears and the Senate so submerged in business that it could not hope to cope with the college system of administration. Not surprisingly the *dvorianstvo* insistence on reform of provincial administration sapped Catherine's will to make the central administration more efficient, and she did not complete her creation of a Council of State. The reform of the Senate into six departments was all that she had accomplished by 1780.

Such was the growth in the *dvorianstvo* power that the attempt to revive town life and independence was fore-doomed. The *Charter for Towns* (1785) gave the right of appealing to the sovereign to the restored magistracies and attempted to sort the townspeople into categories according to their education, profession, membership of guilds or their wealth. Voting according to these categories, the townspeople were to choose a mayor and council to manage the financial and other affairs of the community. But since con-tributions to finances were voluntary and the attitude of the provincial gentry hostile, these towns remained stunted growths, and though Catherine claimed to have created in her reign over one hundred towns, many of these, like her *Charter*, existed only on paper. If this was an attempt to use the town to counter-balance the power of the nobility, it failed. Like all East European monarchs, Catherine suffered from the lack of a reform-minded middle class.

Catherine's so-called enlightenment was thus largely a paper project. Yet it is hard to blame her for this since the odds, historical, social, economic and political, against progress of any kind were too immense. She indulged in the usual anti-clericalism of the enlightened in secularising church lands (1764) but encouraged the orthodox in her plans for a new Empire based on Constantinople. She tried to introduce liberal economic laws but for a backward country like hers there was little point. Long 'sparkling' talks with Grimm and self-publicising letters to Voltaire were almost the sum of her enlightenment in its practical effect.

Meanwhile the economic effects of her attitude to the *dvorianstvo* were seen in the continued backwardness of Russian agriculture, the worst in Europe. The gentry were frequently absentees with their land in the hands of stewards. Serfdom's stringency prevented migration to the rich soil of the Crimea and Black Sea littoral, and increased taxation held back the growth of industry. The number of factories continued to rise yet not as a result of Catherine's endeavour but rather as a result of long, expensive and inflationary wars and increased population. The stunting of urban growth enabled foreigners to control trade. Meanwhile the *dvorianstvo* grew further away from their serfs and aped French manners, since western ways no longer implied a diminution of their powers as they had under Peter the Great.

Joseph II said of Catherine that she was 'a woman who cares only for herself and no more for Russia than I do'. Of herself she said 'I desire the common good'. Joseph, as usual, was going by results and there is no reason to doubt that Catherine did intend the common good. The importunity of the *dvorianstvo* and the needs of an expansionist foreign policy however, stifled her more humanitarian instincts. When the French Revolution came she termed the deputies of the National Assembly 'Pugachevs' and it is strange that as France destroyed the apparatus of the *Ancien Régime* and swept away the privileges of the nobles, as Joseph II attempted his one-man revolution in Austria, Catherine in Russia allowed the nobility to reach the zenith of their power and influence and drove the peasantry to the depths of despair. In 1796 when she died, beloved of the *dvorianstvo*, she already seemed an anachronism.

Of the monarchs of eighteenth century Austria, Joseph II was undoubtedly the most courageous and most interesting. He dared far more than any other monarch yet his problems were greater than those of his contemporaries. The King of France knew that his people were, for the most part, French, with a common ethnic background; Frederick the Great of Prussia in 1780 knew that his state was, despite the Poles, predominantly German speaking; Catherine the Great ruled an Empire which was largely Slav, and whose separate peoples, apart from the Poles, had no very recent history of nationhood, but Joseph II ruled a complex polyglot empire in which the dominant German race were nevertheless a minority people. Germans, Poles in Galicia, Czechs and

Slovaks in Bohemia, Italians in Lombardy, Magyars, Slavs, Croatians, Rumanians in Hungary, and Belgians in the Austrian Netherlands were the races and ethnic groups comprising his Empire. The Empire was largely governed through the towns where, even in Bohemia, the Germans predominated, the other nationalities largely forming the peasant population. However, although since the Battle of the White Mountain, Bohemia had ceased to have a history separate from Austria one Hapsburg territory, Hungary, had preserved, and continued to preserve, a corporate and national identity all its own.

To a certain extent, Maria Theresa, Joseph's mother, had assimilated Hungary more closely into the Hapsburg administration; she called the Diet very rarely, enticed the rich nobility to Vienna, pursued policies of immigration and patronage, but Hungary's real separateness had hardly been touched. Her gentry were so poor themselves that they could not afford to submit to the reforms and centralisation of the dynasty. The abolition of serfdom would ruin them as would taxation by outside agencies. Thus they clung to their privileges and to self government through the country Estates. These Estates continued to meet even when the Diet did not since no Hapsburg had dared to risk causing a rebellion by abolishing them. The situation was further complicated by the racial differences between the Magyar aristocracy and the Slav serfs. Unless Hungary could be 'Germanised' such differences would, in the nationalist atmosphere of nineteenth century Europe, result in conflict.

In 1780, therefore, Hungary was still a separate kingdom which happened to be ruled by the Hapsburgs; a situation an orthodox absolutist could hardly tolerate. Separate status preserved Hungary's backwardness, kept her within a separate tariff wall and prevented the Hapsburgs from collecting from Hungary the revenues which a province of such a size ought to have given. This increased the burden on the other provinces, particularly the peasants, because after the loss of Silesia the Hapsburgs had needed revenue badly.

Joseph's mother, Maria Theresa, had by no means allowed the states of her Empire to remain unreformed, but she had, in a famous phrase, 'merely added new wings to a feudal building'. Thus she had helped the serfs and restricted the powers of the nobility by limiting feudal labour services and by destroying, outside Hungary, the powers of the Estates and implementing a system of centralisation both at the centre and in the provinces on a Prussian model. She had stimulated commerce and began under Tchotek to break down tariff barriers. Finally against her own will she had expelled the Jesuits and thus paved the way for ecclesiastical and educational reform.

Nevertheless in 1780 in Bohemia and Hungary where serfdom existed most notably (it did not exist in the Netherlands, nor everywhere in Austria) the condition of the serfs was appalling. Although their dues and labour services were restricted they were still excessive, and payments to the lord prevented them from paying more taxes to the state. In 1777 thousands of Bohemian peasants died from starvation. The nobility remained practically untaxed. Such over-taxation on a section of the community held back agricultural and industrial progress: no serf would work hard on land not his own and peasant poverty restricted sale of manufactured goods. Despite Maria Theresa's reforms, the administration, still largely in the hands of the nobility, was slack and inefficient, and still not applicable to Hungary. The power of the Church restricted education and the spread of new ideas, prevented toleration and caused the emigration of Protestants whose talents were eagerly accepted in industry and the professions by the Hapsburg's rivals and neighbours. There was no common tariff wall round the Empire and tariff restrictions slowed up economic advance by strangling trade.

Joseph II brought to his immense task qualities and failings in roughly equal proportions. Above all he was impatient. Much as he admired his mother, the years of joint rule between 1765 and 1780, when his eagerness for reform had been baulked by the clerical and aristocratic clique surrounding her, had gravely tried his patience and he felt the need to accomplish everything immediately. These years had also imbued him with a dislike of the nobility amounting to hatred and an anticlericalism which however did not amount to a loss of faith. Above all he was a fanatic who lacked a sense of proportion. While it was true that uniformity was needed in the administration his straitjacket conformity and Germanisation took no account of reasoned objections and historic differences. He had an invincible belief in the rightness of what he was doing; he believed it was forged by reason and as such must work and be obeyed. Joseph himself said:

Every proposal ought to be based on the irrefutable arguments of reason.

His belief in the power of reason places him clearly in the enlightenment tradition of the eighteenth century. Those who opposed reason were foolish, superstitious or criminal and thus their views were not to be taken into account, and since his opinions were the product of reason the bureaucracy must obey without question or deviation. The drab uniformity which he tried to impose is one of the more distressing aspects of his reign, but taking into account the palimpsest of conflicting nationalities, rights, laws and administrative systems with which he was faced his methods seem less foolish. He tried to introduce reason, system and organisation into his régime and for that he deserves perhaps more than any other ruler the title 'Enlightened Despot'. But although he was enlightened, certainly read the *philosophes* and accepted the concept of the Social Contract, it was the problems of his Empire and his own character not the enlightenment which dictated his methods.

He was a cold man, lacking affection from others and having difficulty in giving it, but he took a genuine interest in the lives of his less fortunate subjects, was prepared to listen to their complaints and, risked his position in fighting for them and his own power against the vested interests of the privileged classes.

His first aim was to create a centralised, uniform bureaucracy directed to the service of the state and his ideas. He wished to abolish provincial distinctions which stood in the way of honest, efficient, and cheap government. He insisted on obedience; no one could feel immune from his scrutiny and from his own hand poured an avalanche of instructions, edicts and reprimands. The Chancelleries lost their last vestiges of independent action and by 1786 only Hungary remained outside the new uniformity. A secret police kept an eye on the activities of state functionaries and reported dishonesty or disobedience.

Besides Hungary two major obstacles seemed to stand in the way of his national system: the different legal systems of his realm, and the organisation within his patrimony of the Church, the boundaries of whose sees seemed rarely to correspond with secular administrative or even national boundaries. Joseph set up a commission to produce national criminal and civil codes. When it seemed to be working too slowly Joseph anticipated its decisions and he soon lost patience with its innate conservatism in the face of privileged powers. His new Criminal laws abolished the death penalty and torture and abolished the crimes of witchcraft and apostacy.

Where possible Joseph re-organised the boundaries of bishoprics and resisted the installation of foreigners in German sees. But such measures were part of a general attack on the ultramontanism of the Papacy. Joseph held that since he was absolute the Pope had no temporal power in his dominions. The church in the Hapsburg territories was a state church with spiritual allegiance to Rome only. Joseph was not different in his attitude from other Catholic monarchs who had already destroyed the chief weapon of ultramontanism, the Jesuit order. But Joseph went further and his demands presaged the Concordat of Napoleon with the Papacy in 1801. He forbade the publication of Papal Bulls without his permission, demanded that Bishops swear loyalty to the secular authorities, and not even the visit of Pius VI in person to Vienna could alter his attitude.

His Church policy however ran more deeply than this. He granted toleration to all religions including the Jewish. 'Our country is not a monastery'. 'Nobody should be forced any longer to put up with state proselytism if it is against his principles'. He was not however a free thinker. He had Deists whipped, for to him the Church was a social servant, a spiritual police force and people who did not believe in reward and punishment, or a personal God would not heed the law. Spiritual policing did not extend to censorship which was removed from the Church's hands so that Protestant books and scientific works could circulate freely. However books which were deemed 'superstitious' were banned. Only in 1787 was press freedom withdrawn.

Joseph's view of the Church's role had no place for organisations which he did not see as fulfilling a useful purpose. Monasteries were wealthy but not productive, and thus in 1781 all those either too small or not engaged in charity or educational work were abolished and the proceeds of 700 monasteries were used to set up schools, to try to increase the number of parishes and educated priests and to pay pensions to monks too old to do useful pastoral work. Begging orders were anathema and were not allowed to recruit new members.

Such reforms were undoubtedly useful but they intensely annoyed conservative churchmen and toleration was not yet an idea which was acceptable to most Catholics. When Joseph interfered with church customs he alienated the broad mass of catholic peasantry. The introduction of German litanies seems sensible but his attempt to restrict pilgrimages and processions and his removal of decoration in churches were interferences with the spiritual life of the peasants who were perverse enough to love their superstitious practices in the way that the English in the seventeenth century had loved their maypoles. It is symptomatic of his type that Joseph was unable to leave the relatively unimportant abuses alone. Indeed where reason dictated, a sense of proportion was out of place.

It is his work for the serfs which however is the most remarkable feature of Joseph's reign. In September 1781 he abolished serfdom everywhere but in Hungary, guaranteeing the serfs the freedom to move and work where, and at what occupation, they wished, and allowing them to pay in instalments for the land they held which was theirs inalienably. He did not however abolish Robots or cash payments to the landlord. The corollary of this was his tax law based on the Physiocratic belief in land as the source of wealth. Ordering a survey of all his lands in 1785 he equalised taxes on the basis of the amount of land owned and ended aristocratic immunity. The resulting tax decree of 1789 faced the poorer

C

nobility with ruin and led to the revolts which disfigured the
end of Joseph's reign. Unfortunately they also encouraged
peasant revolt for the peasant, serf or free, still had to pay
twelve and two ninths per cent of his income to the landlord
as well as seventeen and seven ninths per cent which landlord
and serf paid to the state.

His economic principles were those of the absolutist — mercantilist. He encouraged commerce and industry
but feared private enterprise. His high tariffs led to smuggling
and his refusal to set up a Bank restricted industrial expansion. The attempt to create a trading company based on the
Austrian Netherlands was sixty years too late.

Like Frederick then, Joseph was afraid of individualism.
Both church reforms and bureaucracy aimed to create the
habit of obedience. He could never appreciate the arts,
though Vienna was the city of Mozart and Haydn; he disapproved of writers as 'pen cattle'. The Masonic societies
which flourished and which supported his policies he tried to
regulate because they were secret and therefore difficult to
control. Unfortunately for Joseph, although the desperate
need for many of his reforms can be appreciated, his
territories were so diverse, so different in history and ethnic
character that it was virtually impossible for one man to
create a unity in the space of ten years.

It was to be the two areas possessing a strong local
tradition and recent historical identity which were to signal
the end of Joseph's revolutionary experiment. The Hungarian
chancellery had already protested against Joseph's dissolution
of monasteries in Hungary and Hungarians had been mortally
offended by Joseph's refusal to be crowned separately as
King of Hungary and by his removal of the historic St
Stephen's Crown from Budapest to a Vienna museum. Such
actions, insignificant in themselves, though wounding,
showed that Joseph intended to treat Hungary as just another
province and not as a separate kingdom with special rights.

The German language is the universal language of my
Empire. I am the Emperor of Germany. The principalities
which I possess are provinces which form one whole with
the state of which I am the head. If the Kingdom of

Hungary had been the most important of my possessions, I should not have hesitated to make all other countries speak Hungarian.

This movement was enforced by Joseph's insistence that German should replace Latin as the official tongue of Hungary and that those unable to speak the language should not hold office. This struck at the gentry's control of local administration and was fiercely resented.

The extension of conscription to Hungary followed, striking at Hungary's right to raise its own army. In 1786 serfdom was declared abolished and the administration remodelled on the lines of his other territories; the Estates lost most of their administrative functions. Already the nobles had been beset by peasant revolts in 1784 led by an ex-soldier named Hora, and now the King/Emperor seemed to be acquiescing in the destruction of their ordered privileged society. The Magyars prepared for revolt.

Their chance came after 1787 when Joseph's centralising reforms threatened the Austrian Netherlands, an area not backward like Hungary but with traditions of self-government, prosperous commerce, a large middle class and a powerful but popular church. Joseph's attempted reforms, particularly those directed against the church led to open opposition from the people which in 1787 became armed rebellion.

Revolt in Belgium triggered off Magyar revolt in Hungary and with the country engaged in war with Turkey, despite all efforts Joseph was unable to stem the tide. 'In many places the German hat was thrown away and they put the Hungarian fur cap and shako on their heads'. Faced by such patent hostility and horrified by the new threat posed by the French revolution Joseph began to dismantle his revolutionary Empire. Serfdom in Hungary was not abolished until 1836 and when Leopold ascended the throne most of the other reforms were rescinded; the privileges of the nobility were not wholly swept away, the reforms of church usage were abandoned, Hungary resumed its privileged position, Belgium had its rights restored, censorship was reintroduced.

At Joseph's funeral his coffin was stoned by the people he

had tried to help. Yet all was not failure. The bureaucracy continued to function well; serfdom in all his dominions could not be reintroduced, nor could tax exemption; the church never regained full power. But Joseph's centralisation paradoxically strengthened the separateness of Hungary and made the task of nineteenth century Hapsburg statesmen even more difficult. On the eve of nationalism Joseph had failed to 'Germanise' his territories. Above all Joseph's reign shows the impossiblity of one man, however absolute, succeeding in revolutionising his lands against determined opposition by the privileged orders. Joseph was too afraid of the German middle classes to take them into his confidence and their numbers were too small. The attempt of absolutism to reform, without mass support, was bound to fail.

CHAPTER FOUR

Despotism in Western Europe:
The Eve of Revolution

'So long as a People is constrained to obey, and does, in fact obey, it does well. So soon as it can shake off its yoke, and succeeds in doing so, it does better'. *Rousseau*

In Italy and the Iberian peninsula the problems facing the reformers were particularly acute. The centres of power had shifted with the centres of trade, northwards to France, the Netherlands and above all, the United Kingdom. From the seventeenth century onwards the peninsula had sunk into cultural and economic stagnation reinforced by religious obscurantism. Italy's great days were even further in the past. In the South, in Naples as in Portugal and Spain the population declined as the peasants sank to depths of wretchedness undreamed of almost everywhere else west of the Elbe. Fortunately as in the rest of Europe the situation seemed to provide the man.

The Marquis de Pombal who was dismissed from office in 1777 is discussed in an earlier volume of this series. He had created in Portugal an absolutism based on fear and the police but which in a personal vendetta expelled the Jesuits, fatally weakened the legal and social privileges of the church and terrified into submission the great secular grandees whose legal and social position was likewise permanently damaged.

He had done much to stimulate trade, to free the peasantry from the vast latifundia of the church and nobility and rescue the bureaucracy from aristocratic maladministration. But from 1782 the reaction in Portugal grew ever more open and successful, and although neither church nor aristocracy regained all their privileges most of Pombal's work was undone.

The meagre results of Pombal's labours are hardly to be

wondered at. The lack of trained administrators, the dearth
of an educated middle class and the hereditary privileges of
large sections of the population which Pombal inherited,
threw all the burden of reform on one man, and as in the
Hapsburg lands, the strain was too much. An under-
developed agricultural country, like Portugal, could not be
projected forwards at the speed Pombal hoped while the
fierceness of the absolutism which obstruction provoked led
to the even fiercer reaction which followed the death of its
sole protaganist.

Similar problems faced Charles III of Spain, undoubtedly
one of Spain's greatest monarchs, but he had at least had
experience of the difficulties which faced him as King of the
Two Sicilies. Faced by an ecclesiastical control which had
stifled the economy and cultural life, a corrupt bureaucracy,
unchecked particularism in the provinces and municipalities,
the deadening effect of vast entailed estates, a declining
population and peasant poverty, he had gathered around him
men of the calibre of Floridablanca and Jovellanos, men
influenced by the French philosophers and physiocrats.

Centralisation was the first essential culminating in the
Council of State (1783) which co-ordinated effectively the
work of the Intendants and corregidores in slowly weakening
dearly defended local privileges. But the characteristic feature
of Charles III's reign as might be expected from a man whose
servants were physiocrats, was economic reform. The attempt
was made to weaken the privileges of the Mesta sheep
ranchers whose vast herds wandered over private land and
made agricultural improvements pointless. The vast entails of
the church and the family trusts of the nobles were attacked
in a largely successful attempt to prevent the further growth
of the territorial agglomerations in the hands of the church or
of families whose vast wealth made agricultural improvements unnecessary and whose lands could be put to better
use by the desperately poor peasantry. Local tariffs were
reduced or abolished, internal colonisation encouraged, roads
and canals built. The monarchy bought land in the Sierra
Morena, built model farms and encouraged immigration in an
attempt to open up new land and arrest the population
decline.

When Charles died vast improvements had been made and foreign visitors remarked on the apparent prosperity of the towns. But Charles was succeeded by the indolent and stupid Charles IV under whom Spain began to sink back into an obscurantism which the French revolution's anti-clericalism was only to enforce. Even Charles III had not dared to touch the legal and, above all, tax privileges of the nobility. Nevertheless Charles' reforms were not forgotten and they stimulated new forces, especially in the towns, which Joseph Napoleon's reign was to encourage and which would reach temporary fruition in the constitution of 1812.

In Italy little could be expected from the Papal States or from those areas south of Rome under the Bourbons. After the reign of Charles (1734—59) the monarchy of the Two Sicilies lapsed into a vulgar ignorance and superstition totally unrelieved before its extinction by Garibaldi. Such qualities appealed to the *lazzaroni*, the beggars of Naples, and to the peasantry of the mountains whose semi-human existence seemed to fit them only for domination by the last feudal aristocracy in Europe, and its related ecclesiastical aristocracy whose ignorance was that of the tribal witch doctor.

Enlightenment had a fertile soil on which to grow only in Northern Italy closer to the main arteries of thought and trade. Here, in Tuscany, the future Emperor Leopold ruled (1768—90) in a manner which his brother must have envied. Like his brother, Leopold was affected by the writings of the philosophers and physiocrats and these influences can be seen in the abolition of guild controls and internal trade restrictions. Beccaria's influence can be seen in legal reforms which abolished torture and the death penalty and restricted the judicial rights of landlords. In church policy he refused clerical interference in secular matters. Unfortunately, like his brother he tried to alter church ritual with the same results as obtained in Austria. Thus he thrust the peasantry into the arms of the reactionary church, and although the towns and propertied classes supported him they were not enough to stem the tide of reaction which set in well before 1796. Besides Leopold had never intended to upset the social hierarchy of Tuscany and although all his plans led him towards a constitutional form of government, with an elected assembly, he could never quite bring himself to abandon absolutism for constitutionalism and the aristocracy for the bourgeoisie. If enlightened absolutism led towards the sharing of power might it not have taken the wrong road? Leopold hesitated.

Nonetheless in Northern Italy important seeds had been sown, even in Piedmont where after a century of quiet progress clerical reaction had set in. Germination waited on Bonaparte. Unfortunately, in Italy as elsewhere, the lines of future bitter dissension were being laid by the obscurantist opposition of the church backed by a privileged nobility and superstitious peasantry.

In France the superficial picture was much brighter. Much more advanced socially and economically than Italy, Spain or Portugal it possessed few serfs, and those practically free compared to their eastern counterparts. It had a large prosperous and diverse middle class ranging from the *rentier* through the professional men to the *commerçants*. Trade had revived after the Seven Years war, though the trade treaty of 1786 was to cause some dislocation. The population was large and the country ought to have been happy.

Unfortunately neither the system of government nor the organisation of society was suitable for a relatively advanced nation, and standing in the way of reform were the weaknesses of the monarchy and the strength of the vested interests.

Louis XVI was a man of pious intentions but little political acumen. In the opinion of his brother-in-law Joseph II.

> . . .this man is a little feeble but not stupid; he has ideas, he has judgement but with these a physical and mental apathy. He converses reasonably and has neither taste for self-education, nor curiosity. . .

He had already tried once, with Turgot, to remedy the ills of his country. A major weakness was the power of the nobility. Its main areas of power lay in the Court, in the provincial assemblies of the semi-independent *pays d'état*, and in the *Parlements*, particularly that of Paris. The latter had from the beginning of Louis XV's reign led the aristocratic opposition to the Crown's absolutism and had cemented the irresistible alliance of its own administrative and legal *noblesse de robe* with the *noblesse d'épée* and particularly the powerful court nobility (*noblesse de cour*). The *Parlement's* right to register royal edicts and its right of remonstrance against them had been the basis on which the *Parlement* had built the whole philosophy of opposition to the King. It claimed that it was mediator between king and people and that in it reposed the guardianship of the 'fundamental law of the Kingdom'. In fact the *Parlements* used these specious claims to protect aristocratic privileges against royal reformers and had done so with conspicuous success in 1775 when it caused the downfall of the great reformer, Turgot. The legal fees culled from cases concerning gilds led it to protect the interests of these out-dated bodies which stifled trade; those obtained from cases of feudal law were reason enough for the protection of feudal rights and tax exemptions. The monarchy's own financial incompetence and administrative weakness caused many people, anxious for reform, to believe the Parlement's claims and to applaud its resistance to absolutism. Thus both the *Parlement's* opposition to reform and the monarchy's attempts to provide it were obscured, while new ideas, inimical to absolutism, gained currency.

The administration of the country was chaotic. Louis XIV's centralisation had consisted of overlaying existing bodies with the Intendant system. Basically this system still stood but while the Intendants continued to function as before, the old organisation in the eighteenth century gained new vigour, particularly the provincial *parlements* and the assemblies of the *'pays d'état'* (privileged areas of the country which had retained a measure of self government, unlike the pays *d'élection* where the Intendant was more powerful). Some towns had more self-government than others; Orléans for example was exempt from the taille (poll tax). Ecclesiastical districts bore no relation to secular ones and different taxes were collected on different territorial and organisational bases. Feudal privileges, toll rights in the hands of individuals, corporations or towns added to the total confusion, prevented effective administration and delayed tax collection.

France, in fact, was not so much a country as a collection of vested interests. The aristocracy with its many tax exemptions, feudal privileges, provincial powers and the advantages of its social pre-eminence; the *noblesse de robe* with its *parlements,* its privileged legal position, its financial rewards; the church with its legal and tax privileges; *Fermiers-Généraux* who collected indirect taxation and who had taken advantage of royal weakness to make their posts hereditary; the master-craftsmen of the gilds who retained for their family privileged positions in industry; even some of the peasants relying on the continuance of old methods and common rights, all of these groups had a vested interest in preserving some element of a society which was static. Equally nearly all these elements had quarrels with the vested interests of others; for example the peasant resented the feudal rights of the aristo-crat. More important was the rise of a class which resented the privileges of the aristocracy, resented the inefficiency of taxation, coveted the wealth of the church, required the freeing of the labour market and urged new agricultural methods. Perhaps there was not one class which required these things, but it was an attitude of mind associated mostly with the professional and commercial sections of the bourgeoisie. Unfortunately by 1780 it had learned to distrust the monarchy as a possibly ally.

Turgot's attempt to reform had been defeated by the organised vested interests led by the Court nobility and the *Parlements.* His failure was to be repeated by Calonne in even more trying circumstances and the failure of both points to an essential fault in the logic of absolutism. When faced by the vested interests Louis XVI, like Catherine, Frederick and Joseph in their several ways, gave way. Turgot had told Louis that the main weakness of his monarchy was that it lacked a constitution. He pinpointed a great truth. If Louis was to reform and defeat the vested interests which surrounded him he had somehow to reach out over their heads to those who might support him. Such people existed and Turgot, rather like Calonne later, planned a hierarchy of provincial assem-blies, advisory not executive who, though lacking power, could give moral support. Such a situation was fraught with dangers and Turgot himself, like Calonne, had always feared the idea of a States General which he felt sure the monarch would be unable to hold in rein. An Estates General on the old model would give power to the two privileged Estates, aristocratic and clerical, while any new system would involve giving suitable representation to the Third Estate, which might not take the monarch's lead. Provincial assemblies would be a half-way house. Turgot understood that the position of a reforming monarch who was himself the nexus of the whole privileged organisation of the *Ancien Régime* was immensely difficult. The links between the monarch's own position and that of his nobles and others were so wide that the likelihood of the monarch's powers remaining untouched by reform were slim. Reform would unleash a flood of unknown and perhaps uncontrollable forces. No monarch had yet been revolutionary enough to cease willingly to be absolutist, not even Joseph II. In fact the Bourbon's fitful reforms had been in the direction of greater absolutism, not less. Thus it would be difficult for the monarch to reform and already in 1775 Louis XVI had shown that he was afraid of being a revolutionary king. Reform, when it came, was likely to be, not with the King against the vested interests but might drive the King towards the vested interests in an alliance disastrous to both. In a small degree this process had already begun.

Rather than decline, the privileges of the aristocracy, and above all the Court aristocracy, had increased. Not only did it have to fear the reforms of the monarch but also the rising economic power of the talented, wealthier bourgeoisie with its more liquid financial assets. In reaction the nobles became increasingly exclusive; in 1781 commissioned entry into the army was reserved for those who could show four generations of nobility and in 1788 for Court nobility only. As 1789 approached the episcopacy grew more exclusively aristocratic as did the roll of Intendants. Such exclusiveness stood in the way of the advancement of the bourgeoisie which already resented aristocratic tax privileges. Along with increasing social exclusiveness went the feudal reaction, as financial considerations forced the nobility to extract more from its land. This took the form largely of exploitation of feudal rights, some rediscovered, protected by the Courts. Moreover the leasing of rights or of whole manors or entrepreneurs accentuated this feudal pressure and stirred up the anger of the peasant in increasingly violent '*jacqueries*'.

Faced with an apparent conspiracy between the court nobility and the king, the tempers of the middle class rose steadily through the eighties. They resented the tolls, gilds and aristocratic government which held back expansion and demanded civil liberties in the language the *parlements* had taught them. Increasingly they realised that royal absolutism was no way to achieve what they wanted and looked for the opportunity to fight for themselves. Above all they resented their inability to get recognition of their social position.

The largest class remained the peasantry. Like the aristocracy and middle class this was by no means a homogeneous group. It included peasants who owned property of varying amounts, some who share-cropped it *(métayers)*, some leaseholders, some who were landless and others who were leaseholders and freeholders.

The property-less peasants were the most volatile and the poorest, but many peasants had too little land to live on because of the rise in population and division of inheritances. Other peasants were wealthy and the source of much jealousy. Land hunger made the poorer people cast greedy eyes on the lands of the church and nobility. The feudal reaction increased the burden on the peasant, whether through feudal services or payments. The peasant was about the only person to pay the *taille* and had to work on the *corvée*, or road works, which was often misused for the seigneur's advantage. *Gabelle,* or salt tax, and the tithe to the church were other hated payments. Meanwhile new ideas of estate management on capitalist lines encouraged by physiocratic propaganda challenged old ways. Enclosures, though by no means on an English scale, were serious where they occurred, since they prevented the peasant from gleaning, destroyed the old privilege of grazing cattle on land in fallow, and ate away at the commons. However sound such ideas were economically they were disastrous for a peasant relying on common rights to preserve his family from starvation.

Finally in the towns there lived that class which came to be known as the *sansculottes;* small shopkeepers, artisans and journeymen. Even before 1789 the latter had shown signs of unrest as they perceived the master-craftsmen securing the exclusiveness of the gilds. At all times the financial security of this class was precarious, particularly so when harvests were bad and the price of bread high. The price of bread well before 1789 was the most reliable barometer of social unrest.

In the 1780s France, though outwardly calm, was in fact facing grave difficulties; a monarchy which seemed not to have the nerve to reform when revolutionary reform was required, and a class structure far more volatile and complicated than the static hierarchical social organisation provided for. The rivalries of class with class and the rivalries within classes in conjunction with the administrative complexity and web of vested interests provided a situation which was uncontrollable.

In 1787 it was discovered that largely as a result of the American War, the deficit would be 112 million livres and short term loans were falling due for repayment. While the Crown was unable to raise loans because of the *Parlements'* opposition and afraid of calling an Estates General, its chief minister, Controller-General Calonne, prepared a series of reforms resembling those which Turgot and the King had abandoned in 1775. He summed up the abuses which he was hoping to eradicate:

> ...the general inequality in the distribution of subsidies (taxes) the enormous disproportion found in the contributions of different provinces and in the imposition on the subjects of the same sovereign.

He planned to reduce expenditure and, like Joseph in Austria, impose a Land Tax on all. Internal tariffs would be abolished to provide an internal free market, the *Gabelle* would be reformed, *corvée* commuted, *taille* reduced and Crown lands leased to peasants to meet the land hunger. A hierarchy of assemblies at parish, district and provincial levels would be introduced with local executive powers under the Intendant's wing and in which the nobles would sit on equal terms with the Third Estate.

The threat to the social and economic position of the

aristocracy and the implied threat to other interests elicited a storm of protest. Unable to risk any wider assembly Calonne put the plan to an Assembly of Notables consisting of prelates, court nobles, parlementarians, ministers, Intendants, provincial representatives and others. They settled down to frivolous and damaging criticism, while outside the *Parlement* called for an Estates General, which it fondly thought would be controlled by the two conservative Estates. Calonne was unpopular with middle class opinion; his morality and his economic ability were suspect and thus the Notables were able to pose successfully as protectors of the whole nation, and not just themselves, from increased taxation.

> . . .mingling with men of purely liberal views they made common cause with the nation which feared all taxes of whatever kind. *Calonne*

Calonne's failure was patent. Both he and the Assembly were dismissed. The deadlock set the scene for revolution; the aristocratic revolution had begun. Once again the monarchy had failed to take the reforming initiative and there was little that it could now do but submit to the suicidal demands of the privileged orders for an Estates General.

The Failure of Absolutism

Absolutism monarchs achieved much in Europe but in 1790 they were nearly everywhere in retreat — in Austria, Italy, Spain, Portugal and France while in Russia and Prussia the monarchy had come to an arrangement with privilege which smothered future reform. The French Revolution was to lead to a panic among absolutists which drove even those most opposed to privilege and open to enlightenment into an alliance with those forces, lay and ecclesiastical which they had been opposing. In the eighteenth century absolutism was progressive, in the nineteenth it was merely reactionary.

For reforming absolutism was a fatally illogical form of government, as the failure of Louis XVI above all was to demonstrate. Louis XVI might have been envied by other monarchs for the size of the French bourgeois classes and the advanced economic state of the country, the lack of which advantages prevented the fruition of many of their own reforms. But Louis showed the failure of absolutism only too clearly. Unable to combat the privileged groups without the support of that section of the community which shared its opposition to privilege, it feared even more the threat to its own power from those whose help it needed, and thus allowed itself to be driven back into the arms of the privileged. The threat of revolution stifled the reforming desires of the absolutists who had not the nerve to become real revolutionary monarchs. It is too easy to criticise them. No one ever willingly surrenders power or admits the philosophy on which a life's actions have been based to be erroneous, but the absolutists discovered that the logic of reforming absolutism led to radical conclusions involving a diminution of monarchical power. Yet the whole movement of the eighteenth century was towards stronger monarchical power. The full logic of the situation was discovered only in those countries, like France, where there existed a class large enough to replace the privileged orders. Where such a class did not exist the monarch found himself faced with an articulate and hostile privileged order without himself having an articulate mass of support to counteract it. The result was usually reaction, as in Spain after Charles III, Portugal after Pombal, Austria under Joseph and Leopold, Tuscany under Leopold. But Joseph's own attitude to the Masonic societies showed that he feared his articulate support as much as he did the opposition and Louis XVI showed on two occasions that he could not face the risk of using the support of the unprivileged to attack the common, privileged enemy. For he realised that the almost certain outcome would be a sharing of power with that large, articulate and economically vital class; an end to absolutism. Louis was to be the first monarch to experience the dilemma and his answer would be, as the revolution showed, resistance. Such was to be the answer of all European monarchs. It is interesting to note that the most stable countries in Europe in the first part of the nineteenth century were to be those, Russia and Prussia, which never experienced the hand of the truly reforming monarch, or subsequently, of Napoleon.

Perhaps only in England, however, did the monarchy accept the logic of the situation and, after tribulation, find a fruitful way out of the dilemma. George III escaped from the clutches of a narrow Whig aristocracy by hitching the fortunes of the monarchy to the younger Pitt and public opinion, and by abandoning its own pretensions. The parallel is of course as dangerous as it is enlightening since Britain had a parliamentary tradition and a 'Glorious Revolution' behind it, but it is salutary to be reminded that this country, too, faced to a lesser degree, the problems confronting the continental monarchies.

While secular monarchies centralised and tightened their discipline the Papal monarchy suffered growing slackness and loss of prestige. Discipline among the clergy was rarely enforced:

> The bishops easily and without a sense of guilt violate the law of residence leaving the post assigned to them by the holy laws. Boredom drives them from their dioceses.

The church was looked upon as a convenient source of employment for the younger sons of the nobility in all countries, particularly where an exclusive aristocracy shunned trade. Thus although an agnostic, Talleyrand could become a bishop and a majority of French bishops were in fact aristocrats by 1789. The spritual qualifications of Talleyrand might be judged from the words of Mirabeau:

> The Abbé de Périgord would sell his soul for money: and he would be right, for he would be exchanging dung for gold.

The higher clergy were hated for the tithes they took and the land they held and this was particularly the case in Catholic countries where intolerance of other religions added to the tensions.

The pervading intellectual view of religion was both anticlerical and sceptical. A century without religious enthusiasm, especially after the decline of Jansenism, had left churches flaccid and open to criticism. In Russia church lands were nationalised by Catherine without protest and everywhere church wealth attracted unfavourable comment.

Nonetheless the church remained immensely strong. The opposition to Joseph's reform in Austria shows the strength of popular catholicism away from the cynical court and towns. In Russia as the nobility moved towards French culture the rest of Russia strengthened its links with a cultural heritage founded on orthodox christianity. Even in France hatred of the hierarchy by no means implied similar feelings towards parish priests who shared peasant hardships.

Reform movements were not absent. The influence of Febronius in the German lands and the work of Wesley in England showed the ability of the church to renew itself from within.

The Roman Catholic church was then as now the major religious force in Europe. The Pope, by virtue of his Papal lands was a temporal as well as spiritual prince and the Papacy saw its temporal independence as the best protection for its spiritual sway. The Papal rule could hardly be called effective since the Papal lands lapsed into greater poverty during the century and it is doubtful whether the Pope's spiritual power gained anything from his temporal rule: on the contrary it probably diminished as a result. The claims of an exclusively Italian body stirred up an anti-Papal movement within the German churches led by Febronius. Certainly Papal pretensions in many fields had suffered severe blows in the past century. The rise of non-catholic powers like Russia and Prussia and the decline of Spain and Austria weakened its international influence.

> The Pope is an old neglected idol in his niche. He is at present the chief almoner of kings. His thunderbolts are no more. . .

Italy itself lay far from the real centres of international power and conflict. Everywhere, too, Catholic monarchs attempting to reform their patrimonies found that the church was a major obstacle.

The absolutist monarchs denied the Pope temporal power within their lands not only because such authority was an insult to their absolutism but because it stood in the way of major reforms. Most would have agreed with Voltaire;

No law made by the Church should ever have the least force unless expressly sanctioned by government.

The greatest victory of the Catholic powers had been their joint insistence on the dissolution of the Jesuit order. Absolutists with pretensions to enlightenment saw the church as a privileged target which the aristocrats would not defend and they themselves saw it simply as a spiritual police force, a state department of absolutism. They might agree with Rousseau in the Social Contract that

> . . .there is purely civil profession of faith. . .fixed. . .not with the precision of religious dogmas but treating them as a body of social sentiments without which no man can be either good citizen or faithful subject.

Or they would echo Napoleon, 'Men who do not believe in God, one does not govern them, one shoots them'. Leopold of Tuscany, Joseph's brother, had abolished the Inquisition, suppressed some monasteries, taxed the richer clergy for the benefit of the poorer and forbidden appeals to Rome without permission. Charles III of Spain reduced the Inquisition's power, prevented the publication of Papal Bulls without permission and, like Joseph, claimed the right to choose bishops in his territories. Thus in 1789 the Papacy and its powers were probably weaker than for several centuries.

Absolutists ruling over non-Catholic territories naturally found their problems less acute but their attitude to the Churches was similar. Frederick the Great, a non-believer, plagiarising Voltaire said, 'man is. . .an unnoticeable atom in relation to the universe'; but he saw the churches as useful adjuncts to the state. He tolerated all religions on the grounds that all were equally foolish and because such toleration encouraged immigration. Joseph too was tolerant:

> Half and half methods are not my line. Either full liberty of worship or the expulsion of all who do not share your beliefs. . . That souls may not be damned after death, it is proposed to expel them and to forfeit all the advantages

we could derive from excellent cultivators and good subjects during their life. (*Joseph to Maria Theresa*)

Catherine shared Frederick's attitude to religion and had used
the proceeds of secularised church lands not, like Joseph, to
set up schools, asylums and hospitals, but to reward her
favourites.

The weakness of the church among the educated classes
made it particularly vulnerable as revolution approached and
the success of sustained attacks on the church were splendid
examples to those who wished to see the destruction of other
privileged bodies. But the real danger to the church lay not so
much in the threat from the revolutionaries since its mass
support was unquestionable; the real danger lay in the possibility that the church would, under attack, seek refuge with
those other privileged classes and organisations in mere
reaction, rather than seek to find a new link with those
sections of the community which were drifting away from it.

Part Two :
The Revolt of The Individual

CHAPTER FIVE

Ferment of Ideas

Ideas, like societies, are in a constant state of flux and although the eighteenth century is often characterised as an almost classical period of order in its social, political, philosophical and artistic aspects, this order was being questioned long before 1780. Questioning of this order sprang from the lines of thought opened up by the Enlightenment, and long before the French revolution signalled the triumph of bourgeois individualism in its political and legal aspirations, other developments in other fields had shown how the individual was breaking out of stultifying conventions in the composition of music, the painting of pictures and the writing of poetry. Even in the sphere of economics the individual was being freed from the checks and controls of another era.

The Physiocrats were men of experience in business and administration and many, like Turgot, worked for the absolutist governments of their states. But although they worked for absolutists, in attempting to remedy financial ills by creating a better fiscal system and breaking down the whole system of tolls, tariffs and fiscal privileges which hampered trade, they aided the individual capitalist, the man of enterprise who was not a privileged guild member, or landowner with toll rights. The Physiocrats reasoned, and in this they were direct heirs of the Enlightenment, that society, and thus its financial arrangements, should be based on the nature of man and that the basis of the natural order was the right of property. The king must ensure the protection of this right and that of free competition. The link between king and people must be an equitable taxation system. Hence the fundamental tenet of the physiocratic creed was the Land Tax which being based on property was the only natural tax. From this flowed the tax reforms which we have seen those imbued with physiocratic ideals trying to carry out, rescuing the individual from privileged and feudal imposts on his enterprise.

Thus although the physiocrats served 'despots' their main effort was directed towards the individual in his effort to be free, and physiocratic ideals naturally appealed to the industrial and commercial sections of the bourgeoisie who were not themselves members of privileged trading or guild bodies. Naturally, too, the corollary of this economic freedom was the granting of other freedoms since the new ideas put a premium on initiative, self-help and self-education. The physiocrats hoped thus to establish individual freedom under absolutism. The fact that this could not occur was hardly the fault of men like Turgot. The physiocrats had the greatest influence in Great Britain through Adam Smith who read le Mercier de la Rivière's work *L'ordre naturel et essentiel des sociétés politiques* of 1767.

The attempt to find the 'natural and essential' order of society was not confined solely to economists and without doubt Rousseau, who died in 1778, had the most lasting effect on the philosophy of individualism, liberalism and the Romantic movement which was its artistic counterpart. Rousseau had rejected the 'artificial' society he saw around him, a society based on the civilisation of man through artifice, by accepted rules, conventional ways and the improvement of what nature had left so unreasonably unfinished. He broke away from the immediate past by his optimism about man's nature, and his perfectibility if correctly trained. His book *Émile* is an attempt to suggest a system of education capable of producing a man able to live a perfect life within a civilised society. The education, and Rousseau's ideal society, are based on Rousseau's reading of man's character as it naturally was, just as the physiocrats based their fiscal system on their reading of man's real nature. In the *Contrat Social* Rousseau was not describing a blueprint for a society but a political system which might have justified men giving up their natural freedom. For Rousseau, it often seems, believed that even his perfect society was inferior to a state of nature. His state was an attempt to solve the age-old problem of the relationship of the individual to the state by the novel 'general will' by which the sum of all individual desires can be transformed into a general desire without damage to the individual will.

> Some form of association must be found as a result of which the whole strength of the community will be enlisted for the protection of the person and property of each constituent member, in such a way that each, when united to his fellows, renders obedience to his own will and remains as free as he was before.
> ...the complete alienation by each associate member to the community of all his rights. For since each has made surrender of himself without reservation, the resultant conditions are the same for all; and because they are the same for all, it is in the interest of none to make them onerous to his fellows.

For Rousseau the important thing was to preserve the inviolability of the individual and some of his own ideas were to be taken up by the theorists of the French Revolution, by St Simonian socialists, and English Unitarians and Utilitarians like Bentham and James Mill. The insistence on the goodness (more akin to innocence), perfectibility and inviolability of the individual is the prime element in Rousseau's thought and he was, unlike Voltaire, an enemy to absolutist systems of government, Kingship above all;

> Everything, it is true, works to one end, but that end is not the public happiness, and the very strength of the executive continually operates to the disadvantage of the state.

Thus he was in a sense an enemy to the physiocrats yet in a more fruitful way he was their counterpart, and although he would have hated the idea, for he believed that commerce led to enslavement, his theories were to materially aid the attainment of power by the bourgeoisie.

The other most useful aspect of Rousseau's thought was his insistence that the most valuable aspect of man's psychology was his emotional capacity. For Rousseau the fault of the eighteenth century lay in over-civilisation so that the natural goodness of which man was capable was warped and smothered. 'Sensibility' was the new key word. Rousseau was not, of course, entirely a pioneer. The 'noble savage' was a commonplace and men have often believed that man nearest to nature was man nearest to goodness. The myth has been popular from the time of Captain Cook to D. H. Lawrence and beyond. The 'back to nature' movement even affected the Court of Versailles where it became popular for the Queen and her ladies to live like Dresden shepherdesses in 'Le Petit Hameau'. It was Rousseau, however, intoxicated with virtue, who really inspired the development, helping to unleash a whole new artistic movement which broke away from tradition and based itself on the sensibilities of individuals rather than on acceptable poetic and musical formulae. The movement was to gain sway in the nineteenth century reaching its apogee in the romantic Paris Bohemians. But it was already present in the *Sturm und Drang* poets and playwrights of Rhineland Germany. Here the revolt against convention began amongst the young, and the young Goethe, Herder and Schiller whose play *The Robbers* (1781), with its insistence on the goodness of 'natural' man symbolised the whole movement, were its leaders. D'Holbach's *Système de la Nature* contains the words:

> Return, truant child, return to nature, humanity and yourself strew flowers along the road of life.

This insistence on the importance of what the individual had to say in art is visible in the careers of Haydn, Mozart and Beethoven, for in a crude way we see in their careers the coming of age of the artist as individual. Haydn (1732—1809) spent almost all his musical career in the service of aristocratic patrons who largely dictated the nature of his output, but towards the end of his life he was establishing himself as a favourite of the middle class public. Mozart (1756—1791) was for a very short time in the service of the Archbishop of Salzburg but he felt even more than Haydn the need for that freedom of expression denied him by the demands of a single patron. Hence Mozart's financial position was always unstable and he died in poverty, but his musical style heralded the Romantic period. Even in his private life Mozart was a standard bearer of the new individualism, for he was a member of the Masonic societies of Vienna and his Opera *The Magic Flute,* besides being a great work of art, is an allegory of the Masonic movement, attacking the forces of superstition and tyranny, and asserting that the individual's character, not his background, is the only ground on which he should be judged. Finally with Beethoven (1770—1827) the beginnings of the Romantic movement proper in music can be seen particularly in a perspective that looks back to Haydn and Mozart. His music contains a new freedom of expression and subject matter. Beethoven applauded the French Revolution and even, for a time, Napoleon, whom he temporarily saw as the Messiah of European liberalism. A discussion of the Romantic movement is not in order here but it will be seen that the artist was not only developing a more individual style but was also freeing himself from the aristocratic patron. The nineteenth century artist was to rely on a wider public and hence was to become at one time more individually free and more dependent.

The year 1781 is important, not only because it saw the publication of *The Robbers*, but because it saw the emergence of Immanuel Kant's *Critique of Pure Reason*. Kant attempted to reconcile two philosophical schools opposed for centuries: the rationalists' insistence that reason was the basis of knowledge and provided the answer to all problems, and the empiricist principle that direct observation was the basis of a knowledge which could never therefore be absolute. Kant admitted that personal experience is the basis of knowledge but that we possess a capacity for reason which imposes patterns on our thoughts.

When we abstract from all the personal differences of rational creatures and equally from all the content of their private ends, we get an idea of a complete and systematic-

ally connected whole of all ends. . .in other words a
kingdom of ends.

These patterns become reality only with experience and
observation. Thus Kant, again like his contemporaries and
immediate forbears, broke through barriers to progress by
putting man 'as he is', both a reasoning and observing animal,
at the centre of his thought. His works on moral and political
philosophy owe much to Rousseau and like Rousseau's work
they are part of a general reappraisal of all thought which at
the end of the eighteenth century completed the work of the
enlightenment and opened new vistas into the nineteenth
century.

There was yet another way in which the new individualism
of Rousseau, Kant and others was materially to alter the
European world. Rousseau's 'general will', which Kant
accepted in modified form, enabled the state to exert a greater
hold on its members since the obligation to obey the 'general
will' was morally more compulsive than the obligation to
obey a mere monarch, who had been deprived of the
sanctions of Divine Right by the decline in religious feeling.
In Rousseau this obligation becomes almost fascist when he
talks of the civil articles of religious faith.

> Though it has no power to compel anyone to believe them,
> it (the state) can banish from the state all who fail to do
> so, not on grounds of impiety, but as lacking in social
> sense.

Such a sense of obligation was extreme, and Rousseau's
community is hardly a nation-state but the growing national
consciousness of Europeans when wedded to the Rousseauist
obligation of associate members of the community was to
greatly heighten the concept of the 'fatherland' and to make
serving it a 'religious' duty.

Meanwhile Kant's assertion that rights could belong only
to rational beings destroyed the foundations of a society
based on hereditary rights or status, the society of the Three
Estates, and obliged men to look for new *raisons d'être* for
society's existence.

These trends converged in the concept of the nation state which was to be one of the most potent forces for change in the Europe of the nineteenth century. The burdens imposed on individuals in its name should not blind us to the fact that it also is a result of the revolt of the individual.

In studying the individual as he is, the thinkers of the late eighteenth century prepared the way for the essentially practical rather than philosophical nineteenth century. The nineteenth century hero was the man of action. His individualism was, however, difficult to control and the nineteenth century man was to travel in many different and contradictory directions.

CHAPTER SIX

The Fall of
The French Monarchy

After the fall of Calonne the monarchy attempted once more to avoid an Estates General, but the failure of de Brienne, Calonne's successor, to accommodate the Notables and the intransigency of the *Parlements* precipitated a crisis. A royal edict struck at the power of the *Parlements* too late. Throughout the provinces *parlements,* officials of royal courts and royal financiers, rebelled. The Assembly of the clergy offered a smaller 'free gift' than usual and demanded a States General. Intendants and commanders of the army expressed doubt as to their ability to keep order, though whether from policy or fear is questionable. The King agreed to call a States General for May 1789, and recalled Necker as Controller-General because the latter was popular, though he lacked any other qualification.

When the *Parlement* was recalled by Necker it declared that the States General should meet according to its old constitution, giving equal representation to the three Estates, which as before should meet separately. This demand exposed the spuriousness of the *Parlement's* claims to stand for the people, for had the States General met according to the old 1614 constitution, the two privileged houses might have been expected constantly to outvote the Third Estate. The opposition to the *Parlement's* demands set the seal on the nature of the revolution as a struggle between privileged and unprivileged.

During the months preceding the States General censorship was suspended and the release of ideas thus occasioned showed for the first time an apparent universality of demands and ideals. The most significant pamphlet was the Abbé Siéyés *What is the Third Estate?* which proclaimed the importance and ambition of that bourgeois section of the Estate which was to largely dictate the future of the revolution. The monarchy seemed to recognise the importance of the class by doubling its representation to 600, so that its numbers would equal the combined vote of the other Estates. Unfortunately the King's action was reluctantly taken and would remain meaningless unless he also declared that the Estates should vote by head, by a single count, instead of by order, by Estate, which would perpetuate a privileged majority. Such half-hearted moves and weakness of principle were soon to destroy all confidence in the King.

The suffrage was granted to all those over twenty-five paying taxes but as voting was indirect in the Third Estate only the wealthier were really represented. Few nobles were chosen by the Third Estate though Mirabeau was an exception, as was the Abbé Siéyés. In the Clerical Estate, the lower clergy, and in the Estate of the lay aristocracy, provincial nobles predominated, in protest against the growing pre-revolutionary exclusiveness of the *noblesse de cour*.

During the elections committees were permitted to send *cahiers* or lists of grievances and demands for discussion, but as these were sorted out at each stage of the complicated election process, the grievances of the poorer people were ignored. Some were heard in August 1789 during the agrarian revolution but many remained unread until this century. The delegates never intended that revolution should reach the lowest orders.

The causes of the French Revolution are manifold and complex. Many of the causes were well-known; the inefficiency of the government; the inability of the monarch to reform because of the opposition of privileged interests; the aristocratic reaction, which threatened the social position of the middle class and the financial position of large sections of the peasantry; the divisions within the classes. In 1789 the price of grain fell and this hit those peasants who farmed for the market and who also paid rents since these continued to rise. This hurt the lessee farmer badly but it also reflected on the labourer for fewer were being employed. Finally in 1788/9 a bad harvest was followed by a fierce winter which swelled the already considerable influx of poor and un-employed into the towns. The towns could offer little work but the price of bread increased disastrously. Thus in the towns, already hit by the Free Trade Treaty of 1786 with England, a revolutionary situation existed.

At the start of the States General there were at least four dissatisfied broad groups; the aristrocracy, divided against itself between Versailles and the provinces; the bourgeoisie, which was soon to display alarming divisions; the *sans-culottes*, highly volatile, concentrated and with immediate 'bread and butter' demands which might conflict with the economic liberalism of the bourgeoisie; the peasantry, land-hungry and internally divided, whose demands could hardly be satisfied without interference with property. It was obvious that the revolution would have a tendency to swing to the left and it is clear that there was not, and never could be, a single French Revolution.

Much in 1789 depended on the character of Louis XVI, but he lacked nearly all the qualities demanded by the hour. He had already, on more than one occasion, shown his unwillingness to risk a break with the privileged orders or to support a reforming minister properly. The monarchy, if it was to survive, had to lead, or at least work with the leaders, but Louis was unwilling to give up his hunting. His idea of firmness was to be stubborn, of flexibility to turn tail and run. Physical courage he had, but not moral courage, which left too much to be supplied by a woman, who, because she was Austrian, would have been unpopular whatever her character.

The King's weakness soon became apparent. No lead was given on whether the Estates should vote by head or by order, and when the nobility attempted to settle the matter itself the Third Estate declared itself the National Assembly on June 17th. The King, urged by the Queen and the court nobility, asserted himself by closing the Estate's meeting place 'for repairs'. The result was the *Tennis Court Oath* in which the Assembly, already joined by many clergy, declared that it would not separate before France had a constitution.

When the King, three days later, again tried to regain the initiative by ordering the Assembly to vote by Estates and outlined a legislative programme obviously influenced by the nobility, the Assembly refused. Louis, unwilling to use force himself, ordered the Estates to meet together on June 27th realising that a majority of the clergy and a sizable minority of the nobility had already accepted a *fait accompli*.

This incident is symptomatic of why the monarchy failed. Louis convinced enough people that he could not be trusted to accept the changes willingly. He had shown that he was open to court influence, but more dangerously he had shown great weakness. When a body in power loses its nerve, and fails to use force to sustain itself, it is in danger of defeat. Moreover, Louis weakened considerably that conciliatory section of the Third Estate which hoped for reform under monarchical aegis.

The deputies of the Third Estate, two thirds of whom were men with considerable legal training, generally aimed at a society based on enlightened principles of legal equality, the inviolability of property, a share in power and an end to local particularism and economic controls. Members of the Third Estate differed in method rather than in principle. Such divisions as there were concerned the question of whether the king and the privileged could be trusted to compromise or whether they must be treated as enemies. The early stage of the revolution was something of a blow to those who believed in conciliation. Already the Assembly was dividing and the Breton club, later to be the Jacobin club, was showing radical teeth.

It was soon clear that the court was preparing another coup. Troops were moved up to the vicinity of Paris, and, although the Assembly petitioned for their recall, it made no other move. The decisive action came from Paris. On July 11th Necker was dismissed and the petition rejected. Three days later the Bastille fell and, again fearing to use force, Louis withdrew his troops. Louis blessed the revolt in person when he rode into Paris and accepted the new government of Paris, which had created itself from the Paris Electors, and the bourgeois police force, the National Guard, which it had set up, and which in August achieved permanency under

D

Lafayette.

The significance of the Bastille itself is largely symbolic, but the importance of what happened in Paris that July is not. While the Assembly had done nothing, the middle classes of Paris had seized the initiative and used the mob to defend the revolution from counter-revolution. The provinces had simultaneously done the same and Bordeaux, Poitiers, Marseilles, Nancy and many other cities similarly created out of middle-class revolution and *sansculotte* starvation a whole new system of provincial government, and saved the Assembly. Everywhere royal government collapsed; the new town governments became semi-autonomous units, exercising control over not only the urban, but also the rural community, which supplied its food.

Once the Assembly saw that the middle class had assumed control, and that property would be defended by a bourgeois militia, it accepted the revolt, but in the rural disturbances of July and August it saw more dangerous events. The sporadic outbursts of early summer soon grew into serious agrarian revolts affecting Northern France, the Île de France and Provence. Attacks were made on châteaux to destroy the charters which gave the landlords their feudal rights. Where enclosures existed they were torn down. This *Jacquerie* was followed by the 'Great Fear' of late July and early August, when rumours of bands of brigands roaming the countryside and destroying the harvest became widespread. They were only rumours but they increased the hatred of the aristocracy who, many believed, were involved in a plot to destroy the revolution.

The Assembly greatly deprecated the rural disorders as likely to lead to an attack on property. They dared not use royal forces against the insurgents, since to do so might put a weapon in the King's hands and to use the National Guard would be to risk dividing the nation. In the end the situation was saved by the 'spontaneous generosity' of August 4th, when first the Vicomte de Noailles, then the Duc d'Aiguillon rose to abandon their feudal revenues. In a night compounded of generosity, calculation, self-abasement and cynicism the nobility gave up those privileges they had so long defended; privileged provinces, towns and corporations followed. In the end the generosity was to become a little less spontaneous; compensation was to be paid and some burdens were left to be abolished by the Jacobins.

Thus by August the absolute power of the King had been destroyed, as had many of the privileges that absolutism had striven to end. It remained for the revolutionaries to build, and for that, confidence, co-operation and quiet were needed.

The story of the Assembly is one of a constant shift to the left and of an effort on the part of the succession of groups which controlled the Assembly to come to an accommodation with the King. But events had already demonstrated the King's unwillingness to compromise with even the most moderate revolutionaries, whom he feared more than the demagogues of Paris, or the reactionary émigrés. The more the King procrastinated, the more the deputies distrusted him so that the ministers found themselves as little trusted as the King, even though he himself refused to work honestly with them. Such a situation eventually led to the Assembly's impotence which opened the door to control of the revolution by force. Most of the deputies were agreed on the essential aims of the revolution, which hardly differed from 1789 to 1794, but political opposition was always tempted to dally with the Parisian mob. Yet, if neither the King nor the aristocracy could be trusted, the Assembly had to rely on the masses.

The first trial of strength after August 4th centred on the royal veto. Those, like Mirabeau, who wished the monarchy to have an active part in the new constitution urged that the King have an absolute veto, but such was the general distrust of the King and his Queen that his veto was merely suspensive. When the King refused to promulgate the 'Declaration of the Rights of Man' which the assembly had been busy preparing from late July to late August, and also refused to promulgate the decree of August 4th, the situation grew tense. Radicals in the Assembly were already linking up with elements in Paris and when the Flanders Regiment seemed to insult the revolution at a banquet Paris again, as in July, took a hand. On October 5th demonstrators, mainly women, poured out of Paris on the road to Versailles. Louis was

forced to return to Paris with his wife and son. More significant, perhaps, was the fact that the Assembly followed.

Henceforth co-operation between the King and the revolution seemed impossible. Marie Antoinette and Louis began
their clandestine negotiations with Vienna. The Assembly
transferred to the heady atmosphere of Paris where already
moderation seemed criminal. Over twenty deputies, those
who had failed to secure co-operation between the conservative and revolutionary forces, left the Assembly. Their
predicament was appreciated by Mirabeau, the next to
attempt to save the situation for the monarch without com-
promising the revolution. Mirabeau was a sincere revolutionary, but to him it was vital, if the social order was not
to dissolve and the monarchy collapse, that the King must be
given a role in the new constitution and therefore in creating
it. In August 1789 he secretly entered the King's service,
determined to build trust between King and Assembly. He
knew that, without that trust, opposition would seek aid in
Paris, with consequences which none in the essentially conservative Assembly wanted. But the King never worked
sincerely with Mirabeau and the latter's own reputation
awakened unhelpful scruples in the minds of the deputies.
Thus Mirabeau failed to secure the King's right to choose his
ministers from a majority in the Assembly, and the new constitution of 1791 reverted to the old orthodoxy of separation
of powers. When the new constitution came into being the
ministers were treated as lackeys of an untrustworthy King,
while the King's control over the Assembly was limited to a
suspensive veto, the use of which antagonised the deputies.
Mirabeau's plea,

> Ce n'est point donc pour son avantage particulier que le
> monarque intervient dans la législation mais pour l'intérêt
> même du peuple

went unheeded.

The Assembly itself, however, was in difficulties. Unrest in
the country continued, most dangerously in the towns where
bourgeois revolutionary forces faced the old oligarchical
municipal authorities. Incidents were rarely punished by the

Assembly, which could hardly defend the old order against the new. But insults to the King's officers, civil or, as in many cases, military and naval were insults to the King, who grew more offended with the Assembly. Such failure to deal effectively with violence must also have actively encouraged it.

Meanwhile during discussions of the constitution an attempt had to be made to reduce the National Debt, and the Church reaped the reward of its unpopularity. The question of what to do with church property created new schisms in French society to add to those class and political ones already appearing.

In December 1790 four hundred million livres worth of Crown lands and church property were put on the market and these assets were used to back the issue of credit notes, or *assignats*. The land itself was largely bought up by wealthy middle class men rather than the peasants who really needed it. Later the religious orders were abolished (February 1790).

The church opposed these measures bitterly and some laymen were shocked by the anti-clerical feeling behind measures they conscientiously accepted, but the Civil Constitution of the clergy in May was looked upon as an attack, not on the church's temporal power, but its spiritual power. Redistribution of dioceses and parishes, even the election of clerics were little opposed, but the clergy insisted that a priest's induction must be conferred by a spiritual authority. The Assembly opposed Papal 'interference' and rejected the clergy's alternative of a synod which might be a rival to the Assembly. The clergy asked the Pope to allow them to accept the Civil constitution which in August received royal assent. Papal delay led the Assembly to exact an oath of allegiance to the state, which split the church for ten years into jurors and non jurors, and added religious schism to the burdens of moderate revolutionaries. The King was smitten with remorse, while in the provinces the Assembly's attempt to conciliate opinion and preserve unity foundered on the non jurors' reactionary royalism, the revolutionary antagonism to non jurors and Papal opposition to the Civil constitution.

So, as the Assembly worked at its new constitution the country divided into ever more fiercely antagonistic groups.

Moderates of all kinds became increasingly worried and the radicals of 1789 became the conservatives of 1790 and 1791. Talleyrand and Siéyés formed the 1789 club and tried to organise support for the King; further left the still moderate Jacobin club was largely controlled by men of conservative opinion, but in Paris in 1790 the Cordelier Club was formed, named after the Cordelier district of Paris, which under Danton had already challenged the 1789 government of the Hôtel de Ville. Through such cheap and open clubs as the Cordeliers, through newspapers and cafe-table demagogues the principles of the 'Declaration of the Rights of Man' were absorbed, and acquired a tinge of poor men's aspirations. That 'Men are born and remain free and equal in rights' was accepted without the restriction of those rights to 'liberty, property, security and resistance to oppression' which the wealthy lawyers at Versailles had intended. In fact the poorer people of Paris put different interpretations on many things. To the deputies, for example, the Le Chapelier Law of June 1791 was simply a measure to abolish guilds, of either capital or labour. To the poor it was to become a piece of class legislation.

However, much of the unrest was still below the surface and between October 1789 and June 1791 the revolution seemed to assume a fruitful quiet. The National Assembly, which because of its duties became known as the Constituent Assembly, was engaged on the rebuilding of France and was consciously aiming to create a united nation, trying to avoid schism or recrimination.

The new constitution, accepted by the King in September 1791 created a single chamber legislature, the Legislative Assembly, which was to sit for two years and which could not be dissolved by the King. The isolation and independence of the Assembly was further guaranteed by the refusal to allow the King to choose ministers from the Assembly. The powers of the King, now 'of the French' rather than 'of France', as commander of the forces and treaty maker were weakened by the necessity for the ministers' participation and the ratification of the Assembly. Finally the King was allowed a suspensive veto which earned him the pejorative title 'M. Véto'.

That the Assembly was moderate was demonstrated by the suffrage provisions which made the electorate smaller than that which elected the Assembly itself. The vote was confined to men over twenty-five who paid the equivalent of three days wages. But these 'active' citizens' votes, over four million, were diluted by the system of voting and this was closely connected to the organisation of local government.

The events of August 1789 forced the creation of a decentralised system of local government. France was divided into eighty-three *Départements,* which were divided into Districts, themselves divided into *Communes* dealing with local affairs. Officers of the *Commune* were chosen by all active citizens but elections to the district, departmental and National Assemblies were indirect. Active citizens chose an electoral college which picked the deputies, and these electors had to be paying the equivalent of ten days wages in taxes. Potential local office-holders had to be similarly endowed. More important was the fact that election meetings were usually held when poorer people were working.

As might be expected, the *Communes* proved more radical than the *Départements* and this was to be particularly true of Paris, but the chief importance of the local government system was the autonomous power enjoyed by these local government bodies.

The lawyers, who formed the majority of deputies in the Third Estate, were to crown administrative with legal reform. The old system of overlapping jurisdiction was swept away and a new uniform organisation was put in its place. Many legal appointments became elective and the barbarism of punishments, already falling into disuse, was abandoned. Capital punishment was not abolished but it was at least to be expedited according to the scientific principles of 'Madame Guillotine'.

Further valuable work was achieved in the creation of a single direct tax to replace the old multiplicity of indirect taxes. Unfortunately growing disorder, peasant unwillingness to accept that a revolutionised society required taxes, and administrative incompetence, meant that little money was actually collected. Finally the Assembly swept away aristocratic exclusiveness in the armed forces, though aristocratic predominance was only ended with the war and the republic.

Unfortunately the new constitution had a very short life, for by the time it came into force the monarchy had committed suicide. Schemes for the flight of the King had been planned by the Comte d'Artois and the émigrés for over a year but Louis had resisted them. Mirabeau urged the King to flee to the provinces and raise their conservatism against radical Paris in order to win back the initiative, but Louis instead fled towards Austria, demonstrating his guilt. The Pope's opposition to the Civil constitution of the clergy led to the royal flight on June 21st, 1791.

The Republican movement became widespread and a major crisis point of the revolution was reached. The Assembly, equating Republicanism with attack on property, and determined to end the revolution by introducing its moderate constitution, pursued the absurd fiction that the King had been kidnapped, and voted to exonerate him. Thus both the monarchy and the Assembly now merited the odium of the left. In July, Republicanism acquired its first martyrs. The popular clubs of Paris organised a petition for the King's deposition. The meeting on the Champ de Mars was peaceful but the government of Paris, nervous, sent a detachment of the National Guard which opened fire, killing about fifty people. Repression followed and in its wake the apparent unity of the nation collapsed in further class divisions.

The leaders of the bourgeoisie, even those who had been the radicals of the Assembly like Barnave now sought an accommodation with the Crown. Symbolic of this change was the open split in the Jacobin club, which the great majority of deputies left to form the Feuillant club. Barnave now negotiated with the King on the basis of the conservative revision of the constitution, but the majority of the Assembly despite its fears, rejected most of Barnave's suggestions, since in a choice between revolution and counter-revolution they knew there was no choice.

The new constitution was already doomed. Varennes had killed the monarchy, Champ de Mars had set Paris against the new constitution, the events in Paris had opened a wedge between the classes and there was no possibility that

Feuillant leaders, driven by fear of social revolution to negotiate with the Crown, could find common ground with the *sansculottes* and their popular leaders like Danton, Desmoulins, and, behind them, Hébert, Chaumette and Hanriot. Moreover, the ordinary deputy had shown that while he feared social revolution and dictation from Paris he feared royalist reaction more, and without a doubt his instincts were correct. The final act of the old Assembly was to pass the self-denying Ordinance, preventing any of its members from sitting in the new Legislative Assembly and denying that body experienced leadership.

The new Legislative Assembly met on October 1st 1791. Although it had shed the extreme right wing of the Constituent Assembly its attitudes were largely those of the majority of the body it replaced.

Of the 745 deputies 334 joined the Feuillant club and 136 the Jacobin club. Others lined themselves up behind a group calling themselves Girondins whose leaders were members of the Jacobin club. The Girondins, also known as Brissotins because of their association with Brissot, had many very talented leaders such as Mme. Roland, Gensonne, Ducos and Vergniaud.

Such groups were rather illusory, however, for the majority of deputies were remarkably untrustworthy in their voting, even if they did belong to a club, and the majority of members, the Centre or Plain, attached to no group in particular, voted as a result of many pressures. But, like their predecessors, they feared reaction more than revolution and hence would not trust any group which had the King's apparent support. As the groups which achieved power needed the King's support they in their time became conservatives. Thus the shift to the left continued and the Plain supported the group to the left which looked the most dangerous or best organised. The group which commanded these attributes was that centred around the Jacobin club, with its closely linked provincial counterparts, its uncompromising ideology and its close links with the leaders of sansculottism, entrenched in the electoral assemblies of Paris.

In the Assembly the Brissotin wing of the club predominated, in Paris the Cordelier wing. The Brissotins soon took the offensive in the Assembly, leading the votes for the deprivation of non-jurors and for the declaration of all émigrés as traitors, both of which Louis vetoed. It was noticeable however that in areas controlled by Jacobins Louis' veto was ignored. The Girondins were attempting to put pressure on the King for their installation as ministers, but their major weapon in this game was war.

Brissot, and particularly Vergniaud, began a campaign for war against, not only the émigrés, but also against Vienna and for territorial gain. 'Aux armes: citoyens, hommes libres, défendez votre liberté'. 'Notre revolution a jeté les plus vives alarmes autour de tous les trônes'. The anti-monarchical tone of such propaganda was damaging to an already threadbare throne for the fear of an aristocratic reaction was widespread and no one trusted King or Queen. Such fears were justified, for Louis and his wife were in constant contact with Leopold.

To the Feuillants war, as the quickest way to a republic, would be disastrous but the King did not listen to them and their influence over public opinion was destroyed by the propaganda of the Girondins who persuaded moderate men that peace was counter-revolutionary. It was the King, however, who helped the Girondins by declaring war in March 1792 on the Elector of Trier in whose territory the émigrés were concentrated. Believing that war might unite his country behind the throne and that a war against an Elector of the Holy Roman Empire would involve Leopold, the Court attached itself to the Girondins, and in April war was declared on Austria.

The Feuillants were now in disarray, the Girondins took over some ministries and joined the establishment, the Jacobins alone remained pure and undefiled. In April they were unpopular, for the left wing element of the Jacobin club, the 'Mountain' as they came to be known, led by Robespierre, Desmoulins and Danton saw the war as a royal trap. The Jacobin club divided for the second time, and the Jacobins as history knows them, prepared to assume the revolutionary leadership.

The war was a disaster. Feeling rose against the 'Austrian committee' at the Tuileries palace. Fanned by rumours that the King was in touch with the enemy and that aristocratic officers were betraying the common soldier, feeling in Paris grew to fever pitch. In June the King dismissed his Brissotin ministers, with the result that a mob swarmed into the Tuileries and forced the King to wear the cap of liberty. In July the invading general, the Duke of Brunswick, issued a declaration threatening vengeance on Paris if harm should come to Louis, and promising to restore him to full power. The return of the Feuillant Lafayette to Paris from the front in an apparent attempt to save the King by use of the army led Girondins and Jacobins to call for the removal of the King. 'Enfin tous les maux qu'on s'efforce d'accumuler sur nos têtes . . . c'est le nom seul du Roi qui en est le prétexte ou la cause'. The Brissotins' republicanism was merely tactical but that of Paris was not. On August 10th a mob seized the Tuileries and the Assembly, not daring and probably not willing to protect them, imprisoned the King and his family in the Temple prison.

The rising was largely the work of the forty-eight 'sections' into which Paris was divided and each of which contained an electoral assembly of active citizens. These had become controlled by caucuses of men able to spare time for radical politics. Moreover in July they had begun admitting passive citizens to their deliberations. The arrival of provincial National Guards in Paris, including the famous Marseillais, and the fear of counter-revolution which affected the most moderate property owners after the Duke of Brunswick's declaration, completed the revolutionary situation of August. The belated attempts of the Girondins to prevent the fall of the monarchy, which they had done so much to bring about, were fruitless and only succeeded in poisoning relations between Girondins and the Revolutionary commune which the sections had created to plan the uprising and which now became the undisputed master of Paris.

To what extent August 10th was Louis' own fault is a matter for endless and fruitless debate. Certainly he lacked all the necessary qualifications for leadership, and totally failed to distinguish his true friends from his courtiers and his enemies. But the role of the monarchy in a revolutionary situation was almost impossible, since any attempt to preserve untouched any freedom of action was bound to be treated with suspicion. The revolution created such divisions in society that only the armed victory of one side could cover over the wounds, and it was the left in France as in Russia in 1917 which was best organised under a banner of almost religious fervour. The Jacobins were the political Methodists of France. Such were the conditions in France in 1792 that these men were able to assume an importance greater than their numbers should have permitted. The fear of counter-revolution so potent that it almost delivered bourgeois France into the hands of the Paris *sansculottes,* the Jacobin shock troops.

The Convention which met in September had 750 members. The majority of them were from the same class as its predecessor, but moderates had found it difficult to vote in the elections and partly for this reason, partly because of the Girondins' new policy, the Girondins formed the conservative section of the Convention. To its left was the Mountain which met at the Jacobin club. The majority of the Convention however remained in the Plain, looking with disfavour on anything which suggested counter-revolution and with fear and disfavour on the Paris radicals. Usually fear overcame disfavour.

The real differences between the Girondins and Jacobins were slight. They were divided by personal rivalries and by the irreversible link of Girondins with monarchy. The Girondins became associated with the idea that the revolution had gone far enough and were forced to seek allies to their right. In this way they lost Paris, fell foul of Danton and allowed the Jacobins to use the *sansculottes'* grievances to get into power.

After the massacres the King's trial next exacerbated the quarrel. The Girondins divided on the issue but gave the Jacobins the opportunity to accuse them of royalism by attempting unavailingly to postpone the execution which occurred on January 21st 1793. Danton, who might have brought the two sides together, found his position increasingly difficult.

CHAPTER SEVEN

The Rise and Fall of The Jacobins

In September a new Assembly, the Convention, was to meet to create a new constitution. But before then a period of confusion ensued. The Girondins asserted themselves quickly, Le Brun, Roland, Servan and Clavière forming a provisional government with the addition of Danton. Such a government was nearly powerless for the Commune overshadowed all. The threat of Brunswick after the fall of Verdun accentuated the panic and fear for the revolution. The rivalry between the Girondin ministers and Paris and the fear of a monarchist fifth column lie behind the massacres of September, when nearly a thousand inmates of Paris' prisons were slaughtered. Whose fault this was no one knew. The Commune, if it started the massacres dared not stop them, the assembly dared not intervene, nor dared the government which at one point was under direct threat from Robespierre and members of the Commune. Danton saved the ministers and also saved France. His leadership and organisational ability sent hundreds of men to the front and although neither the victories of Valmy (September 20th) nor Jémappes (October 6th) were the direct result of Danton's efforts without doubt his spirit helped to save the country.

Sadly, Valmy and Jémappes made it safer for revolutionaries to quarrel and the massacres had envenomed the relations between the Girondins and Paris. In consequence the Girondins moved towards the right and the Jacobins sought closer links with the *sansculottes*.

The Girondins mismanaged their advantages in the

Assembly. The majority of deputies feared Paris and this gave them a predisposition to support the Girondins. But they disliked the attitude of open hostility evinced towards Paris because it threatened the country in time of war. Moreover the Girondins, although never sure whether they were a party or not, alarmed the Plain by insisting on monopolising offices. The constitution put forward by Condorcet was disliked, not only because it was complicated, but because it seemed designed as a class measure to perpetuate Girondin rule.

The war after the successes of the post Jémappes era began to turn sour again. The involvement of Holland and England overstretched resources and soon after a royalist revolt had broken out in La Vendée in March 1793, the commander of the French army, Dumouriez, a prominent Girondin, defected to Austria. The effect was considerable, for in the fevered atmosphere these two events were enough to make accusations of Girondin royalism stick and to make the Girondins commit the error of striking in self-defence at Marat, a critic, revolutionary hero and Jacobin leader. Marat became a martyr, though acquitted of treason, and the Jacobins reverted to street action to get rid of the Girondins. The sections and clubs planned their uprising.

The urban poor were, as in 1789, in distress. Prices rose as the value of the *assignat* plummetted at an increasingly alarming rate. Although the government had temporarily issued decrees for price control in September, these affronts to economic liberalism had soon been removed. The Girondins were loath to retreat from this cardinal revolutionary principle, but the *sansculottes* demanded controls on prices and action against speculators and hoarders. Nor were these demands solely confined to Paris. In Lyons thirty thousand were unemployed and, with war making exports almost impossible, there was no hope of improvement. Demands of provincial *sansculottes* were encouraged by the commissioners sent out in August of 1792 by the ministers and, more significantly, the Commune. In Paris the chief revolutionary force was Jacques Roux and his supporters, known as the enragés, who led the demand for controls.

In many cities throughout France the struggle broke out

between the rich and the poor, in Lyons and Marseilles particularly, and everywhere the rich were called Girondins the poor Jacobins, even where such terms hardly applied. Thus in appearance the struggle between two parties, essentially similar in aim, assumed the colour of class war. In Paris the Jacobins were forced to treat the Enragés with respect. Fearing counter-revolution, seeing that the Girondins were weakening and that a real danger of social revolution existed they joined in the sectional preparation for a coup d'état. On June 2nd the Convention was surrounded and, under protest, it voted to deliver up twenty-nine leading Girondins.

The Jacobins were not social revolutionaries; their principles included economic liberalism. Their political sense, their fear of the Girondins, their realisation that the Girondins prevented the achievement of national unity so necessary to fight the war, all told them to unite with the *sansculottes* to oust the Girondins. But they were determined not to be the servants of the *sansculottes* and their enragé leaders. They knew that Paris was not France and determined to prevent the city from controlling the executive or the Convention. The Convention was only too pleased to accept their protection. Thus the Jacobin period assumes the appearance of a tightrope act in which the government endeavours to win a war by galvanising a nation's resources, to preserve unity yet conciliate the *sansculottes,* and to satisfy Paris yet preserve the control of the Convention.

There was little room for manoeuvre. Not only was there an external war to fight, but the revolt in La Vendée was accompanied by a 'Federalist revolt', part Girondin inspired, in which Brittany, Franche Comté and Normandy seceded, in which Toulon handed itself over to the British navy until December 1793 and in which conservative forces in Lyons and Marseilles held the revolutionaries at bay until August. Meanwhile the economic situation deteriorated without hope of reforms as prices rocketed.

Although a new constitution was introduced it was never implemented, for the situation called for extreme centralisation. The system employed was a development of that used by the Girondins. Two committees of twelve men, those of 'Public Safety' and 'General Security', chosen by and from the Convention, were the effective government. Under them the ministries were mere commissions of civil servants. The Committee of Public Safety soon assumed the chief role and it was to be the jealousy of the other Committee which was to aid in the downfall of the Jacobins. Linking the Committee of Public Safety to the provincial governments, now simplified by the excision of the conservative Departments, were resident *agents nationaux*, and temporary, but more powerful, *Représentatives en Mission*. Their role was to enforce government decrees, help revolutionary forces, curb reactionary forces, conscript and feed the people. Some like Fouché acquired considerable, if not pleasant, reputations. At their disposal they had carbon copies of the Paris Revolutionary Tribunal, a body progressively freed from the irksome duty of having to prove the guilt of the accused.

At the beginning of the Jacobin period conciliation as a way of ending revolutionary strife had to be abandoned and Danton's dismissal from the Committee is a sign of this. The pressure of the enragés and their Jacobin supporters led by Hébert were considerable, as were military and economic pressures.

The Convention, needing Jacobin protection, unwillingly therefore gave in to Committee pressure and step by step gave up economic liberalism via the closure of the Bourse, the abolition of joint stock companies and measures against hoarders and the rich. Later in September Committee and Convention were forced to agree to the 'Maximum', control of prices, while simultaneously the terror deepened as the work of the Tribunal was simplified and the trials of Queen, Girondins and others began. From October to December executions accelerated.

Nevertheless as these steps were taken they were counterbalanced by the execution of enragé-leaders Roux and Varlet, the curbing of the sectional assemblies, wage controls, and first steps towards closer controls of the *Représentatives en Mission* in December (Frimaire by the new revolutionary calendar).[1]

Such measures widened the gulf between the Indulgents,

---

[1] For explanation of the revolutionary calendar, see p.323.

including Danton and Desmoulins who, after the defeat of the Federalists by the end of 1793, felt that conciliation should be tried, and the Hébertist enragés who demanded further attacks on the rich and new controls. Their dissension threatened the Committee and in March and April of 1794 (Germinal) first the Hébertists then the Indulgents were tried and executed, Robespierre, a Dantonist by nature having stood clear of trouble. Such a move to curb the Paris hotheads pleased the Convention but that same body heartily deprecated the charges against Danton, whose conciliatory policies they themselves approved of.

The defeat of the Hébertists was followed by the disbandment of the revolutionary army, the curbing of the clubs and the popular societies, (*sansculottes* heirs to the Jacobin clubs) and the dismissal of inspectors of food hoarding. Then the Jacobins destroyed the army of the *sansculottes;* by striking at the clubs as they had earlier weakened the sections they undermined the organisation of the *sansculottes;* by execution they rid themselves of the rivalry of *sansculotte* leaders. The Committee might now seem to be totally in control. Unfortunately by obliterating the political power of the *sansculottes* the Committee had rescued the Convention from the obligation to accept the Jacobin protection while annoying it by the execution of Danton. It only now required the two Committees to quarrel and the dictatorship would break.

Although La Vendée was never wholly quietened by the end of 1793 the Federalist revolt was over and the *raison d'être* of the government by committee rested chiefly on the war. Here too success was undermining its position. The organisational ability of Carnot, the success of the *Amalgame* which had united successfully the old professional and the new citizen armies and the weakness of the Coalition constantly threatened by squabbles over Poland, allowed the Revolutionary armies to cross into foreign territory in late 1793, to defeat the British at Tourcoing in May 1794 and achieve the great revolutionary victory of Fleurus in June which secured Belgium. On the Rhine, in spring, Prussia was angling for peace in order to secure her part in the third Partition of Poland.

Yet the terror continued. The Committee, despite its victories, did not consider the war won, was not convinced of its victory over the *sansculottes* and feared the effects of continuing economic crisis. *Above all, however, the Committee increasingly saw the Revolution as an agency for imposing virtue. The Jacobins had always possessed an air of virtuous proselytism, reminiscent of Methodism, but now Robespierre and St Just had the machinery of the state at their disposal. Robespierre imposed virtue by religion, St Just by institutional methods. Robespierre had always feared the dechristianisation policies carried out by *Répresentatives en Mission* and by Paris sections, and twice had attempted to curb it, but the churches had remained obstinately shut. Thus in *Floréal Year II* (May 1794) the festivals of the Supreme Being were instituted. Meanwhile under St Just the terror was made more institutional, efficient and 'virtuous'. The Terror had existed since the first riots of 1789, but had reached new heights with the September massacres. It had gone unchecked in the provinces under men like Fouché and had been accompanied by dechristianisation. As dechristianisation was replaced by the Supreme Being so indiscriminate terror, which had cost over thirty-thousand lives, was replaced by centralisation. The *répresentatives* were recalled and provincial revolutionary tribunals suppressed. In their place came the *Law of the Twenty Second Prairial* (June 10th) which excused courts the necessity of hearing witnesses and refused the accused the aid of counsel. The Terror deepened further and into the net were swept those who worked against the government or spread rumours, those who were defeatists, dishonest contractors or who spread sedition. *The Laws of Ventôse* (February) threatened the confiscation of property of 'recognised enemies of the revolution'.

Under such an onslaught the Convention could hardly stay silent and Fleurus convinced many people that the time was ripe for change. The Committee had alienated too many people. The *sansculottes* could never forgive it for the destruction of its power. Moreover the 'Maximum' on prices was never fully successful and hurt those *sansculottes* who were traders. It only helped wage-earners, but their wages were controlled and strikes forbidden. Although in their search for the virtuous society Robespierre and St Just aimed at creating a society of small independent producers, and ending disparities of wealth, the sale of land from such measures as Ventôse only helped those with money. Plans for national relief and education could not meet the problem created by the appalling inflation. Meanwhile such schemes as these and the social policy of the 'virtuous' men, angered and alarmed the Convention deputies whose social and economic beliefs hardly differed from those of the men of 1789. The Terror frightened them and the Festival of the Supreme Being was interpreted by many as the beginning of a return to catholicism and reaction.

Moreover, thankfully, people do not like to be forced to be virtuous, nor did the Committee possess the institutions of the modern totalitarian state whose precursor it was. Yet no one dared move for fear of denunciation and execution. It was to be a division within the Committee of Public Safety itself which was to lead to the Thermidorean reaction and end Robespierre's 'tyranny of public opinion'.

The Committee of General Security was jealous of the police powers assumed by the Committee of Public Safety after 22nd Prairial. They disliked the extreme centralisation which threatened their power and these views accorded with those of recalled *Répresentatives en Mission* like Fouché. Elements in the Committee of Public Safety led by Carnot, Barère and Lindet disliked the terror and the excessive virtue of Robespierre who after several quarrels ceased to attend the meetings. Such absence was frightening and when Robespierre on 8th Thermidor (July) denounced 'enemies' to the Convention the threat was real. But Robespierre's typically totalitarian tactic of not naming his enemies frightened the Convention who would not give him the blank cheque he desired. His enemies struck back and he was arrested. The Commune's attempt to rally support for Robespierre failed and on 9th Thermidor (July 27th) he was executed.

Revolutions are easy to start, but very difficult to halt. All those who had tried between 1789 and 1794 to end the revolution had been defeated. With the fall of Robespierre, however, it became obvious that the revolution was over.

Fouché, Barère, Carnot and others had merely acted in self defence and had not intended to lose control of the situation. But once the Convention had seized the initiative it determined never again to let go. Backed and hurried by a relieved public opinion it proceeded to dismember the terror.

The Committee of Public Safety was not allowed to continue, as Barère had hoped. It was put under strict control and its personnel changed completely each year. Prisons opened their doors, 22nd *Prairal* was repealed, and the forty-eight sections of Paris were regrouped to give control to more respectable elements of society. Even had the Convention wished to retain any of the men or institutions of the previous period, public opinion would have prevented it. People began to enjoy themselves again in theatres, at balls and in brothels. Instead of the *Marseillaise*, the reaction battle hymn *Réveil du peuple* was the popular song and young, rich men, the *Jeunesse Dorée* now not afraid to flaunt the fact that they were rich, and that their parents were *nouveaux riches*, picked quarrels with well known Jacobins. Sensible Jacobins kept out of sight or denounced their friends, as the 'White Terror' gained momentum.

The policy of the majority of the Convention was to grant amnesty to Jacobins, to preserve the essential work of the revolution but to remove those excrescences interfering with economic freedom, which seemed inimical to the spirt of '89. Unfortunately Jacobin turncoats, popular pressure, desire for revenge and the activities of the *Jeunesse Dorée* made such a sensible policy impossible to operate. Slowly the amnesty was extended, first to the Girondin survivors, then as the need for pacification seemed more urgent, to the Vendée rebels, royalist and clericalist though they were. Toleration in February 1795 (Ventôse Year III) was granted, if grudgingly, to the church.

Throughout this period the attacks on the 'terrorists' increased. Carrier, the butcher of Nantes, was executed; in the provinces gangs persecuted and attacked Jacobin sympathisers and known members of the popular societies. As the amnesties were extended to more and more groups so the force of this reaction grew and, as if in despair, in Germinal and Prairial, 1795 the *sansculottes* made a last effort whose failure sealed the fate of the remaining Jacobins.

Continuing price rises following the abolition of the 'Maximum', the re-opening of the Bourse and a dearth of food provoked risings on 12th Germinal (April 1795) and 1st Prairial (May) which were beaten off by National Guardsmen. Each rising led to the sacrifice of more Jacobins; Barère and others after Germinal, more obscure Jacobins after Prairial. After this the 'White Terror' was uncontrollable, especially in the Rhône Valley, and in towns like Lyons, Marseilles and Toulon where old scores were brutally settled.

The 'White Terror's' ferocity, the re-appearance of émigrés and the open royalism of many people alarmed the Plain who had no intention of sacrificing the republic to reactionary royalism. The new constitution was hurried on, in order to stabilise a difficult situation.

The Constitution of Year III differed greatly from that which the Jacobins had introduced but never operated. Its 'Declaration of Rights' made no mention of equality; the social welfare aspects of the previous constitution were omitted and universal male suffrage abandoned. Economic freedom was enshrined. The new executive was entrusted to a Directory of Five, of whom one retired each year. The Directory's control over the re-established Departments was minimal and it could initiate no laws. The resolutions which initiated the law-making process began in the Council of Five Hundred, the lower house of a bicameral legislature whose upper house consisted of two hundred and fifty *Anciens*.

In the provinces the Department was re-introduced, the District was abolished and Communes became municipalities under direct Departmental control. There was a conscious reaction against the centralisation of the Committee of Public Safety and an attempt to revert to the true revolutionary tradition.

The Directory was a rather poor instrument for the work in hand. Its essential task was to consolidate the gains of the revolution but the Directory found that this was akin to building a castle of sand. This was difficult enough, but with both hands tied, and under attack from rabid dogs it was impossible. The Jacobins and Bourbons between them had implanted a fear of strong executives, so the Directors, being five in number, and prone like normal men to quarrel, were prevented from exercising proper control over local government, or from initiating legislation required to safeguard the revolution. The Revolution had seen the emergence of, and given scope to, large numbers of fanatics. It created royalists, transformed by Louis XVI's martyrdom into worshippers of absolutism; there were Jacobins who through the 'White Terror' became social revolutionaries, clericalists who espoused ultramontanism. Likewise there were groups of constitutional monarchists, clergy who accepted the revolution and moderate Jacobins, who found themselves cut off from those with whom they most sympathised, yet unable to accept a government which, through weakness, was forced to depend on the Plain. This latter majority feared royalism or clericalism of any kind as reactionary and Jacobinism of any kind as opposed to economic liberalism.

The retiring Thermidoreans did their best to secure a Directory to their liking by destroying *sansculotte* power and revising laws against émigrés and clergy. They had even troubled to take upon themselves the burden of the Directory by insisting on re-electing two thirds of the old Convention. Selflessness could go no further. Thus the last leaders of the first republic prepared to walk the tightrope again, with only themselves to applaud the act, for it must be admitted that few Frenchmen were any longer entertained by it.

The five initial Directors consisted of a turncoat Vicomte, a mediocre Girondin, a Jacobin, Carnot from the old Committee of Public Safety and a friend of the latter. Thus the Directory began as it meant to go on, quarrelling. The initial threat being from the forces of reaction the Directory gave succour to the Jacobins in its appointments and subsidised their press. However when the *assignat* reached less than one per cent of its face value and food became scarce the first serious attack appeared to the left.

Gracchus Babeuf's 'Conspiracy of the Equals' in the spring of 1796 was the first fruit of enragé Jacobinism and the first truly proletarian uprising. His communism terrified respectable men but the threat was overcome and Babeuf was executed. From him however, through his companion

Buonarrotti, arose a tradition of French social revolution which is not yet dead.

Although the Directory made moves against Jacobins in the civil service it did not go far enough to please a public which, as the election of Year V approached, grew more openly royalist. When the election results were seen to show a right wing majority the left wing of the Directors in Fructidor (September), led a *coup d'état* against the right wing led by Carnot and annulled the elections of 198 deputies. Priests were deported and censorship of right wing newspapers tightened.

Yearly elections forced the Directors to prepare for the possibilities of Year VI and considerable efforts were made to secure a revolutionary majority. The Directors, however, discovered that the pendulum had swung too far towards the Jacobins. The Floréal 'coup' adjusted the balance. Unfortunately as the election of year VII approached (1799) the war took a turn for the worse, business stagnated, conscription created social disturbances and people were openly calling for a return to a Jacobin dictatorship. The elections showed wide left wing gains and this time the coup (of Prairial) was directed by the Council of 500 against the Directory and reinforced by a forced loan on the rich and a Law of Hostages reminiscent of the terror.

The alarm of the moderates was however short lived. Siéyés, now a Director, was preparing to dissolve a constitution which signally failed to produce stability. He was backed by the army which was as tired of extremism as it was of the Directors, and most important, Siéyés found in Bonaparte a national hero of suitable grandeur. Having secured the co-operation of two other Directors, the turncoat Vicomte, Barras, a man whose capacity for survival suggests that the Almighty was under some obligation, and Ducos, he planned the *coup d'état* of Brumaire (December) which scattered the Jacobin resurgence at bayonet point and achieved the military dictatorship which Burke in his *Reflections* had forecast.

In short, the Directory cannot be described as a glorious episode in the history of the revolution. Nevertheless, despite its own instability, it did much to ensure the stability of

Consulate and Empire, and despite the cost of war a real attempt was made to put the economy on a sound footing.

The problem was huge. The *assignat* was almost valueless, war, which the Directory failed to end because peace was thought to be royalist-inspired, became more expensive, taxes were years in arrears and no one knew what the normal budget should be. War time needs called for controls, but these were politically out of the question, with the result that the Directors came under the control of government contractors whose activities gave the Directory, justly, a reputation for corruption. The attempt to restore the economy began after *Fructidor* Year V. The declaration of a two thirds bankruptcy and the return to a metallic currency, the new tax administration and the acceptance of new indirect taxes paved the way for the relative stability of the Consulate. The Directory itself was never strong enough to benefit from its measures or to survive the unpopularity of the deflation they caused. So the Directory was forced to rely increasingly on spoils of foreign conquests which made it difficult for them to curb the independence and ambition of men like Napoleon. Only peace could do that. But peace, popular with the right wing, was unpopular with the left and after Fructidor the *coups d'état* were left wing *coups*.

In other, less edifying, ways the Directory prepared the way for the dictatorship of Napoleon. *Coups d'état* against the legislature, and simultaneously in provincial government, prepared men to accept the control of elections and the weakness of the legislatures which characterised Napoleon's period. Censorship and police activity similarly began under the Directory or even before. In 1799 the French did not give up liberty; they had not had it for several years, if at all during the revolution. What they were surrendering was inefficient dictatorship, lawlessness and uncertainty. The countryside was beset by brigands, unemployment was rife, political passions higher than since 1795. Nowhere was the Directory's failure more apparent than in its religious policy. The church was still merely tolerated, its buildings taken from it and its clergy suspect. But it suffered most from the leftward lurches of the Directory. No attempt was made to solve the deep divisions in the church and to resolve the problem caused by the fact that, while the legislature might be anti-clerical, the country was overwhelmingly catholic. France wanted peace at home and abroad; and the guarantee of those economic and social freedoms which had been won since 1789. The Directory could not provide these.

Brumaire was accepted with relief. The strong man could protect the gains of the revolution from Jacobinism on the one hand and reaction on the other. For the revolution had been fought by and for a particular class. The unwillingness of the Committee of Public Safety to submit to *sansculotte* demands, the Thermidorean reaction and the crazy gymnastics of the Directors had all been attempts to secure the benefits which the bourgeoisie had won from the revolution. Not all the bourgeoisie, Government-stock-holders suffered badly during the revolution, some importers and exporters must have been hard hit and no doubt businesses went bankrupt, professional men's practices were damaged and many suffered from revolutionary excesses. But generally the revolution had aided the entrepreneur, the embryo industrialist, the man able to take advantage of economic freedom, the sale of property and inflation. The *jeunesse dorée* were the sons of such people daring to show themselves again, and it was such people for whom the Directory had failed to secure stability. The revolution, which was their revolution, had made so many enemies, to the right of the royalist and catholic, to the left of the thwarted poor, that it was based on too narrow a support in unstable times. The hope was that the strong man would impose order and reconcile the rest of France to the narrowness of the revolutionary class.

CHAPTER EIGHT

The Revolution Abroad

(1) WAR 1792–1802

It would be a delightful convenience to be able to accept the myth that the war between Europe and the revolution was caused by frightened conservatives attempting to stamp out a dreadful contagion. In fact, of course, the absolutists rarely went to war unless this was completely necessary, and they did not fear the revolution in France because the revolution had to happen before anyone knew the nature of the contagion. Besides, history taught that a country going through a revolution was to be discounted as a force in international affairs, and from Pitt to Kaunitz Europe's statesmen wrote off French power for the next few years. Naturally, while France was otherwise occupied, other powers took advantage of the situation but no one presumed to interfere with French territory; even before 1789 France had been ignored by powers occupied with affairs of Turkey and Poland.

So although Burke might rage, Gustavus Adolphus III of Sweden threaten to descend in a fiery chariot to rescue a Queen in distress and the first royal émigrés led by the Comte d'Artois, Louis' brother, plot darkly, European statesmen in general remained singularly cool and depressingly prosaic. Austria in 1790, for obvious reasons, needed peace. Britain had no allies and although Prussia might initially hope to embroil Austria in French affairs the successes of Catherine made Austria a necessary ally, as Reichenbach showed.

Thus Leopold from 1790 studiously ignored the pleas of Artois and the émigrés and he was urged to refuse help to them by the Court at France, which feared Artois as much as it feared Paris. Nonetheless there were increasing causes of friction. The most important was the traditional hostility of Frenchmen for Austria. The loathing men felt for Marie Antoinette increased the feeling that Austria must be an enemy to France and in league with the émigrés. Already in 1790 the application of revolutionary decrees to Alsace, French but part of the Holy Roman Empire, without consulting Leopold, had caused considerable friction. The French increasingly felt a desire to spread their ideas to other parts of Europe, to introduce the revolutionary heaven to other suffering mortals. The encouragement given to the Belgian revolutionaries was capable of considerable expansion. Nor did the revolution curb French expansionism; on the contrary it encouraged it. The traditional covetousness towards Belgium, the hostility to England and Austria acquired new force.

Only after Varennes would Leopold, however, make a gesture, despite appeals from his sister for over a year. He had become increasingly willing to intervene in France but only if Louis and his Queen escaped. The Declaration of Pillnitz of August 1791, by Austria and Prussia was only a gesture. The declaration that they would intervene in France if all Europe agreed was tantamount to saying there would be no intervention, but French public opinion unlike French diplomats, failed to appreciate the subtlety of the 'if' and when the Declaration was published in Paris it had attached to it, unknown to Leopold, an émigré manifesto. When Louis accepted the new constitution in September 1791 Leopold saw there was no further need for action of any kind, but by then French public opinion was aroused.

The Girondins in the new French Legislative Assembly were eager for war with Austria and Vergniaud's oratory had its effect. Brissot in 1791 declared that Louis XIV had declared war because an ambassador had been insulted '. . . and we who are free, should we for a moment hesitate?' These attitudes are not however merely a result of party demagoguery or over-confident chauvinism. Fear of counter-revolution, hatred of the émigrés and ingrained attitudes older than the revolution all played their part. Certainly war was more likely to be declared by France than by Austria while Leopold remained Emperor. But in February 1792 he died and was succeeded by the less circumspect, less talented Francis II.

Francis' adviser was not the cunning Kaunitz but Spielmann who had negotiated the defensive alliance with Prussia in February 1792. Spielmann was almost eager for war, hoping for territorial gain. Similar eagerness was evinced on the other side of the Rhine where, besides the arguments of chauvinism, arguments of revolutionary expediency added weight to the call for war. War would allow the revolution to take steps unjustifiable in peace and would unite the people. Discussion of Austria's crimes began in January and satisfaction was demanded before March, or war was promised.

It was the King, however, who precipitated war for he came to the conclusion that a limited war over the presence of émigrés in Trier would strengthen his position. Accordingly he gave in to Dumouriez's pressure for a request to the Assembly to declare war on April 20th. Simultaneously Austria had been preparing for the conflict which Dumouriez's hostility made inevitable. Prussia entered the war on Austria's side in May.

At their first sight of Austrian troops the French fled and, from the French point of view, the war began disastrously. Fortunately the Allies were disorganised. Prussia was already suspecting that Russia's eagerness to push her into war cloaked sinister designs on Poland and Austria had failed to supply all the troops she had promised. The commander of the invasion forces, the Duke of Brunswick, lacked the qualities of leadership while the Prussian army was cumbersome, unlike the French who had begun to acquire the tactics of Guibert, which Napoleon was to use later to such advantage. The advance was slow and it was not until September that Brunswick met Dumouriez at Valmy. The French republic was saved. It was saved not so much by French skill, however, as by Brunswick's dilatoriness, and Poland, whose imminent partition caused Frederick-William to deprive Brunswick of troops whose use would have proved decisive.

Pitt and Grenville in London continued to view the revolution as a purely internal affair and so recently (in 1790) had Britain become isolated in Europe that there was no eagerness for war. Only a threat to security or commerce could have made Pitt, eager to solve the problem of the National Debt, go to war. Nonetheless the September massacres had revolted public opinion and the execution of the King was to lead to a diplomatic breach. By then however war was practically inevitable.

French armies had crossed into the Austrian Netherlands and at Jémappes (November) defeated the Austrian armies. It became increasingly obvious that they meant to stay and by two decrees the Convention alarmed London. In the first they declared France's willingness to come to the aid of all peoples wishing to assert their liberty and in the second they declared that the river Scheldt should be open to all shipping. As a result of several disputes the Scheldt had been declared closed to foreign shipping and it could only be forced at the risk of war with the United Provinces (Holland). Moreover Britain could hardly willingly run the risk of seeing the shores of Holland and Belgium, which faced important ports and which were important market centres for British goods in Europe, in the hands of a power which showed itself by its pronouncements, and a hostile commercial policy, increasingly inimical to European peace, and to Britain in particular. It was obvious that the new republic had acquired all the diplomatic and territorial aims of its aristocratic predecessors without the caution or good manners with which they had been conducted. Britain declared its support for Holland. Even after the French gunboats had forced the Scheldt Pitt sought peace, but the execution of Louis led to the severing of diplomatic relations and on February 1st 1793 France eagerly declared war.

France now faced Prussia, Austria, Great Britain, Holland plus Spain and Sardinia which had also declared war in the first of the great Coalitions. The year 1793 was, in its early stages hardly a successful one for France. The Belgians learned quickly to hate their liberators who despoiled their church, plundered their economy and annexed their lands. Dumouriez, in violent opposition to such a policy, was ordered to advance into Holland. The battle of Neerwinden (March 1793) drove the French from Holland and caused the disillusioned Dumouriez to defect to the Austrians. The retreat began as Prussia occupied Alsace, the Dutch, British and Austrians took Condé and Toulon gave itself up to Admiral Hood.

Once again France was to be saved by Poland. Ever since the Prussians had first withdrawn troops earmarked for France in 1792 Austria and Prussia had engaged in mutual recrimination: the final settlement of the second Partition in September 1793 broke the alliance just as victory seemed possible. The new Polish revolt of 1794 made certain that a Third and final Partition would be necessary and both Prussia and Austria began to make the necessary troop deployments. The see-saw battle moved into its decisive stage. The Duke of York was defeated at Dunkirk in September 1793 and the French crossed the Rhine again. In June 1794 Jourdan won the great victory of Fleurus one month after Frederick-William had moved large concentrations of troops to Poland. By the beginning of 1795 the United Provinces were in French hands. The final blow to the First Coalition came in April of 1795, when Prussia, piqued at being left out of the negotiations for the Third Partition of Poland, made peace with France by the Treaty of Basel, which gave France the left bank of the Rhine. A month later the satellite state of Holland made peace with France and declared war on England, and in July Spain, never a sincere ally of Britain, made her peace.

The First Coalition had shown many reasons why the war with France would be long and difficult. There was no real similarity of interests between the Allies. England's aims were limited to making the North Sea coasts friendly again, with the result that her Allies never trusted her to stay in the war any longer than was necessary to secure this aim and they therefore rarely gave the British all the help required in that sector. Increasingly the Allies saw the war as a Holy War while England never saw it as more than a war for the territorial *status quo ante bellum*. Moreover French superiority on land and British superiority at sea secured by Howe's victory of the 'Glorious First of June' in 1794 guaranteed that the war would stagnate. For however many victories the French might win on land, without sea power Britain could not be invaded nor her commerce effectively dealt with.

Britain's commerce provided the cash which had kept the First Coalition together and which would subsidise many more. On the other hand, as the First Coalition demonstrated, Britain's cash did not secure Allied co-operation or trust. Unless either France or Britain was prepared to give way on the Netherlands question peace was impossible. Britain could not risk her sea power and no French government would dare to give up land won by the glorious armies of the people. That fundamentally was why war continued until 1815.

In 1795 Austria and Britain alone remained at war with France. The Directors, like Danton in earlier times, wished for peace and attempted in the first two years of their existence to secure a general settlement. But not only were they prevented by expediency from giving up conquests in Belgium, Savoy and Nice but the constitution specifically forbade such a surrender. Nor could they easily sacrifice Holland and Spain from whom England had quickly seized colonies, including Ceylon and the Cape of Good Hope.

Nonetheless in 1796 the main aim was to demolish the forces of Austria by a main attack through Switzerland and Germany supported by a subsidiary effort in Italy to be led by the young artillery general Bonaparte, friend of Director Barras. Napoleon's campaign soon became the most important. His inspired leadership transformed his ramshackle army into an effective force. His incessant activity and speed constantly surprised the over-prudent Austrians. By April 1796 he had forced Sardinia-Piedmont to an armistice at Cherasco and, ignoring the Directors' prohibition, crossed the river Pô, defeated the Austrians at Lodi, took Milan and later forced Mantua to surrender. He went further however and began to organise his new conquests in Lombardy, promising independence and liberty, and fraternising with members of the popular societies.

Unfortunately for the Directors the war in the north was a failure and by the autumn of 1796 they were prepared to negotiate with England whose commerce was suffering. Negotiations however could not get past the obstacle of Belgium. In the summer of 1797 England seemed more willing for peace but misunderstanding among the plenipotentiaries and the *coup d'état* of Fructidor brought the negotiations at Lille at an abrupt close.

Austria had proved more tractable. Having imposed a peace on the Pope in February 1797 Napoleon had risked a march towards Vienna. So successful was he that in April he was able to force the Austrians to make a preliminary peace at Loeben which six months later became the Treaty of Campo Formio.

The Directory had by no means enjoyed Bonaparte's successes, for it did not wish to be permanently involved in Italy nor did it wish to set up republics in that area. It resented the high-handed way in which Bonaparte had organised the setting up of the Cispadane (and later the Cisalpine) republics of Northern Italy in 1797 and it resented the growing mystique surrounding his name. It could hardly refuse the victories he offered, however, and accepted them with a bad grace, for it needed the generals even more after the failure of the Lille negotiations not only to carry on the war but to protect the constitution from its enemies.

The peace with Austria, finally ratified at Campo Formio, had been hard won. The Directors wished to give up Italy and Austria wanted Milan and Mantua back, but Bonaparte was prepared to accede to neither request. So Venice ceased to be an independent republic, her Dalmatian territories were occupied by Austria and the Ionian isles came to France.

Hard won though the peace might be it could not last long. Austria could not willingly accept the presence of the Cisalpine republic in Italy and although almost eager to get rid of Belgium, its incorporation into France kept the war with England simmering. The peace terms which concerned the Rhine frontiers flatly contradicted the peace of Basel for it was agreed that Prussia should not receive compensations on the right bank of the Rhine promised her in 1795 for losses on the left. A congress of interested parties at Rastatt failed to solve the complicated problems of compensation and territorial arrangements necessitated by France's new acquisitions on the left bank.

'The treaty is not a peace, it is the call to a new war'

As yet, however, the war was not to begin; only Great

Britain and Portugal were belligerent and a new way had to be found to weaken the British war effort. Although not entirely effective the blockade against British trade pointed the way to an attack on Empire and trade. The result was Bonaparte's Egyptian expedition (May 1798), a romantic crusade which was to bring home to Britain the critical importance of Egypt to British routes to India. The victory of Nelson at the Nile in August 1798 destroyed the effectiveness of this rash stroke of genius, and eventually Napoleon cut his losses, returning home as French disasters mounted. He arrived to be welcomed as a deliverer, just as the tide of arms swung in France's favour.

The Egyptian expedition alarmed more than just Britain. Tsar Paul whose reversal of all Catherine's policies at home and abroad now made him the protector of Turkey, whose territory seemed violated, was affronted. The French seizure of Malta, of whose Knights Paul was Grand Master, further alarmed him and if Napoleon was to pursue a romantic crusade in the East Paul was determined to pursue a christian crusade in the West. Moreover Bonaparte's Cisalpine republic and the new republic of Holland needed proper defence. The Directory, therefore, invaded Switzerland and formed the Helvetic republic to secure alpine communication with Italy. Even worse, the French had seized upon the pretext of the death of General Duphot in a street scuffle to take over Rome, expel the Pope and create a Roman Republic. Austria had always viewed Italy as her sphere of influence and felt called upon, as did the Orthodox Tsar, to defend christianity. Britain could not accept a slow seizure of Italy which, with Malta, could have provided France with an effective way of cutting off the British fleet from the Eastern Mediterranean. Italy was added to Belgium as a permanent source of friction between Britain and France.

The Second Coalition formed in the autumn of 1798 contained the powers of Britain, Austria, Russia, Portugal, Turkey and Naples which also felt itself threatened by French activities in Italy. Sadly Naples caused the first defeat for the coalition. Promised help by Nelson, and desiring to acquire Papal territory, Ferdinand IV invaded the Roman republic. Within a few weeks he was in Sicily and Naples was

E

the Parthenopean republic. Luckily the Austro-Russian armies had more success. The Cisalpine republic fell and France left the Parthenopean republic to the mercy of its enemies, internal as well as external. Italy was lost but Massena in Switzerland saved the French position north of the Alps and the 'Grand old Duke of York' after many fruitless manoeuvres embarked for England, leaving Holland and Belgium in French hands. Then Napoleon returned.

Once again the coalition failed. Before the campaign of 1799 opened Russia had withdrawn. Paul had acquired his Ionian isles and soon lost interest in the war. His relations with Austria worsened and he could not forgive Britain for holding on to Malta. He had no trust in Britain's willingness to carry on the war after the recapture of Holland and in this he was supported by Austria. Thus the Allies failed to work together and in 1799 only Austria and Great Britain remained.

Napoleon quickly marched to Italy where Massena, besieged in Genoa, expected rescue. Napoleon ignored Massena however who surrendered. After he had taken Milan Napoleon met the Austrians at Marengo (June 1800) one of his greatest victories, wrested from defeat by General Désaix. After Moreau's victory at Hohenlinden the Austrians made peace at Luneville (February 1801) by which the Empire lost all territory on the left bank of the Rhine.

Britain alone remained. Napoleon's attempt to create out of Prussia, Russia, Denmark and Sweden a naval power of neutrals, inflamed by the British use of her claimed right of search, to overwhelm the British navy, foundered at Nelson's victory of Copenhagen. Eager for quiet in which to settle the internal divisions of France, Napoleon made peace with a weary England at Amiens, March 1802.

Amiens solved no problems. Great Britain was to restore her French conquests and Malta, whose independence was to be guaranteed by five great powers. There were no stipulations about Belgium and Holland. The Helvetic republic remained as did the Cisalpine and Ligurian (Genoa) republic in Italy. Such a settlement, which settled nothing, could not last.

(ii) REVOLUTIONARY PROPAGANDA AND RULE
1792–1802

The lasting effects of the Revolution were to be most felt in those areas occupied by France, Italy (the Cisalpine, Ligurian, Roman and Parthenopean republics), Switzerland (the Helvetic republic) Holland (Batavian republic) and Belgium. But even before these countries were overrun, the effects of the revolution had been felt.

The news of the fall of the Bastille had nearly everywhere been welcomed as the breaking of a yoke of tyranny, a sign of hope for humanity. 'Bliss was it in that dawn to be alive . . .' Interest in the proceedings of the Assembly was great and men were pleased to see the institutions of the greatest cultural influence in Europe undergoing the scrutiny of Enlightenment's reason.

In 'Germany' the influence of the revolution was felt in those areas near to France and most akin to her in social composition. The city states of the Rhineland archbishops with their educated middle class acquired the sign of revolutionary respectability, in Jacobin clubs. The peasantry of this area had much the same needs as their French equivalents and this area was easily absorbed into France after Basel, Campo Formio and Lunéville. In Prussia the effects were minimal for the middle class was too small, serfdom was still a living institution and the aristocracy largely immune from French thought. The revolutionary party was miniscule in size and influence.

Within Austria's territories 'revolutions' had broken out in 1788 but they were by no means of the French type, except in so far as they possessed the common element of aristocratic reaction. Hungarian 'nationalism' was class nationalism, owing nothing to France. In Vienna there were certainly members of Masonic societies who welcomed 1789 but their influence was small and they disliked the Hungarian uprising as much as did Joseph. Only in Belgium, an economically advanced area, did the French revolution have any significant effect. Here the Vonckists were francophil and radical, and it is significant that they fled to Paris when order was restored in Belgium, after its revolt against Joseph. Perhaps more significant is the fact that they were driven out by a clerical-ist-aristocratic victory, supported by peasants and workers who disliked the Vonckist merchants. That co-operation of church aristocracy and lower classes was to remain a potent anti-revolutionary force in much of Catholic Europe.

The real impact of the revolution came, however, when war transformed it into a crusade. This crusade was carried to Europe not only by the armies but also by minority groups from within the countries, who received encouragement from France. But France's revolutionary ardour like Russia's in our own times, hardly cloaked her straightforward annexationist tendencies. France sought her 'natural frontiers'. This phrase, meaningless in itself, appealed to men who had been taught by Rousseau and the physiocrats that what was natural was good and right. Savoy, the small mountain country ruled from Turin in Piedmont had active French sympathisers. Nice had not. But both fitted neatly into the new republic in 1792.

In Belgium the pattern of annexation has a sad familiarity. Behind the armies of 1794 came the Jacobin clubs organised in the large cities, filled with Frenchmen and sympathisers who through the Convention petitioned for annexation. The pro-French elements were always a minority, but Belgium endured French armed occupation with eventual resignation. Initially the opposition had been great for the economic weakness of France itself forced the army of Dumouriez in 1793 to live off the land. There was opposition to the despoiling of the nobility and, more particularly, the church. The extension of anti-clerical policies to Belgium encountered bitter opposition but the social and legal changes were, on the whole, accepted. The new French models reformed the legal system, the remnants of feudalism, such as they were, were abolished and privileged corporations and guilds were rooted out. But after 1793 the French never again claimed to be spreading revolutionary benefits to a conquered territory. This was straightforward annexation, which despoiled the country of art treasures, milked it of money by taxation and used it to provide and feed troops.

Elsewhere north of the Alps save in Holland the war hardly affected the day to day affairs of the people. Prussia, having escaped from war in 1795 stayed out for ten years. Such revolutionary influence as there was was confined to Masonic-type societies and merely called for a slight tightening up of police control. The rest of Germany was altogether too subdivided, and too backward to be capable of absorbing new political ideas except for mild liberalism among educated merchants and lawyers. The Hapsburg lands, besides being under a fierce police system, were also too backward to accept new ideas and such 'revolutionaries' as there were tended to bear aristocratic names. Even so Viennese 'Jacobinism' was harshly treated. The fear of the rulers was already out of all proportion to the size of the danger. In Russia, Paul banned two Russian words because their French equivalents were *citoyen* and *patrie*. Mild liberals like Radischev were exiled and Masonic lodges closed by Catherine.

It was in Italy following Bonaparte's successes that the revolution was to make a real impact and find fruitful soil. Italy might only be 'a geographical expression' but it had almost rid itself, except in the Kingdom of the Two Sicilies, of feudalism, and possessed a lively articulate bourgeoisie, already participating in political power. The revolution had soon made itself felt in Italy through the ubiquitous clubs, which though persecuted, had a membership of aristocrats, professional men and men of letters.

The revolutionary war in Italy began and ended with exploitation. The Directory rejected the ideas of Italian Jacobin exiles for the setting up of revolutionary republics, and even Bonaparte, who was to create such a republic at first restricted himself to pillaging church and nobility. The removal of arts treasures and confiscation of church property led to riots of peasants and clergy, which foreshadowed the hatred for all things French which occupation was to foster.

The commissaire of the army, Saliceti, had from the first made it his business to encourage 'patriots' in Milan, Modena, Bologna and Reggio. Napoleon saw the military advantages of Italian support and in October 1796 the Lombardic Cispadane Republic was created which, with the addition of Milan in January 1797, became the Cisalpine Republic. Campo Formio extended it further into Papal territory. It acquired a Directorial constitution, though its Directors were chosen by Napoleon.

To the Cisalpine republic another was added. In June 1797 Genoa succumbed to public opinion and Napoleon's threats to become the Ligurian Republic. Rome, 'cette Babylone, gorgée des dépouilles de l'univers, doit nous nourrir et payer nos dettes', wrote the Directory in a curious mixture of non-conformist imagery and annexationist honesty. General Duphot's death provided the pretext for the Roman Republic which soon acquired a constitution and, poetically, seven consuls. Unfortunately Rome was also subjected to a savage pillage which, besides Papal intransigency, was the real excuse for its seizure, and which provoked a popular rising in February 1799. Finally the Parthenopean Republic was established in Naples in January 1799. Although a constitution was established the sole aim of its conqueror, Championet, was exploitation.

These later republics were the work of mere military and financial expediency and could hardly outlast the withdrawal of France. The Cisalpine Republic had been created and then deserted by Napoleon. The Directors destroyed its constitution and exploited its wealth. It fell as quickly as the rest. Rome was despoiled of nearly eighty million francs and the revolt in Rome showed the hatred which the invaders aroused. As the Allied armies approached the Italian republics the mass of the population, which did not live in the towns where 'patriot' strength lay, rose against its persecutors. In Turin the hostility of the inhabitants forced the French out; in Rome Cardinal Ruffo's peasants marched on the republicans. Only in Naples was much help offered to the French and there the republicans must have known how outnumbered they were in that priest-ridden land.

Yet the influence of the revolution was considerable. Enough Italians could separate republicanism from French hegemony to continue to support the former, and the Cisalpine Republic had shown, before the Directors despoiled it, some vigour and independence. Moreover the reaction against what was naked exploitation created an anti-French nationalism which never died. A less happy legacy was the bitterness which had been created by the opposition of the church which had such support among the peasants. That dispute was to continue and severely hinder the birth and growth of the Italian state.

The French revolutionary armies had demonstrated only too clearly the gap between revolutionary principles and aggressive nationalist practice. Even before the Empire's legions rolled across Europe all idealism had dissipated itself. Already the French revolution was showing that its greatest legacy to Europe would be nationalism fostered by hatred of France. Its greater ideals took root where the seeds already existed, in those areas where a middle class was already interested in new liberal ideas. There was no great French desire to proselytise the rest of Europe, except half-heartedly, where it was militarily helpful, for by 1796 the French had almost lost faith in the revolution themselves. Europe might see a Jacobin lurking behind every new idea, but if there was, France had not put him there.

CHAPTER NINE

Napoleonic Rule in France

'To be in God's place? That I would not wish;
it would be a *cul de sac. Napoleon.*

The main difficulty the historian encounters when called
upon to assess the rôle of Napoleon is the sheer historical
grandeur of the man and the resulting legends. He is tempted
to worship with the rest of humanity rather than coldly cut
the colossus down to the size of ordinary mortals. Yet legend
must be separated from fact though the legends are innumer-
able. There is that fostered by Napoleon himself on St
Helena; that he secured the true aims of the revolution, rid
France of fractious faction and endemic disorder, and forced
the monarchs of Europe to respect a revolutionary monarch.
'*La Gloire*' from Louis XIV to De Gaulle, has been a potent
element in the French psychology, and *La Gloire* without
doubt played a huge part in the legend. It was fostered by
Louis Philippe and extended by Napoleon III. Napoleon
became the peaceful monarch betrayed by a vengeful Europe,
the liberalism of the Hundred Days was presented as a natural
growth, not a sop to necessity, and the Empire became the
only régime to have represented all France and not just the
narrow class interests of the Bourbon restoration and July
monarchy.

The reaction against such legends has stressed the authoritarian nature of the régime and the centralisation and control
which seem to have more to do with the *Ancien Régime* than
revolution. Napoleon's constant wars are seen as largely the
result of greed or nemesis, not of Europe's jealousy, and her
régime is portrayed as based on narrow class interest. As
usual all the legends, both for and against this man, contain

an element of truth, and this is no doubt confusing. Of course Napoleon was the heir of the revolution, but since he is ruling the same country as his Bourbon pɪedecessors he will rule in very much the same way with the advantages wrought by ten years of revolution. No war is ever the fault of one side only and Napoleon is no doubt sinned against as well as sinning. Perhaps if Napoleon is seen as an enlightened absolutist, what Joseph II would have liked to be, he will be best understood, for enlightened absolutists were revolutionaries afraid to risk a revolution. Napoleon was the heir to a revolution, and could be an enlightened absolutist without risk.

The Constitution which Siéyés had planned was not that with which Napoleon ruled. Siéyés had planned a balanced constitution, a return to the ideals of 1789, and he had never intended that the First Consul should be overwhelmingly more powerful than the second and third. Bonaparte's idea of his role won the day and the central power was allowed to increase at the expense of the balanced constitution. 'Gentlemen you have a master — a man who knows everything, wants everything and can do everything'.

The executive, then, consisted of three consuls, two of merely advisory power. The Legislature was divided in two bodies, the *Tribunat* and the *Corps Legislatif* while alongside them was a *Senat Conservateur* which was to act as a cross between the American Senate and Supreme Court, deciding disputes between the executive and legislature and guarding the laws and constitution. Unfortunately the increased power of the executive made the Senate's role largely illusory, and Napoleon used it as an adjunct of his own power. The *Tribunat* was the more radical of the two legislatures and had one hundred members whose minimum age was twenty-five. It was the most troublesome house to the executive and was abolished in 1804. The *Corps Legislatif* of three hundred members, all over thirty, though purged, survived and had at least one deputy to represent each Department. All members of both houses were chosen by the Senate, for, as was becoming almost traditional in French constitutions, elections were indirect.

The Constitution gave to France universal male suffrage but the practical effect of this was small. The basic electoral

unit was the commune which elected one in ten of its population to a *liste communale*; this in turn elected the same
proportion to a *liste départementale*. From each *liste* local
government officers were chosen by a variety of authorities.
The Consul and later Emperor chose the most important
officers and they in turn chose the less important. The Senate
appointed the two legislatures from the men on the *liste
nationale* which contained few more than six thousand
names.

As might be expected from a régime centred on one man,
to whom the nation looked for order, the watchword of local
administration was centralisation. This was hardly new, for
even in the revolution the Jacobins had centralised through
their *agents nationaux* and *Représentatives en Mission* and
even the Directory had had its agents, and had interfered
constantly with the personnel of local government. In 1800
Napoleon based his administration on the Department, which
was divided into districts (*arrondissements*) and further
divided into communes. In each area was placed an official,
more or less directly responsible to Napoleon; in the Department the Prefect, in the arrondissement the Sub-Prefect and
in the Commune the Mayor. Prefects and sub-prefects were
appointed directly by the Consul as were the mayors of
Communes with large populations. Otherwise mayors were
appointed by the Prefect. None of these functionaries were
permitted any discretionary power.

At the hub of the great wheel was Napoleon aided by a
Council of State, resembling the old *Conseil du Roi,* under
whose authority were the ministries. The Council was merely
advisory but at least in his early years, Napoleon was
prepared to take its advice, even when it conflicted with his
own opinion.

Nevertheless, subordination to a central will is the obvious
characteristic of the régime's organisation. The personnel of
the Consulate and Empire must be studied to see the nature
of its servants, whether they were servile or not, or of one
particular group. The Council of State was a body remarkable
for the variety of its members' political allegiances. As might
be expected from a body succeeding the Directory, extremes
of royalism or Jacobinism were eschewed but otherwise

republicans and royalists of most political colours were there. The political tone is, however, Feuillant, for Napoleon seems to have realised that despite their early demise as a party it was the Feuillants who best represented what the revolution stood for. The Prefects are perhaps the most obviously Napoleonic legacy to France. Again Prefects were drawn, not from extremists but from the revolutionary moderates, as were the sub-prefects. Like the Councillors of State they were intelligent and hard working, imbued with the philosophy of the enlightenment, somewhat anti-clerical but they were not terrorists nor men chosen simply for their ability to say yes. They had usually had political experience in one of the revolutionary legislatures, and if they were far enough away from Paris, they might even manage to use some personal initiative in their Department.

The Prefects changed little under Napoleon and few were removed; it would anyway have been difficult to find very many men of sufficient calibre, but there were changes in personnel elsewhere. The judicial personnel was, in the beginning, chosen from the same class as the other servants of the régime, but after 1807 when the independence of the judiciary was curbed many judges were replaced by personnel recruited from old parlementarians or their families. It would have been easier, in a country where a legal education was *de rigeur,* to find replacements for legal, than for administrative, personnel.

Napoleon's régime was authoritarian and tended to become more absolute as it grew older. Censorship was strict and only thirteen of the seventy-three political journals existing in 1799 remained in 1800. A *Bureau de Presse* was installed at the headquarters of the police. Censorship, it was said, 'intéresse la politique et dès lors la politique doit en être le juge'. The theatre too was subject to censorship and as a result the arts suffered badly. Dictators usually have abominable taste. But it could hardly be said that censorship was a Bonapartist invention. The police rule became more oppressive with the change from Consulate to Empire and agents entered all branches of society. Under the ubiquitous Minister of Police, Fouché, they acquired a rôle in the provinces, independent even of the préfects. Political opponents were imprisoned without trial, arrests were often unjustified. Napoleon's prisons undoubtedly contained more unjustly incarcerated victims in 1814 than did Louis XVI's in 1789. The *lettre de cachet* system, almost obsolete under the Bourbons, acquired a vigorous new life. With the re-organisation of the Judges' bench in 1807 criminal law became more harsh and arbitrary, while such safeguards as juries, acquired from the revolution, were frequently not used. The class nature of justice became more obvious and good bourgeois juries were encouraged to inflict harsh punishments, particularly where worker organisations were involved.

France therefore accepted a régime which grew increasingly authoritarian. But it at least gave order and even prosperity. If a French businessman had to choose between revolutionary anarchy and Napoleonic order there was little real alternative. He never had any other choice. Napoleon's régime was increasingly arbitrary, but until conscription after 1811 led to increasing rural disturbances the countryside was rid of brigandage; even La Vendée was almost quiet. Above all Paris was peaceful, not only because Napoleon prevented strikes and combinations of workers but also because he made sure Paris was fed with cheap bread. His frantic efforts to feed Paris in the 1811 harvest crisis were even allowed to interfere with the principle of economic liberalism. So Paris was kept quiet. His centralisation worked, and repaired the collapse and discredit of the administration endured under the Directory. France's armies were paid for by conquered territories, whose markets were until 1812 at the service of French trade.

Such measures pleased most Frenchmen but above all they satisfied the urban middle class and particularly the '*commerçants*'. Without a doubt Napoleon's régime was based most securely on the support of that section of the bourgeoisie which had gained most from revolution. The personnel of the régime reflected it, the administration of criminal law reflected its economic and social prejudices. His new education system gave a sound, if over authoritarian, technical secondary education to its sons. But Napoleon's régime did far more. The *Codes Napoléon* were among its most lasting monuments.

The revolution had dismantled much that was wrong with the legal system of the *Ancien Régime* but had had little time for rebuilding. The civil code of Napoleon (1800) synthesised the best of Roman and customary law into a coherent system. Its provisions were distinctly pleasing to the bourgeoisie. It re-affirmed equality before the law, reinforced economic liberalism and made property inviolable. The family was strengthened, divorce made difficult and the father and husband was made dominant. Napoleon believed deeply in moral behaviour for lesser mortals. The code regulated the laws concerning marriage and the bequeathing of property and enforced civil as opposed to religious marriage. Besides being a measure bound to satisfy the bourgeoisie it also satisfied the country which is basically conservative and the civil code, like Napoleon's administrative re-organisation, has lasted. In 1801 the criminal code was published, though it was less than strictly adhered to by the police.

The middle class might have lost its political freedom but its social pre-eminence was secured; its economic liberty, social equality and moral teachings were enshrined in the constitution. Very important, too, Napoleon guaranteed the possession of land bought as a result of the sequestration of property whose former owners were now returning to France. But this bourgeoisie was a small class; France remained overwhelmingly a peasant country and although the peasantry in 1789 had achieved the destruction of feudalism they were not yet satisfied. Napoleon could not give them what they really wanted, land, since what had been sold in the revolution had been bought by the bourgeoisie. They remained very attached to their church. If Napoleon could achieve a settlement of the religious question he would gain the support of this conservative class. To Napoleon, as to Joseph II, religion was the 'cement of the social order' and though not himself religious, 'If I were governing Jews I would rebuild the Temple of Solomon'. He approved of the teachings of the church, particularly those concerning obedience. 'Men who do not believe in God — one does not govern them, one shoots them'.

The Concordat of 1802 with Rome was arrived at with difficulty, for the Pope had no reason to feel well disposed.

Moreover the division in the French church between jurors and non-jurors had been widened by too much blood. The Directory had waxed hot and cold on the church question and many people's faith had lapsed altogether. In France opposition to a concordat came from the intellectuals, the army and politicians. The negotiations lasted a year, beginning in 1801, but eventually an agreement was signed. The church accepted the loss of its property, agreed to receive non-jurors, accepted state salaries and agreed to religious toleration. Napoleon attached to the concordat, unknown to the Pope, *Organic Articles,* which restricted the church's relations with Rome, curbed the freedom of movement of churchmen, imposed an oath of allegiance and allowed state interference in church disputes. It was an attempt to subject the church to the state, but it failed, for by the end of the Empire the church's power and freedom of movement had increased. Nonetheless Napoleon's concordat with Rome temporarily healed the worst festering sore of the revolution and pleased the vast majority of the French people.

Napoleon became first Consul for life shortly after the Peace of Amiens, and Emperor in 1804. The Pope hastened to Paris for the coronation, but Napoleon crowned himself. He also crowned in 1804 the achievement of four years of real progress for France and it was as well that he had accomplished so much so quickly, for from 1804 his business was to be mainly military. His defeats in 1814 and 1815 explain the main reason why he fell from power but even before 1814 his popularity was slipping. He seemed unable to stop the war; the British blockade was starving French trade and industry for which not even control of half Europe could compensate, while the long withdrawal after 1812 finally showed Frenchmen how expensive was the war against which they had been cushioned. Expensive not only in money, for the countryside was in revolt against fierce conscription. It was impossible for the Prefects to obey Napoleon's orders to both quieten the rural areas and get more conscripts. The Napoleonic police system was becoming more arbitrary and many of the *bourgeoisie* feared other signs in the wind. They disliked the purge of the judges, the Imperial aristocracy seemed to be a threat to equality, and where was the career open to talents in a country where a new aristocracy was digging itself in at an increasingly expensive court? Besides, in 1812, who remembered what the Directory had been like? He who wrote 'Passez vite, il va tomber' on a statue of Napoleon in 1813 was not merely thinking of military defeats. If dictatorship was no longer preserving internal peace, social equality or prosperity, perhaps political liberty was the answer.

CHAPTER TEN

Napoleon in Europe

(i) WAR

Amiens could only be a temporary peace. Britain's failure to insist on French withdrawal from Italy, Switzerland, Belgium or Holland and her own consequent refusal to withdraw from Malta were causes of friction. Napoleon's advertised wish to create a Mediterranean 'Mare Nostrum' and the combination, despite peace, of the economic warfare against Britain led to the outbreak of war in 1803.

The war soon brought French troops into Hanover and Naples as both sides feverishly sought allies. Napoleon hoped to gain the friendship of Russia, but Alexander I was not Paul. Not only did the Tsar fear that French activities in Italy threatened his interests in Greece and the Balkans and his possession in the Ionian isles, but he was also annoyed that he had not been consulted in the negotiations for the settlement of Germany which had been proceeding since the conference at Rastatt in 1797, and which reached fruition in February 1803. He feared for the safety of the Vistula and Elbe areas and posed, with some real concern, as the defender of the interests of 112 dispossessed German princes whose states were absorbed by larger neighbours.

Russian concern for Italy coincided with Austrian and British fears but it was not until the kidnapping of the Duc d'Enghien from Austrian territory and his subsequent murder that the final rupture came, though Napoleon earlier in the same year (1804) had offended all three countries by his proclamation of the Kingdom of Italy.

The Alliance was a fiasco. Prussia, though afraid of

Napoleon's intentions, would not join the Coalition: Russia, concentrating on Italy, would not work properly with Austria who was in turn afraid of Russian intentions. Although Britain secured herself from defeat at Trafalgar and prevented France from achieving the decisive blow which would have ended the war at Ulm, the Austrians, and at Austerlitz the combined Austrian and Russian armies, were vanquished with the aid of Bavaria, Württemberg, Baden and Hesse-Darmstadt. Austria made peace at Pressburg and abandoned Venetia and some German territory to Napoleon and his allies.

In July 1806 the Confederation of the Rhine was created, dividing Germany on lines familiar to the nineteenth century. Prussia would continue to rule in the north, Austria in the south and east but in the south and west a confederation of states under French protection would be in control. This was no sop to German nationalism, which still did not exist. Napoleon was really in control, particularly of its armies. The Holy Roman Empire, however, was dead.

The war still had life, and Prussia now blundered belatedly into it. She had not gone to war in 1805, resisting the blandishments of the Coalition and of Napoleon who had offered the bait of Hanover. The action of Napoleon in crossing Prussian territory to reach his eastern enemies had given the victory in the Prussian court to the 'German' rather than to the 'French' party. A visit by Alexander to Berlin impressed the dull Frederick William III and in a moment of Wagnerian romanticism the two monarchs swore an alliance on the tomb of Frederick the Great. Austerlitz sent the Prussian King back into a state of panic and he accepted the bait of Hanover which Napoleon was simultaneously offering to Britain as a gage of peace. Unfortunately Prussia lost Cleves to Napoleon's general, Murat, and the war party gained the advantage again. War was declared. In October 1806, at Jena and Auerstadt, Prussia was crushed. Russian resistance ended at Eylau and Friedland in February and June 1807.

By 1807 Russia was positively eager for peace as also was Napoleon who had no wish to invade Russia and hoped to divide Europe between the two colossi. The Tsar was angered by Britain's refusal of a loan and was not sorry to leave the coalition; but perhaps more important was his desire to secure his position in the near East. As usual Russia's geographical situation interested her in the affairs of Northern Europe and the near East simultaneously and while Alexander had been engaged in Northern Europe Napoleon had been endeavouring to foment war between Russia and Turkey. Russian activity on the Venetian Dalmatian coast, after the defeat of Austria which had hitherto held it, worried Turkey. Napoleon had succeeded in creating a Russo-Turkish war out of this situation in 1806.

So in 1807 Russia wanted a settlement; but it could not be permanent for a French presence in Turkey was inimical to Russia's interests, while the peace terms of 1807 were only acceptable as the price of a breathing space for Russian re-organisation. The Treaty of Tilsit was planned by Napoleon as a great Partition exercise, with Prussia and Turkey as the prey. But Russia found that the scheme of partition did not promise her Constantinople, and without it French presence in the near East on the Dalmatian coast was insupportable, so Turkey was saved. Neither was Alexander prepared to see the destruction of Prussia if a French Poland was to act as a new barrier to Russian expansion. Tilsit was therefore less world-shaking than Napoleon had hoped, but Russia was hardly in a position to make too many demands. Prussia had to be sacrificed to some extent. Poland re-appeared as the Duchy of Warsaw under the King of Saxony, almost entirely at the expense of Prussia who also lost sole control of Danzig. Such a manoeuvre could hardly be accepted by Prussia for ever, nor could Russia really wish to see all the troubles of the Polish partitions revived. Tilsit could not last. Even the Poles were dissatisfied. They had believed that Napoleon was to re-create Poland for them, and so he would have done had it been diplomatically desirable. In effect they were betrayed.

For the moment Russia was obliged to fall in with France's plans. She still had a war with Turkey to fight, and after 1808 at Erfurt, when it became obvious that plans for the partition of Turkey were impracticable, Napoleon encouraged that war even more. It ended only in 1812 just before the French invasion of Russia. Alexander was requested to accede to the Berlin Decrees of 1806 by which Britain was declared in blockade and all trade with her was forbidden. With Russia's agreement the coast from Finland to Southern Italy would be closed. Britain countered with the Orders in Council prohibiting all trade between any two ports from which Britain was excluded. This harmed the neutrals more than Napoleon, but neutrals were permitted to trade between blockaded ports if they did so via a British port and warehouse. This clearly worked, for Napoleon in the Milan decrees (1807) threatened confiscation of the property of anyone resorting to British ports. Although the Continental system did Britain harm, the Continent needed British goods and did much to get hold of them. The severe economic crisis which hit Britain in 1811 and which convinced Napoleon that the British were about to close down their shops was caused chiefly by harvest failure and damaged Europe more than it did Britain. The harm was seen even before 1811. King Louis Napoleon of Holland abdicated because his brother would not relax his policy, and Holland like North-West Germany was annexed in 1810 to plug the leaks in the system.

It was not in Northern Europe however that Napoleon was to receive his first real check, but in Spain. Since 1795 Spain had been a client of France and had fought with her at Trafalgar. Her monarchy under Charles IV had sunk into a corruption and ineptitude, rivalled only by that of its Neapolitan cousin. The country had deteriorated since Charles III's attempts to rescue it from economic, social and intellectual torpor, and a small section of the population desperately wished for reforms of the French type. Since 1807 French troops had already been in Spain, engaged in a war against Portugal, when an internal squabble allowed Napoleon to capture the entire Bourbon royal family. But Spain was not Italy; it had a tradition of greatness and it had three centuries of existence as a nation. The spontaneous resistance of the people that was easily dealt with in Italy was inextinguishable in Spain, where the church, provinces, cities and people declared a war. For the first time in Europe nationalism was actively at war against France. Joseph

Bonaparte, in name King of Spain, was never so in fact. The real rulers of Spain were the popular bodies, the national committee of 1808, the Cortez of 1810, the Constituent Assembly which created the liberal constitution of 1812, and the catholic church which, rather to its surprise, found itself, for once, on the side of the angels.

Britain immediately offered help to Spanish nationalism, which after its early victory at Baylen in July 1808 was soon in retreat, as Napoleon himself came to Spain. Sir John Moore fell poetically at Corunna, but Napoleon could not give to Spain either the attention or the troops which it needed and Marshalls Ney and Soult found their task appalling. The peasant population reacted to the French with a savagery which only extreme poverty could breed, and under Wellington the British after Talavera (1809) proved impossible to dislodge. Spain became the running sore of the Empire.

Elsewhere Napoleon's grip was slipping. At Erfurt the Tsar had been peculiarly elusive, complaining about French possession of Dalmatia, and as unwilling to make joint plans for the defence of the European *status quo* as he had earlier for the dismemberment of Turkey and Prussia. Francis of Austria and his Chancellor, Metternich, sensed the groundswell as did Napoleon's servant Talleyrand who already smelled a change in the wind, and passed on information to Vienna. In the event Austria moved too quickly and at Wagram (1809) was defeated, though Napoleon's victory was itself wasteful and seemed to suggest a decline in the master's touch. Britain's covering expedition to the continent collapsed in a diseased fiasco at Walcheren, but the significant aspect of the 1809 campaign was Francis' call 'To the German Nation' which seemed to reflect a new mood in Europe. At Schönbrunn Austria lost the last of her Illyrian provinces (Dalmatia, Croatia) and Napoleon married Marie-Louise, to become the nephew of Marie Antoinette.

The fate of Europe lay in the hands of Alexander and Napoleon. 'At bottom the great question is — who shall have Constantinople?' wrote Napoleon. Napoleon was determined that it should not be Alexander, Alexander was afraid that with French troops in Illyria it might be Napoleon. Initial attempts to partition Turkey had foundered on the rock of Constantinople and Alexander had resisted all further plans to prepare a joint attack on the Porte. Napoleon hoped that Alexander might be too busy in Turkey to worry about Prussia's fate, but even before Erfurt Alexander had disillusioned him. It was known that Russia was permitting the import of British goods and in 1810 Russia refused to abide by the Berlin Decree. The annexation of North-West Germany in the same year dispossessed Alexander's brother-in-law, the Duke of Oldenburg. Warsaw continued to offend the Russian outlook while in 1810 a possible ally for Russia had appeared in Sweden, now ruled by Napoleon's bitter enemy, Marshal Prince Bernadotte.

With Britain's help Russia secured peace with Turkey just in time to meet the French invasion. The history of the war in Russia is too well known to detail here. With losses of over three hundred and fifty thousand Napoleon staggered back to France, to call for a supreme effort. Behind him came the Russian army and alongside it in March 1813 soon appeared the Prussian army called out, not by the King, but by General Yorck's sense of popular feeling. Austria entered in July. Fearful of French activity, wary of expecting success, Metternich had attempted to secure a peace but received from Napoleon no guarantees or concessions. Quickly other German states switched to the winning side. Despite defeat at Dresden the Allies pressed on. At Leipzig's 'Battle of the Nations' the French army was mauled more than it could afford. Meanwhile in October Wellington, victorious in Spain, was crossing the Pyrenees. War at last reached French soil and although Napoleon fought with unparalleled genius to defend himself, overwhelming numbers told, and despite the French resistance to the cruelties of the Prussians and Russians, he was obliged to abdicate at Fontainebleau on April 9th.

To this the Hundred Days, following the return from Elba, are a mere postscript. The Army deserted its new master Louis XVIII en masse and the people accepted Napoleon instead of the Bourbons who had, as yet, failed to inspire confidence. But he was only welcomed back on condition that he governed according to the same liberal rules accepted by the returning Legitimists. Europe would not accept him, however, at any price and at Waterloo the adventure was ended.

(ii) RULE

The effects of Napoleon's rule could never be effaced from Europe. No one attempted to recreate the Holy Roman Empire: no one attempted to reunite those German rulers unseated by the reduction of the number of states in Germany from nearly four hundred to forty. Some things just had to be accepted. Feudalism was not re-introduced in 1815, the church was not fully restored and many of the Napoleonic constitutions remained, hardly modified. The other major effect of Napoleon's rule was revulsion against all things French, and the beginning of German nationalism.

The effects of Napoleon on Germany were the most startling outside France. The territories acquired by the Directory had been quickly organised by Napoleon into four Departments with Prefects and the whole administrative paraphernalia of France. Noble titles and feudal rights, monasteries and church property disappeared, the peasants acquired land in freehold, the Napoleonic codes were introduced, education, taxation and conscription all conformed to the French pattern. Such a pattern of government accepted for fourteen years by the Rhinelanders, could hardly be rescinded when the territory was given to Prussia in 1814.

In 1803 Napoleon signed treaties with various German states at the end of years of negotiation. Ever since 1797 it had been necessary to redraw the map of Germany to compensate princes for land lost on the Rhine to France but the 'recess' of 1803 was far more dramatic than originally intended. The number of German states fell by half and those who profited were the larger states, chiefly at the expense of the ecclesiastical princes and the Free Cities. Bavaria, Baden, Württemberg, Nassau and the Hesse states reaped great benefits and demonstrated their gratitude at Austerlitz, after which they were further rewarded.

Those lands east of the Rhine were combined into the Confederation of the Rhine, containing sixteen states organised with a diet of two chambers. But Napoleon was in real control, using the Confederation as a recruiting ground for his armies. By 1807 he had completed the control of Germany. He had occupied Hanover in 1806 and after Friedland Prussia lost her Polish gains, the Altmark, Magdeburg and Halle. Saxony was drawn into the Confederation, while from confiscated territories of Prussia and her allies a new Kingdom of Westphalia grew, soon to be enlarged by the addition of much of Hanover. The rest, with Oldenborg and Holland was absorbed into France in 1810 as part of the defences of the Continental system.

In large areas of Western Germany the benefits of French ideas were felt. The reforms introduced into the Rhineland provinces were extended to the lands of the Confederation and the way was laid open for the growth of the middle class. Legal systems and administration became rational and efficient. In a similar way the boundaries of states became more rational, or at least the German patchwork had fewer patches; and once the first steps were taken to bigger territorial units others were even easier to take.

Nevertheless the chief reaction to Napoleon in Germany was an unfavourable one. His later territorial changes lacked the sanctions of popular acquiescence or reason. Westphalia was always an artificial creation, like Warsaw, and the attachment of Hanover to France was merely opportunist. The re-arrangement of Germany by Napoleon became part of a huge diplomatic chess match played with either Russia or Britain, and Napoleon switched Kings and boundaries around with a lack of concern which would have shocked the monarchs of the eighteenth century. Conscription was Napoleon's major concern; he cared little for the constitution of the Confederation, much for the number of soldiers it produced. German trade was sacrificed to the Continental system. Danzig was idle, Hamburg profited only by smuggling; Rhine, Elbe, Oder and Vistula were empty of shipping and many merchants must have been bankrupted. Among the German middle classes only the civil servants profited and even their work was constantly interfered with by the needs of war. Coming from the ecclesiastical and free cities they lacked loyalty to their new princes or to Napoleon.

Napoleon had swept away barriers to free trade but what was the use if there was no trade? He had reformed the legal and administrative systems but they were open to constant disruption. Conscription was drawing off the life blood of a nation's prosperity — its young men. Germany felt she was being used and German national feeling, even if it was mainly negative, began to stir.

The new Germany created by Napoleon seemed so artificial and liberty acquired with such little effort that intellectuals who reacted against France did so by trying to dig roots into the past, by a return to tradtion. German romantics were traditionalists, men like Arndt, Brentano, Müller. But others found such exercises futile and with Fichte we see a German welcoming revolution and urging Prussia to lead a German revival. The traditionalists tended to look to Austria, the revolutionaries to Prussia; German dualism was already born.

Prussia suffered the greatest humiliation at the hands of Napoleon, only just escaping extinction; but its King, Frederick William III was hardly the man to pull it together. Without Stein, Hardenberg, Scharnhorst and Gneisenau, none of Prussian origin, Prussia would have lain supine. They urged the King to reform. Stein hated France and wished to use a reinvigorated Prussia to drive France from Germany. His period of office as Minister of Trade convinced him that the bureaucratic organisation of Prussia was the root of all her weakness. Stein's policies had been rejected but after Jena he was made Chief Minister. His aim to make the Prussian people into active citizens by agrarian reform and local self-government ran counter to the whole Junker tradition of Prussia. Stein began the work of emancipating the peasant though later acts of 1811 and 1816 severed the peasant from the land and created a class of agricultural labourers which Stein never intended. He did however end the caste system so that middle class men and Junkers could engage in each other's activities. In the towns he encouraged initiative and citizenship by allowing the middle classes to elect councils and share in the choice of mayors.

Stein's most important period of office lasted only from 1807 to 1808 for he incurred the wrath of Napoleon, to say nothing of the Junkers. The work of Scharnhorst and

Gneisenau, however, in reforming the army complemented his work. The restrictions placed on the size of the Prussian army forced her to find another way of training a large force. Scharnhorst and Gneisenau organised a system of short term military service in the army or the Landsturm (Home Guard) which in 1814 was made compulsory. The Landsturm did not distinguish itself in 1813 but certainly the idea created a strong sense of nationhood. The Landsturm was not least important for giving the middle classes the opportunity to become officers, which in the regular army was still impossible.

Other reformers made Prussia more efficient in different ways. Hardenberg prepared to call an Assembly of Estates, while von Humboldt reformed primary and secondary education and created a University at Berlin. Through all these activities, accompanied as they were by the language of a 'nation in arms' Prussia not only became more aware of herself but Germany became aware of Prussia as a leader of resistance to the foreigner. Prussia did not however become a revolutionary nation; the Junkers remained in control and turned all reform to their own advantage. Frederick William did not lead a nation to the Battle of the Nations; General Yorck allied with Russia without his monarch's knowledge and Prussia's army at Leipzig was largely professional. Nonetheless Prussia was now seen by many Germans as a possible alternative to Austria for leadership of a national movement. Such a movement was still minute in 1813 but Napoleon's career had sown some interesting seeds in the soil of Germany.

In Spain the reaction to Napoleon's seizure of the royal family was a bloody one. Religion and fierce national pride joined together to throw out the infidel, and because Napoleon imposed his brother Joseph without a constitution, which he had promised, the middle classes joined the reactionary forces of church, province, noble and peasant in a truly national movement. It began with popular risings of the 'canaille' which terrified the rich, some of whom, especially local notables, sought safety in channelling this enthusiasm. Thus provincial Juntas were set up which, though conservatively composed, became increasingly liberal, when they met the resistance of representatives of the Old Regime which had been so supine in the face of Napoleon. From the provincial Juntas arose the Central Junta at Aranjeuz and eventually a Cortes, meeting, not in the old way, but, under popular pressure, with a liberal electoral system. It met as a Constituent Assembley at Cadiz and created the Constitution of 1812. This Constitution was to be a rallying cry for liberals throughout southern Europe in the years after the defeat of Napoleon. It was the result of a widespread desire for something new to replace the failed régime, but its weakness was that the majority of Spaniards were too poor to be political or patriotic. The church was their nation. While Spain was at war with antichrist the division did not appear; later the numerical weakness of the enlightened was to be obvious. Sovereignty of the people was declared and the freedom of the individual; a far from straightforward system of elections based on manhood suffrage elected a single chamber; the executive was to be in the hands of the monarchy of Charles III's son, Ferdinand VII, still believed to be a liberal; the Catholic religion was to be the only permitted religion of Spain. Only time was to show that popular sovereignty might demand a government which would overturn the 1812 constitution and rule with a cruelty, inefficiency and obscurantism which would shock even conservative Europe.

The reaction to Napoleon in southern Italy, the Kingdom of the two Sicilies, was somewhat similar; hardly surprising perhaps in view of the equal incompetence of the *Ancien Régime,* the same extraordinary poverty and backwardness, the same strength of the still feudal church and aristocracy.

At the time of the Peace of Amiens Napoleon had troops in Naples which, because of Britain's intransigence in Malta, he did not withdraw. When war broke out, and Napoleon became King of Italy, Queen Caroline of Naples called in Russian and British troops, though she and her husband had earlier declared neutrality. Defeated, the royal couple retired to Sicily where they remained protected, if not loved, by Britain. The French occupation was met by fierce opposition in Calabria where extreme poverty had long made brigandage endemic. The brigands became royalist bands, fighting with an extreme cruelty which did not stop at cannibalism. The first Calabrian revolt ended with the fall of Gaeta in 1806 but further outbreaks troubled Joseph Bonaparte, king until 1808, and Murat, king until 1815. The only welcome was from the middle class which remembered the fall of the Parthenopean Republic with horror. Joseph's policy was subservient to Napoleon's needs, but he did begin the work of abolishing feudalism, reorganising the economy and taxation and giving the middle class a National Guard. Spoliation of the monasteries however made the church into a fierce enemy, and this was hardly helped when the new Naples army was used to depose the Pope in 1809. Under Murat Naples began to slip away from Napoleon's grasp. The Continental system and conscription, as elsewhere in Europe, led even the bourgeoisie to hate France and their need to protect themselves from Napoleon's fall created a bond between the middle class and Murat who wished to keep his throne, and was worried by the marriage of Napoleon to a Hapsburg relation of Queen Caroline. In 1812 he defected and sought the friendship of Austria, but he was never happy about his betrayal. His hopes of becoming King of Italy alarmed Austria, and sensing that Austria would sacrifice him he rejoined Napoleon at Waterloo. He was shot by his own people in 1815. While Murat might have been accepted by the middle class of Naples he never received the loyalty of the church, the majority of the nobles or any appreciable part of the peasants who were too poor to benefit from the abolition of feudalism. Those forces, the popular forces, preferred their dreadful Bourbons, and few of the reforms of the French kings got beyond the paper stage.

If the south of Italy could assume some independence no such ideas could be entertained in the north whose strategic importance was too great to be risked. Northern Italy was richer; it had the fertile plains of the Pô, on which it was centred; it had rich towns and ports. Although poverty was not unknown it hardly reached the proportions common in the south. There was therefore a class which could benefit from the Italian republic which succeeded the earlier republics. While the church and nobility were not further molested a new class of businessmen, contractors, traders and professional men assumed greater importance. The breaking

down of the old boundaries encouraged feelings of unity in
Northern Italy and men became used to easy travel and trade.
The political and legal system, though imposed by France,
was workable and encouraged the ideas of unification which
were beginning to stir. A Polish officer in Italy wrote, 'La
formation d'une seule République Italienne est l'idée favorite
des Italiens'.

Napoleon's vice-president Melzi endeavoured to wean his
country from too close a dependence on Napoleon. It
became obvious that Italy was used as a pawn in the great
diplomatic game and her resources were vulnerable to
Napoleon's trading policies. Melzi had severe difficulties with
Napoleon and endeavoured to persuade Austria to help him
prevent Napoleon from taking the crown of Italy and
subordinating it to his own will. The French army, even
though it needed feeding and helped the agriculturalists, was
high handed and Murat, when its commander, treated Melzi
as a subordinate in an occupied country. War constantly
upset economic plans and brigandage met conscription. When
finally Napoleon assumed the crown in 1804 the country
became entirely subservient. Grain was taken to feed France;
she was used as a dumping ground for French goods; her
economy collapsed behind the wall of the Continental system
and her men were used as cannon fodder — Napoleon's 'small
change'.

Although the Italian army and the reforms introduced by
Napoleon helped to create the beginnings of Italian nationalist, hatred of French 'colonialism' did far more. The republic
had never been given a chance to win the loyalty of Italians.
Those classes which had supported it as preferable to
Austrian control or *Ancien Régime* disunity, were soon
disillusioned, while the rural population always viewed it
with defiant neutrality. The Austrians in 1813 were
welcomed whole-heartedly.

In Italy the treatment of the church would very materially
affect the attitude of the majority of the population to the
new rulers. Reform of the church was of course begun in
Tuscany under Leopold and the middle class sections of the
population welcomed it, but the real strength of the church
lay in the countryside, among the peasants. The Papal terri-

tories had already suffered occupation in 1798 and some territory, the Romagna, had been lost. During the negotiations for the concordat Napoleon encouraged the opposition to the church and this was to prove a frequent tactic of his when pressure had to be brought to bear on the Vatican. As in France he cheated the church by adding the 'Organic Articles' to the concordat, so in Italy he allowed Melzi to introduce measures inimical to the Church's interests, beyond the terms of the concordat made between Italy and the Papacy.

The Papal lands attempted to preserve independence during the Third coalition but Napoleon could not afford to let Rome remain as a centre of intrigue. 'Tous mes ennemis, doivent être les siens'. To Papal claims of independence he answered, 'Votre sainteté est souveraine de Rome, mais j'en suis l'Empereur'. Finally after Tilsit, when the Pope broke off negotiations with Napoleon, after French troops had violated his territory, Rome was taken, the Pope removed and the Papal administration dismantled. But although French administration was an improvement on that of the Cardinals the French received no welcome. Both the nobility and the bourgeoisie depended for their existence on the fabric of church government. Resistance to conscription and passive resistance to the French administration weakened Napoleon's control even before the retreat from Moscow.

Only rarely in Europe did Napoleon's rule succeed in striking a responsive chord among its peoples. The needs of the French economy and Napoleon's diplomacy precluded any real notice being taken of the aspirations of the people he governed, even if he had had the humanity, sympathy or understanding required. But it was also obvious that the vast majority of Europeans were, though grateful for some improvements, on the whole unready for many of the changes. Peasants in Germany cared little whoever ruled over them and certainly were not ready for nationalism. In Spain and Italy they reacted bitterly to the changes wrought in their dreary lives, particularly by attacks on the church. The middle class, besides resenting French interference, as yet showed little sign of mass nationalist feeling except in a negative way. The experience of Metternich's System and economic progress were still needed to germinate the Napoleonic seeds. The System in itself was a legacy of Napoleon and the Revolution, for the experience of over twenty years of war against revolutionary France had created a great reaction which turned the enlightened absolutists of the eighteenth century into the frightened absolutists of the nineteenth. The monarchs no longer sought to weaken church, aristocracy and remnants of the *Ancien Régime* but clung to them in the face of change which they now associated with revolution and French ideas. The middle classes which had fought Napoleon as a conqueror were not prepared easily to put the positive social gains he had brought at risk; they did not wish to replace the irresponsible authority of Bonaparte for the uncontrollable authority of the new despots. They had not fought Napoleon to bring about a return to the *Ancien Régime*. The difference in outlook between the urban and rural population of Europe was to seriously damage the liberal cause in Europe.

The experience of French armed might had the effect of making European statesmen see France as the constant danger to peace, whereas in fact, Napoleon I's reign was the last time France consciously or unconsciously threatened the *status quo*. Britain's failure to see the change was long matched by the fears of other European statesmen before Bismarck. Austria was so shaken by war and by the threat of liberal nationalism that she became a threat to peace only in her weakness. Prussia and Russia were the real victors in 1815, though both were slow in realising their advantage.

The twin fears of the statesmen of the absolutist monarchies in the early nineteenth century were liberalism and nationalism, the children of the revolution. The Revolution had convinced Europe that they were Siamese twins joined at the heart. The first man to realise that they were separable would be able to hold Europe to ransome; but for the moment ignorance kept her at peace.

Part Three :
Uneasy Equilibrium 1815-48

CHAPTER ELEVEN

Vienna and The Congresses

The men who made the Vienna Settlement of 1815, Alexander for Russia, Castlereagh for Britain, Hardenberg for Prussia, Metternich for Austria, and at its later stages Talleyrand for France, have been much vilified. They have been criticised for failure to accommodate the new Europe to the twin forces of liberalism and nationalism, for an outdated policy of legitimism, for failing to take account of the needs of Europe's peoples, for helping to create a system of absolutism and for attempting to turn the clock back to 1789. No doubt there is some truth in all these assertions but they are nevertheless largely unfair as criticism. These were conservative men who no more chose to consult the people of Europe about their fate than had the statesmen of the French Revolution or Napoleon himself. There was no attempt to return to 1789, there was no consistent policy of legitimism, no deliberate flouting of the wishes of Italians, Poles, Germans or any other peoples. Even if the peoples of Europe could have been sounded there is no evidence to suggest that they would have known what to demand beyond minor social changes, and certainly no emergent nationalism would have been uncovered except in some commercial or university towns.

The Holy Roman Empire was not restored; the new states of Germany were not dismembered and their component parts given back to their original rulers; the old boundaries of Prussia were not restored, Poland was recreated; Belgium did not return to the Hapsburgs. The Allies had not insisted that

F

Louis XVIII should return to France; Talleyrand had been the prime mover in that scheme and Napoleon's long delay in surrendering had settled the matter. Bernadotte kept Sweden and Murat might well have kept Naples if he had been sensible. Thus legitimism was not an immutable principle of the men of 1815.

The statesmen who danced the diplomatic quadrille at Vienna were attempting to achieve one aim; European peace. And in that they succeeded triumphantly. France and, secretly, Russia were seen as the real threats. It was felt necessary to contain France by strong border states. Thus Belgium was assigned to the restored King of Holland. Napoleon's German Confederation in a slightly altered form was to form another buffer and to the south-east Italy was protected by a stronger Piedmont-Sardinia and Austrian control of Northern Italy. Such an arrangement well suited Austria. Not only did the multi-racial nature of the Hapsburg Empire make her peculiarly susceptible to the liberal-nationalist menace but Austria saw herself as guardian of middle-European order with Vienna as the centre and Germany and Italy as linked areas. This *Mittel-Europa* would not only preserve Europe from France and her liberal disease but it would also act, with Prussian connivance, as a barrier to the expansion of Russia. Furthermore if this area was protected by the Treaty of Vienna it would preserve Austria from the consequences of liberalism and nationalism and help her to combat those forces. But if this was Metternich's hope it was not the main Allied intention. It was hardly possible to dispossess the German princes who had sized up Napoleon's predicament correctly in 1813 and aided the Allies, and these princes, having received their improved status only in 1803 were loath to give it up. Above all Germany must be organised to remove the threat from Russia, while at the same time it was necessary to face the fact that Russia had the largest armies in Europe and had done more than any other continental power to defeat Napoleon.

It was such practical and immediate problems which faced European statesmen as they began their deliberation in 1813. The squabbles among the allies were constant; defeats made them nervous, smaller powers demanded to be heard and required satisfaction. The wonder is that any progress was made at all.

The Vienna settlement was the sum of four main treaties; Chaumont (March 1814), the first Treaty of Paris (May), the second Treaty of Paris (June 1815), and the Treaty of Vienna (June 1815). Negotiations had been in progress since 1813. At Chaumont the Allies formed the Quadruple Alliance, to last for twenty years, undertook to overthrow Napoleon's dynasty and agreed to preserve the approaching territorial settlement for twenty years. By the first Treaty of Paris Louis XVIII accepted the reduction of French boundaries to their position in 1792, ceded Mauritius, Tobago and St Lucia to England and part of San Domingo to Spain; but France kept her trading stations, retrieved Guadeloupe and retained her fishing rights in Newfoundland. The French paid no indemnity, saved their army and kept those movable spoils gathered in plunder raids on the treasure houses of Italy, Germany and Spain. The second Treaty of Paris was signed after Waterloo and after the Treaty of Vienna. France's boundaries shrank to those existing in 1790. The nation accepted an occupation force until such time as an indemnity could be paid and agreed to restore her war-booty.

The decisions made at Vienna were, of course, the most important. The most successful power in terms of territorial gain was Russia. Alexander had hoped to acquire all of Poland and set it up as an independent kingdom with himself as king. Without doubt his intentions were honourable for he was inspired by liberal ideas, but to Metternich 'his heart and his conscience were honest; his mind was false.' The creation of the Poland of 1772 would deprive both Prussia and Austria of territory. Prussia agreed to accept Saxony in return for giving up Poland but Metternich could not accept this and Castlereagh was determined to prevent such an over-whelming accession of Russian and Prussian power. Talleyrand took advantage of the situation to exert French influence and eventually under the threat of war from Britain, Austria and France, Prussia and Russia gave way. Austria kept Galicia, Prussia retained West Prussia and was given, as compensation for other losses, nearly half of Saxony, the Rhineland provinces, Westphalia and Swedish

Pomerania. At the time Prussia was not pleased to lose three million pliant peasants and gain three million independent prosperous Germans; but in 1815 the Ruhr meant nothing. Russia gained the rest of Poland as a separate Romanov kingdom.

Austria's gains were mainly in Italy which was now accepted as a purely Austrian sphere of influence. Venetia and Lombardy became Hapsburg territory; Tuscany went to Ferdinand of Hapsburg, Modena to the Austrian Archduke Francis, Parma to Napoleon's Hapsburg wife. Naples was returned to Ferdinand but was put under Austrian protection and Ferdinand could not introduce a constitution without Austrian assent. The Papal States returned to their legitimate ruler and, as a bulwark against France, Sardinia acquired Genoa and received back Savoy and Nice.

Other minor changes were made; Sweden lost Finland but gained Norway from Denmark; Bavaria gained territory and ceded other land to Austria; Hanover acquired a few trifles, and Holland acquired Belgium only to lose it in 1830. Finally the four powers established the Quadruple Alliance binding its members to keep the territorial settlement intact for twenty years, to keep Napoleon and his successors from the throne of France and to 'renew their meetings at fixed periods' to discuss matters 'of common interest'. Such was the genesis of the Congress system.

Of course the Vienna Settlement was not a total success. It bore in itself seeds of destruction. The fragmentation of Northern Italy went counter to twenty years of development, and the control of life from Vienna by Metternich was not acceptable, for in liberal institutions and national aspirations Metternich saw only demagoguery. His rule in Italy was despotic without the compensations brought by Bonaparte and it was bound to lead to widespread discontent. Moreover after Vienna Austria became a 'European necessity' for her collapse would create a power vacuum which perhaps only war, or France and Russia might fill. Thus, not only Russia and Prussia, but Britain too, became enemy to German and Italian nationalism.

Nevertheless the Allies could not see eye to eye on the nature of the settlement of 1815. To Britain it was a terri-

torial settlement, no more, and to her the internal affairs of a
nation, so long as they did not actively threaten her
neighbours, were no concern of the rest of Europe. But to
Metternich, attempting to preserve a multi-national Empire,
trying to preserve his own country and all Europe from a
liberal slope which he was sure would lead to anarchy, the
internal affairs of any country were of paramount importance. Liberal revolt in Naples or in Spain was a danger to the
peace of Europe. At first this view of the settlement was not
pressed by Metternich; in 1815 he simply saw the Alliance as
a way of preventing any of its signatories from signing
outside alliances, more exactly a way of keeping France and
Russia apart. Later it was to become a moral principle with
him and the Holy Alliance, about which Metternich made so
many sacreligious remarks, and which to him in 1815 was
merely a matter of humouring the Tsar, became the symbol
of an abstract principle of opposition to revolutionary
tendencies everywhere.

When the Tsar mooted the idea of a Holy Alliance of
monarchs bound in a union of Christian virtue Europe, with a
few exceptions, had signed and laughed. If Metternich had
had any fears about it, it was because Alexander's tendencies
were liberal but any association of absolute monarchs after
1815 was eventually bound to discover what Louis XVI had
felt before the revolution — that no compromise between
absolutism and liberalism was at all possible and that liberals
had a way of wanting more than could reasonably be given,
faster than it could be safely given. Such alliances took on an
increasingly conservative tone and the Holy Alliance and
Quadruple Alliance became synonymous, when Britain
discovered how impossible it was to accept the wide interpretation of the Alliance which Metternich demanded. The
growing fears of the absolutists coincided increasingly with
the pressing needs of Austria's survival. Metternich arose as
the messiah of conservative Europe. And not only did he
have faith on his side, Austrian rule over Italy and Germany,
seen as a way of combating any attack from France, was also
arranged by Metternich to counter any liberal or national
growth. Defence of Austria's strategic role implied defence of
her conservative role, and if Europe accepted that liberal

nationalism in those areas was a danger — and Britain even under Palmerston consistently did — it was hardly logical to suggest that liberal revolt within Spain was not dangerous to European peace, for disease spreads.

Whatever comments may be made about the logic and the failings of 1815 it certainly established Austria as the leading influence in European affairs, not because she was strong but because she was weak and fearful. If to be liberal is to believe in human progress through free institutions then Metternich was the arch-enemy of liberalism for in it he saw only anarchy. The powers must not give way even one jot:

In revolutions those who want everything always get the better of those who want a certain amount.

CHAPTER TWELVE

The New Monarchies

France

The immediate post war period was one of peace and quiet. Liberals, disappointed by Napoleon and tired of war were prepared to give their new rulers a chance and in France at least they had a ruler who, like Charles II of England in 1660 was determined never to 'go on his travels again'.

Louis XVIII was not as inspiring figure. Fat, not even very dignified, and with a family seemingly coarsened by contact with foreign climes he had returned after the Hundred Days in a rather undignified manner. He was not popular with the army, though he is hardly to blame for Ney's execution, he was unfamiliar to nearly all Frenchmen, especially to that generation, now reaching maturity which could not recall what Bourbon rule was like, and he possessed no mystique of legitimism, which Louis XVI had effectively drained from the monarchy in the first years of the revolution.

In his own way, however, Louis was a successful king. He was at all times perfectly constitutional in his dealings with the Chamber, he resisted the White Terror and he tried to curb his foolish brother, the future Charles X.

With the defeat of Napoleon impending Louis had accepted a Constitutional Charter which was a clever compromise between his own legitimist principles, which required him to insist that he had been king since the death of 'Louis XVII', and the revolutionary theory of popular sovereignty. Logically such a compromise is impossible but politically the impossible was acomplished. Thus legitimism 'sat uneasily with the chief political and social gains of the revolution'; legal equality, careers open to talents and freedom of speech and religion, though the Catholic church became the Established church. The Napoleonic *codes* and local organisations were preserved, though its personnel was open to change.

Ministers were responsible to Louis but he usually saw the need for them to be acceptable to the two Chamber Assemblies, the nominated House of Peers and the Chamber of Deputies elected on a franchise restricted to those over thirty paying three hundred francs yearly, in direct taxation — an electorate of ninety thousand. If this figure seems small it is worth remembering that any much larger electorate might well have created grave difficulties. The peasantry if given the vote would have been cowed by the great men of the countryside whose politics tended to be fiercely reactionary while the *sansculottes* might well have swung to the opposite extreme. The friction could have broken the monarchy. It was the right wing of Louis' support which tended to demand an extention of the franchise, the liberal wing which wished to restrict it. It is perhaps a valid observation that in Europe liberalism in the first half of the nineteenth century never, as it did in America, implied democracy since an extension of the franchise was always associated with the destruction, not the preservation, of free institutions.

Some idea of the difficulties facing Louis can be grasped when the results of the electoral law of 1815 are analysed. This lowered the voting age for electors and increased the number of deputies. The result was a chamber of youthful, unknown, ultra-royalists — the *chambre introuvable* — who soon pressed the King to dismiss Fouché and Talleyrand from his ministry and supported the unofficial White Terror then operating in royalist provinces. Louis was a constitutional monarch and obeyed his calling. Fouché was dismissed, Talleyrand retired and repressive measures were taken against, among others, hostile writers and, of course, Marshal Ney. But neither of the two new chief ministers the Duc de Richelieu and Décazes were ultra-royalists. When the Chamber proved increasingly obstreperous Louis, urged by his Allies, dismissed it and a more moderate but reduced

Assembly was elected. Here the King acted against his most vociferous supporters with the weapon of royal prerogative and all the liberals applauded. Now the monarchy having accepted that it must bar the way to ultra-royalist reaction had to win the support of those committed to the Revolution and, as yet, wary of royalism.

Austria

Francis II of Austria, while not an imbecile like his successor, lacked any apparent will, and although the bureaucracy continued to function there was no directing hand behind it. Metternich's remedy for lack of control was to set up an Imperial Council, but, although Francis occasionally blew the dust off Metternich's memoranda, the idea went no further. Nothing could have been more unlike the absolutism of Joseph of Austria, where the imperial will was everything. Nineteenth-century Hapsburgs were to pay for his sad failure. Metternich's answer was to decentralise, to revive provincialism. Thus the Austrian monarchy capitulated to the fear of French revolutionary ideas and threw in its lot with the aristocracy and gentry.

Metternich never intended to give the revived fossil Diets actual power, but he did, by this revival, stir up nascent nationalism and he even encouraged it in a sense. For he patronised a literary renaissance among the ethnic groups under the Hapsburg wing. His support for Czech literary revival, the movement towards a single south Slav language and the revival of the Hungarian language under Kazinczy were entirely spurious, but they might later be useful against German nationalism, which was Metternich's immediate dread. Thus the monarchy turned itself against Germanisation too, though later it was to discover in the Austrian — German fear of other nationalisms one of its greatest allies. In fact the monarchy was trapped. If it encouraged the Germans it threatened its position of control in the German Confederation with German nationalism, and if it encouraged provincial nationalisms it alienated the most obvious allies among the Germans of Austria and the Czech and Hungarian towns. If it did nothing, both threats would grow anyway. Little wonder that the characteristic feature of Hapsburg rule is fumbling indecisiveness. Metternich's system, in internal Hapsburg affairs at least, was not real system but lack of it. Disunity was not so much a theory of government as an alternative to it. Everything was negative; the fiercesome prying police force, the press censorship, the cultural revival and the provincialism. Perhaps it is unfair to see Metternich's internal system in isolation from international affairs, when Hapsburg existence depended so much on international acceptance of her role, but that the Hapsburg monarchy under Metternich was devoid of ideas is indisputable. Only the economic and political backwardness of its peasant peoples preserved it, and even that could hardly survive the century.

Prussia and the German Confederation

If Prussian absolutism had been proud and confident under Frederick the Great, apparently since then it had seen something very nasty in the woodshed, and was not a little fearful in consequence. Under its sad little monarch Frederick William III it jumped at every shadow of 'French' liberalism; it feared the nationalism of the Poles, many of whom it still contained within its boundaries; it distrusted the catholic and liberal areas of the Rhineland acquired in 1815. The backbone of the Prussian state was still largely the Junker aristocracy of the estates East of the Elbe; their authority had been challenged by the reform of Stein but they had turned the the abolition of serfdom to their advantage and still controlled the army and civil service. Like their monarch they feared German nationalism and liberalism for they could not conceive of their survival in a larger unit with its base in a more liberal south and west. They were Prussian nationalists, but their nationalism was a compound of fear as they were to show later with their squeals of anguish when Bismarck was engaged in the very act of saving their influence. The middle class remained relatively important and even the Rhineland could not detach the heart of the country from East Prussia.

Nevertheless in Prussia there was an essential dynamism lacking in Austria. Within her territories and linking the two great blocks of territory which made up Prussia the government built roads, reduced internal dues and customs duties and facilitated trade and economic expansion. Absorbing small enclosed states into her customs system Prussia began the process leading eventually to her control of the Zollverein. Straddling as she did major rivers, Vistula, Oder and Elbe, Prussia was set fair to assume control of much of German economic life.

All this was in the future. In 1815 and for some time after, Prussia was Austria's obedient servant, sharing distrust of German nationalism and sharing, in a minor way, control of the German confederation. The confederation's task was negative. It was to neutralise Germany in two ways; from French aggression and from German nationalism. It effectively fulfilled the latter task without ever being called upon, luckily, to fulfil the first. The German princes were too proud of their new power to give it up, and though many had quite strong middle classes these were no great threat. They were mainly civil servants and centred themselves on the individual courts. Essentially Germany like most of Europe remained conservative: aristocrat and peasant were still dominant. The active nationalists were few and far between but they soon grew vociferous and resentful, and so sensitive were the courts of Europe that when a student sneezed seismographs of revolution registered earthquakes.

Russia

Russia remained, even by east Europe's standards, backward. Alexander I's father Paul had been murdered because he had tried to reverse Catherine's capitulation to the nobility and this power of the nobility, their fear of the towns and the middle class, the continuance of serfdom, and the vastness of Russia were the essential factors of the environment in which any Tsar of all the Russias had to work. No Tsar was absolute, not even the 'Northern Sphinx' Alexander. But Alexander was no ordinary Tsar; he was an idealistic liberal absolutist who spoke of the importance of the rule of law and the injustice of monarchy, and befriended liberals and nationalists like Czartoryski.

But not even Alexander's good will could combat the vested interests. He and his 'private committee' of liberals had already by 1815 given up the idea of abolishing serfdom.

Without fundamental reform of this kind educational reform and mild attempts to extend the right to own land were meaningless.

The Holy Alliance and the Polish constitution are typical of this liberal autocrat: they both contain the idea that humane government by good men, who have only moral responsibility to their peoples will be enough to keep Europe happy. But this was merely old enlightened despot theory with an injection of Christian mysticism and its optimism would hardly outlast the outbreak of popular demands any more successfully than its predecessor had.

Italy

'We treat the maintenance of public order in Italy as a matter of life and death for ourselves', wrote Metternich in 1832. He also wrote that it was 'necessary for the Lombards to forget they are Italians'. On this last matter he wavered between optimism about Austria's failure there and pessimism. 'The Italian makes a lot of noise, but he does not take action'. In 1815, optimism might well have been the predominant emotion. The returning sovereigns had been enthusiastically welcomed back and the new monarchs, dukes, empresses, Pope and kings had eagerly dismantled anything and everything Italian. With the exception of Sardinia's Victor Emmanuel and the Pope, they were only too pleased to accept Austria's protection. Ferdinand of Naples agreed to supply troops for Austria when required, as did Tuscany. Metternich's control of police and postal systems kept him in touch with Italian affairs.

The result of this fierce repression, the new provincialism and the memory of a Northern Italy that had for twenty years known unity was a resistance movement stronger than any other in Europe and with an anti-clerical bent grounded in the church's opposition to the French revolutionary reforms. The chief feature of this resistance was its conspiratorial nature. The spirit of the Carbonari was abroad in Italy, for nowhere was there a greater dead weight of tradition and ignorance to overcome and nowhere had the prospect of a liberal nation seemed so near and yet so far from reach.

CHAPTER THIRTEEN

The Liberal Revival and The Congress System

It was hardly to be imagined that the liberals of Europe, small in number though they were, would be quiet for long. In 1818, when the Allies met at Aix-la-Chapelle to admit France to their number Europe still seemed peaceful and Metternich's attitude to the Congress was one of general hostility, but before the next Congress met at Troppau Europe had changed and so had Metternich's attitude to the Congresses.

In 1815, some students at Jena had founded the first Burschenschaft, or student association, a liberal and patriotic organisation. Such associations were endemic among German students but the liberal, nationalist nature of the phenomenon spread quickly among German students everywhere and the Wartburg festival of 1817 saw the creation of a General German Students Association. The murder of Kotzebue by a German student for criticising German liberals rang the alarm bells in the chancelleries, not least that of St Petersburg where Alexander, already in steady retreat from liberalism, was finally convinced of the need for all good despots and true to come to the aid of the party. Frederick-William and Metternich met at Teplitz and the result was the Carlsbad Decrees of 1819 to which the larger German states ascribed their names. Press and education were rigidly controlled. There was very little opposition, so small was the real threat. For Metternich however the result was admirable. With Alexander now under his control he could view a Congress with delight provided Britain was not too awkward.

Kotzebue was not the only man to be assassinated. In February 1820 Louis XVIII's nephew, the Duc de Berry suffered a similar fate and the King's experiment with the middle-of-the-road government was jeopardised. It was however already in danger before 1819. The Ultra-Royalists could not stomach concessions to the men or principles of the Revolution. Their royal champion, the Comte d'Artois, was heir-apparent, and besides this advantage the Ultras had good organisation. The other opponents of the régime were those to the left, republicans, Bonapartists, Orléanists often organised in masonic societies. The real supporters of the experiment, though they had the advantage of the government machine and administration, the support of the King and leadership of Décazes, were thus assailed from both sides. Already in 1818 Décazes' conciliatory policy towards the left had ended in Richelieu's resignation. The assassination ended the trend to the left; the electoral experiments, press freedom and army reforms came to an end. Décazes was forced out, and Richelieu returned, bringing in his wake fresh curbs on the press, and a new restrictive electoral law which re-introduced indirect voting while giving double votes to the rich. Elsewhere in Europe too there was unrest. The year 1819, and the years immediately following a post war slump, coincided with harvest failures to accentuate political unrest.

In Spain in January 1820 a revolution had broken out in Cadiz combining army officers and liberals under Rafael Riego and which, because of the feebleness of the government, forced Ferdinand VII to re-establish the constitution of 1812. The contagion spread in August to Portugal where army risings in Lisbon and Oporto brought demands for a constitution and for the return of the King from Brazil, of which he was also Emperor. In Naples news of the Spanish revolution arrived in March. General Pépé had long been plotting against the monarchy and had recruited into his army revolutionaries of the Carbonari. After initial difficulties he was able to march on the capital and force Ferdinand to grant a constitution, based on that of Spain in 1812.

The revolution of Naples was of particular concern to Austria as Ferdinand had promised to make no constitutional concessions without Metternich's permission. It was Alexander, however, who suggested calling a congress meeting at Troppau to discuss what to do about the European situation. Metternich had no intention of letting Alexander interfere in German affairs nor, if he could help it in Naples. As to Spain Metternich was wary: Britain was positively hostile to any idea of intervention in the internal affairs of a nation (though Castlereagh would support Austrian action in Naples) while France seemed only too eager to interfere. The combined action of Russia and France would be the last thing Metternich could want. So he agreed to leave Spain and Portugal alone while England agreed to say nothing about Austrian action in Naples or Germany. Metternich however could not entirely resist Alexander's demands for the Congress, which met at Troppau in October 1820, just as Ferdinand of Naples swore loyalty to the new constitution.

Britain and France merely sent observers to the conference which looked likely, despite Metternich, to sanction policies of intervention. In the end Austria's expected intervention in Naples was taken in the name of the Alliance and the principle of intervention was asserted. The Congress re-assembled at Laibach in January 1821 and shortly afterwards the King of Naples was restored by Austrian arms. Austrian help was then requested by Piedmont. A rebellion of army officers in March 1821 was soon followed by demands for a constitution which Victor Emmanual had not resisted. He abdicated in favour of Charles Felix, a known reactionary, who was out of the country, and appointed Charles Albert, a man of vaguely liberal sentiments, as Regent. Charles Albert's capitulation to the liberals forced Charles Felix to call for the help of Metternich, which the latter was only too ready to offer.

In Spain, too, the liberals were faltering. In the face of radical pressure in the provinces the moderates tried, but failed, to gain the support of the King. Ferdinand's own blunderings destroyed any chance of a counter-revolution led by the court and hence it was from the provinces that help came in the form of church-led peasant guerrillas. It was obvious, however, that these alone could not subvert the liberal army and so Ferdinand in 1821 appealed to the Powers for assistance.

Metternich was occupied with troubles in Germany and Italy and disliked the idea of Russian and French activity in Spain. France however was eager to help Ferdinand, not to re-establish the corruption of 1819 but to establish a conservative liberal constitution. Only Great Britain was violently opposed to intervention and since she would send only observers to the proposed Congress at Verona in 1822 she could offer no help to Metternich.

The international situation was further complicated by revolts in Greece and Spain's American colonies. In Greece, Alexander Hypsilantes' revolt in the north and a revolt in the Peleponnese strained relations between Russia and Turkey to breaking point, and while the Greek revolts continued it became imperative for the British and Austrian governments, which had their own interests in the near east, to prevent an actual Russo-Turkish war; Metternich by quelling the revolt, Canning by coming to an arrangement with the Tsar. In Spanish America revolutionaries like Bolivar had been greatly helped by the Spanish revolution in their already quite successful attempt to eject the royal government from America. It remained to be seen whether the Eastern Powers would be able to unite to destroy liberalism everywhere.

Great Britain under Castlereagh had already at Troppau begun to withdraw from the Congress system as it took an avowedly interventionist and reactionary path. Under Canning who had had no part in Vienna and who possessed no personal knowledge of the men of 1815 this process was accelerated. Thus at Verona in 1822 the Alliance took on the nature of a moral crusade against liberalism. But there were practical problems too, for Metternich above all; the Tsar's wish to intervene in Spain; the French eagerness to do the same; the problem of the Greek revolt.

In the end the Tsar agreed not to precipitate matters in Greece and France was not prevented from intervening in Spain, because, for Metternich this seemed a reasonable price to pay for the Tsar's acquiescence in other policies. The French army entered Spain in 1823 and met little opposition. Great Britain was driven into a position which made her eventual recognition of the Spanish American governments a matter of time. Metternich secured an agreement between

Russia, Prussia and Austria to repress liberal movements everywhere in their own spheres of influence. In Prussia the long promised constitution was finally shelved; German princes were prevailed upon to revise their constitutions and take action against students; in Italy Austrian garrisons dotted the country and a network of spies grew up: Alexander in Russia drove the liberals to despair in his repression of the press, universities and secret societies. Switzerland under Allied pressure expelled its liberal refugees.

In 1822, the alliance of Austria, Russia and Prussia was all that remained of the Quadruple Alliance of 1815 and Quintuple Alliance of 1818. France was pursuing an independent policy as was Great Britain, but though the alliance had lost members it had become what Metternich called a 'moral principle'. It was no longer a meeting ground for powers to settle international differences, but a tacit understanding that liberalism should be suppressed. Thus the real diplomatic work of Europe now went on with little or no reference to the alliance system. But Metternich was not disappointed; he had always disliked the Congress system because of the way it allowed potential enemies, like Russia and France, to coalesce. The 'moral principle', however, was a guarantee of the Austrian Empire's continued existence.

The liberal years of 1819—22 were short and sad, but they were also somewhat premature. The number of liberals was still, in most of Europe, minute and the instability of European governments, including the British, in these years was far more the result of harvest failure and trade dislocation than of any prevailing liberal sentiment. In Britain after 1822 good harvests and reviving trade enabled the repressive Tories, with few changes of personnel, to become the liberal Tories until the next wave of depression hit the ship of state from 1829 to 1831. In Europe too, 1822 was followed by relative quiet. The peasantry went back to the day-to-day business of growing crops and they, after all, were the backbone of Europe, not those intellectual middle classes, and artisans in the towns whose proximity to centres of government made them appear more important than they deserved.

In only a few areas did liberalism outside Britain seem to

be making progress after 1822 and that was largely because, in the mêlée of national revival, opposition to alien rule could be confused with liberalism. In America the Spanish colonies, long in revolt against a failing parent, succeeded in 1823 in acquiring their independence under republican governments with the assistance of the United States' 'Monroe Doctrine', British naval power and a Franco-British agreement.

Confusion still reigned in Portugal. While John VI had returned from Brazil in 1821, as requested by the revolutionaries, his younger son Don Miguel took heart from the French victory in Spain and repressed the Portuguese constitution in 1823. The heir to the Throne was not Miguel, however, but his elder brother Don Pedro, Regent of Brazil, where the cold winds of nationalism and liberalism had had their effect on his principles. When his father John VI died in 1826 Pedro renounced his claim to the throne of Portugal in favour of his daughter, eight year old Maria. He aimed to secure her position by marrying her to her uncle Miguel and by promising to restore the constitution. Miguel, however, preferred the role of Wicked Uncle to that of Prince Charming and civil war threatened. Faced by this threat the constitutionalists appealed to Canning, the self-styled friend of liberalism, who, having made sure first that France would hold Spain back from invading Portugal on Miguel's behalf, sent a fleet to Lisbon to defend the liberals from a non-existent French threat. Miguel was to prove more difficult to beat.

The events in Spanish America and Portugal had been relatively easy to sort out. France, in both cases, had been willing to secure the friendship of Great Britain by agreeing not to interfere in either area and British sea power had been a decisive factor. In neither instance had the immediate political interests of Austria, Russia or Prussia been involved, for though Austria would have preferred to see Portuguese and American liberalism stamped out the American contagion was at least now less able to spread to Europe and Portugal, surrounded by reactionary Spain, was none too dangerous. More important perhaps was Metternich's need for British friendship, for the revolt in Greece was a threat not only to the 'moral principle' of the Alliance but to

Austria's territorial and political interests. The Greek revolt was to prove a far more delicate problem than America or Portugal for it involved the rivalry of Russia and Austria and the Mediterranean interests of Britain.

The Greek revolt, had, of course, inspired romantic liberals everywhere, Lord Byron not least among them. Politicians were however more wary about committing themselves. Metternich had succeeded in 1822 in convincing Alexander that the real issue was the spread of liberalism and that in this case the Greeks were the belligerents, a view with which Canning concurred. But the action of the Sultan of Turkey in 1824 in calling on his vassal, Mehemet Ali, to send help in the form of his son Ibrahim and large Egyptian forces, impending Greek defeat and Alexander's death totally changed the situation. Nicholas was in every sense a traditionalist and determined to take advantage of the revolt to embarrass Turkey. Moreover a strong Egyptian force in Greece threatened the *status quo* in the Mediterranean more than did an independent Greece. Russia's ultimatum to Egypt in 1826 therefore was inevitable. War however could be avoided. Canning chose to work with the new Tsar to secure a compromise agreement. Not for the last time Britain would find it convenient to work with her greatest rival in the Near East. France, fearful of Anglo-Russian collusion accepted the dictum that if you could not 'beat 'em' you should 'join 'em' and agreed to put pressure on Greeks and Turks to accept a compromise. The result was the destruction of the Turkish and Egyptian fleets at Navarino bay, shortly after Canning's death. Navarino sharply increased Russia's strength and Nicholas quickly seized on this as an excuse to declare war on Turkey. But Russia, despite Wellington's fears, was not eager to dismember the helpless Porte. The Ottoman Empire was as necessary to European peace as was Austria, for Russia feared the consequences for European stability of the collapse of either. Nicholas could not entirely discountenance Metternich's fears of revolutionary movements and well knew that Austria was a better permanent friend than England whose foreign policy under Canning, and Palmerston later, was to be based on the principle of using the weakness or isolation of a continental power to secure a temporary alliance for immediate British interests. Thus at the Treaty of Adrianople Nicholas made a generous peace, the most important clause of which secured a Russian protectorate over the governments of the Danubian provinces of Moldavia and Wallachia. In 1830, the Greek struggle was crowned with complete independence under a new King, Prince Otto of Bavaria.

The Greek question did not destroy the Congress system any more than Canning did. As a means of settling the affairs of Europe it had ceased to exist in 1821; as a principle, it was still in existence. But the Greek question did show that even the 'moral principle' could be temporarily jettisoned by one of the partners if the immediate gains looked promising. Metternich could hardly have been pleased by the way the Greek question had developed; Austria had been isolated, liberalism and nationalism had been allowed an easy and spectacular victory and Russia had established herself in the Danubian provinces. But for the moment Russia saw in a strong Austria and a weak Turkey guarantees of European stability, bastions against the spread of the liberal viruses and the best way of preventing the all out European power struggle which would follow their collapse. Curiously enough Great Britain, though liberal in intentions, also saw in Austrian and Ottoman strength the best safeguards for the European *status quo* and peace. This common attitude which was to last until the Crimean War, was to be the chief reason why peace was not threatened until 1854, despite the growth of liberal and nationalist forces. That growth by 1830 was centainly visible but it could hardly be called as yet all-powerful. The year 1830 was to again demonstrate both its strength and its weaknesses.

CHAPTER FOURTEEN

The Revolutions of 1830

France

The 1830 revolution in France was not necessarily inevitable though it became more so when the charming but bigoted and unimaginative Duc d'Artois succeeded to the throne. The Bourbon monarchy was always in danger, not only from the left but also from the right. The ultra-royalists had a built-in advantage in provincial elections and only the strictest control from the centre had before 1820 secured the continuation of the government's constitutionalist policy. Décazes and Louis had realised the need for the new government to satisfy the rich, landed and financier bourgeoisie which had emerged victorious from the revolution. This class felt itself threatened by the social exclusiveness of the émigré nobles and was suspicious of any moves which suggested a return to the *Ancien Régime*. It feared the clergy and was nervous of the ultra-royalists. It was however a privileged class, an oligarchy as suspicious of the left as it was of the right. Its liberalism was strictly circumscribed by class interest and its nerves were set on edge by the policy occasionally pursued by the Ultras, of suggesting a broadening of the franchise, not only because it might again give the peasant masses a voice, strictly controlled by the aristocrats, but because it might also re-awaken *sansculottism*. The widening of the franchise was a process which it was difficult to halt.

Further dangers to the restoration were to be found in other legacies of the revolution. Paris always had to be watched, for the tradition of Babeuf was still alive. Even more dangerous was the political fragmentation of society which made the game of 'ins' and 'outs' more alarming than in England. The revolution had created legitimists, constitutionalists, republicans, Bonapartists and even a few Orléanists for whom memories were more than political badges; they were political war cries which the fatal French propensity for logic and intellectual hair-splitting never allowed to grow less strident. A Bourbon government could not employ anyone but a legitimist as Prefect or Mayor and so there were always myriad 'outs' who depended on the total collapse of the Bourbons for advancement. Louis Phillippe was to suffer similar difficulties.

In 1820 however, even after the fall of Décazes, the return of Richelieu, the new press law, the new electoral scheme and the abandonment of the plan to make entry into commissioned ranks in the army easier, the collapse of the régime was not inevitable. Although the richest now had two votes the richest might still be, at least in opposition to the Ultras, liberals. The government of Richelieu, despite Ultra victories at the elections of 1820 had not changed the composition of the ministry and Richelieu was to be brought down, not by the Ultras but by them in co-operation with the left against Richelieu's foreign policy.

Villèle, his successor, enjoyed a period of financial stability which quietened the opposition as much as his foreign policy bored them by its timidity. Even here, however, the government scored a striking success by Châteaubriand's vigorous and successful intervention in Spain where Napoleon himself had failed. The success was soon reflected in electoral results which reduced the liberal opposition to a derisory number.

It was unfortunately at this point that the Ultras' foolishness began to make itself felt. Villèle was attacked for being too liberal by an extremist group to his right, and, despite Charles X's protestations of loyalty to the Charter and his suppression of censorship on his accession in 1824, the chief minister's position was weakening, especially as his former foreign minister Châteaubriand had now joined the right-wing opposition.

The bourgeoisie soon had cause for alarm. Even before Louis' death secondary education had come under church control. Under Charles the *chambre retrouvée* made sacrilege a capital offence and increased the state budget for the church. The coronation itself became a display of medieval theocratic monarchy. Monks and nuns unofficially re-appeared, the Universities came under closer ecclesiastical control and, even more alarming to the class whose ideas were still influenced by the enlightenment, the Jesuits re-appeared.

Two innocent government measures were bound to be misconstrued in the prevailing spirit of unease. The first, an indemnity granted to émigrés to compensate them for loss of land in the revolution, was intended to make the new owners feel more secure in their ownership but in fact had the opposite result. A proposal to modify the Napoleonic civil code to permit primogeniture was interpreted as a plot to restore the old social order.

In the end the government felt called upon to prevent misrepresentation of its policies by curbing the circulation of newspapers. Such was the opposition from the peers, para-doxically by English standards the more liberal House, that the bill was dropped.

An election in 1827 resulted in a House containing as many right wing opponents as previously but many more liberals. A change of ministry from Villèle to Martignac did not solve the problem, despite concessions to the left and a more active foreign policy in Greece and Algiers. The only alternative was to negotiate with the right and severely curtail constitutional liberties. The new government that emerged in 1829 was led by the Prince de Polignac, an émigré and cleri-calist of the most alarming kind. In July 1830 Charles' *Coup d'État* was at last attempted.

On July 26th four ordinances were published empowering the King to make laws by decree, and introducing strict control of the press and a much restricted electoral system. Foolishly the King expected his ordinances to go unchal-lenged and was taken aback by the disturbances and barricades which appeared in Paris. Paris, like other cities in Western Europe, was adversely affected by the harvest failures of 1829 and the expected failure of 1830 as well as by the accompanying trade depression. The revolution therefore took on the appearance of a *sansculotte* rising. Nothing could have been more alarming to the liberal deputies, who wished to secure the position of their class with only the slightest concessions to any popular feeling. Like the liberals and whigs in England they greatly feared the common man.

Quickly the liberals secured their position by contacting the Duke of Orleans, made Lieutenant of Kingdom by the departing Charles X, and offering him the throne. Louis Philippe, though hesitant about taking up so difficult a task and of breaking his oath to Charles and his grandson, accepted in order to preserve social order. In fact social order was not in great danger. The only possible leader of the republican mobs was Lafayette, and though he planned and schemed revolution at the Hôtel de Ville he was vacillating and unsure of himself. When Louis Philippe visited him, therefore, at the Hotel and they both appeared on the balcony wrapped in a huge tricolour, their action, ludicrous as it was symbolic, effectively established the Orleanist monarchy. The middle classes, even those unrepresented by the franchise of the original charter, were anxious for order and stability and Louis, unknown though he was, seemed to guarantee it with his mixture of royal birth and respectable revolutionary background.

Louis Philippe, King of the French, was established. The church was separated from the state, the electorate was widened safely by a reduction in the voting age to twenty-five, censorship was abolished. Otherwise the Charter of 1814 was still intact. It remained to be seen whether Louis Philippe would build on it.

The Bourbon restoration ended in dismal failure. It had not been able to withstand the pressure from the right, nobility and clergy and had thus failed to guarantee the social position of the *haute bourgeoisie*. It had been defeated by the revolutionary traditions which still divided the country so hopelessly.

Germany

The events in Paris had their effects elsewhere, not least in Germany. Hesse-Cassel, Hanover and Brunswick all felt the revolutionary rumblings but only in Brunswick was there any real violence and there the Duke's idiosyncracies had made him particularly unpopular. Not even Metternich could make a great deal of this. It was not until 1832 when the revived Burschenschaften held their festival at Hambach that the princes, many of whom had continued to experiment with mild constitutionalism, became at all alarmed. Metternich was able to use this opportunity to introduce, with Prussia at Münchengratz the Six Articles of 1834 which circumscribed the Federal Diet even more and took measures against meetings, popular societies and educational freedom. Constitutions were nearly everywhere revoked and few signs of liberalism were visible in Germany before 1848.

Italy

Italy since 1822 had continued to plot. Conspiratorial groups slipped across frontiers, tenuous links were forged and risings planned. They were largely the work of Enrico Misley whose travels throughout Europe had put him in contact with many radical revolutionary groups. His plan for a united kingdom in Northern Italy was naive since it depended on Russian acquiescence and risings throughout the Hapsburg Empire. Its weakest link was Francis, Duke of Modena, ambitious to become ruler of an Italian kingdom but too nervous to commit himself fully to Misley or to Metternich. The accession of Louis Philippe, whose first government contained members of the European-wide revolutionary group the *Comitatu Cosmopolita,* gave Misley new hope but Francis betrayed the conspirators and Austria marched in to defeat the liberal army which was protecting a meeting of the 'United Provinces of Italy'. Despite the army Misley's conspiracy was lacking in any real backing; the peasants were hostile or indifferent, the middle classes by no means committed and the revolutionaries divided over the future form which the Italian government would take, monarchy or republic. Piedmont, the wealthiest, largest and best organised of Italian states, held aloof under its unsympathetic monarch. Britain was hostile, fearing french intervention and Austrian collapse and Louis Philippe was determined to pursue a peaceful policy.

Poland

The Polish revolt was to prove equally unsuccessful. Polish nationalism had been kept alive by catholicism, romanticism and disputes between Tsar and Diet. The revolt itself began among army officers but unfortunately it remained a military revolt for the peasantry did not join it and the middle classes hardly existed. Moreover, divisions between the Czartoryski moderates and the radicals exacerbated the great difficulties. Hence early military success was meaningless and when the Russians counter-attacked the revolt collapsed, in September 1831.

Belgium

Only in the west where the middle classes were of considerable size could a successful revolution, like that in France, be expected. The most successful perhaps was that in Belgium. The Belgians had never been a contented part of the United Netherlands created in 1815, and King William I's attitude allowed the creation of none. Dutch was the official language and few Belgians were able to enter either the army or the civil service. Belgium's growing industries needed protection against Britain's competition while Holland's agrarian economy demanded low tariffs.

The revolution broke out in August 1830 and was made possible by the success of the French Revolution and by the beginnings of a compromise between the liberal and clerical elements in Belgian society. The advanced state of Belgian society made possible a liberal uprising but it was not initially nationalist in tone for the *haute bourgeoisie* feared the possible social consequences of republicanism. William I's action in attacking the Belgian capital turned the bourgeois into nationalists but also drove them to look for a king to guarantee their new constitution with its very limited franchise. The future of Belgium depended, however, on the conflicting opinions of the powers who were to remain in conference until 1839. By that time the Belgians had acquired Leopold of Saxe-Coburg-Gotha as King and had already settled down to a period of bourgeois respectability and industrial expansion.

Switzerland was also to undergo a successful revolution in

1830, a revolution of the intellectuals and the businessmen against the particularist and patrician government of the Cantons. Here again the new constitution was to be based on an extended but still restrictive property qualification.

Property qualifications, equality before the law, freedom of the press — these were the signatures of the liberals of 1830. They suggest a common purpose, common attitudes and possibly common backgrounds. Liberals and liberalism in 1830 will repay some careful study for Europe was on the threshold of considerable economic, social and political change which would change men's attitudes almost as much as had the French Revolution of 1789 and its successors.

CHAPTER FIFTEEN

The Threshold of Economic Revolution 1815-48

In 1830, when Europe experienced the first serious revolutions of the nineteenth century, the social and economic organisation of the continent was still recognisably that obtaining in the eighteenth century. True, the aristocracy had seen its powers diminish in parts of Western Europe as a new class laid claim to social equality but in most areas little had changed. In Hungary and Russia serfdom continued to exist; in Prussia and Bohemia the peasant was still not free of obligations to his lord. The Junkers still largely determined the policies of the Hohenzollerns. The middle class could be described as strongly entrenched in only three places; Great Britain, Belgium and France. Even in Great Britain the Reform Act was still two years away and it was not until 1846 that politicians finally accepted that the country's wealth depended above all on the enterprise of its middle class industrialists and entrepreneurs. In France the middle class which secured its pre-eminence in 1830 was essentially an oligarchic *haute bourgeoisie* of financiers and landowners which excluded large numbers of the lower bourgeoisie from political representation or social equality. Industry, the supreme catalyst of social change, was still an embryo growth. From France and the Mediterranean shore to Prussia, Russia and the Baltic the peasantry exerted its conservative influence and provided for the constituted powers a preponderance of popular acquiescence, if not support.

Nonetheless the old order was changing, and by 1870 those states closest to the major trade routes, and benefiting from previously unused natural resources, had undergone a rapid and alarming social and economic transformation which had shifted economic weight, if not as yet the weight of population, from the country to the town. Such rapid changes were to seriously undermine social stability and create revolutionary stresses in societies where only a few decades before revolutionaries had been merely poets or university professors and students, dreaming of their unachievable, logically perfect societies.

The most extraordinary and momentous of these changes was the growth in the size of the population. In 1780, the population of Europe was probably in the region of 160 million people: by 1850 it had increased by 100 million and had passed the 300 million mark by 1870. No society could withstand such strains unharmed and emigration to America was not to reach immense proportions until the last quarter of the nineteenth century; Europe had to absorb the impact. The reasons for the spectacular increase in the number of Europeans are still difficult to fathom. People certainly seem to have lived longer and medical science had rid the continent of many of the medieval scourges, though cholera and typhoid were regular visitors in the first half of the nineteenth century. The land was better utilised in the nineteenth than in the preceding century but whether this is mainly a cause or an effect of change is still not satisfactorily discovered. New techniques were slow to spread, as the example of the so-called 'Agrarian revolution' in England had taught us, and England did not suffer from the stifling effects of labour services and inequitable taxation and had rather better communications than most European countries.

As might be expected Russia was slow to adopt new techniques yet the rate of population growth there exceeded that in England. The Iberian peninsula saw a slower increase in population than either England or Russia as did France whose population grew by only nine million in the century. The populations of Germany, Belgium and Great Britain doubled during the same period. It is thus difficult to ascribe general causes to this great phenomenon.

Nevertheless, one common factor in this demographic explosion is discernible. While the rural areas shared in the general increase it was the towns which everywhere showed the most rapid growth. The overall rate of growth in France was steady rather than spectacular but the towns saw a more dramatic increase, the great industrial towns of Paris, Lyons and Marseilles doubling in size by 1870. In Germany too, and even in Austria, though rather less noticeably in Bohemia and Hungary, the urban centres were expanding. In 1870, the process had still far to go in the lands of the Hapsburgs and Romanovs; but already in 1848 it was to be the towns which were to give the most cause for concern to the monarchs of Europe, for while the rural areas remained conservative the urban areas were increasingly prey to revolutionary ideas.

It remains to be seen how much this economic transformation had achieved by 1848. On the continent of Europe it was Belgium which initially underwent the industrial revolution which was rapidly changing the face of Great Britain. She had rich coal supplies and, especially after 1830 rich veins of individual initiative and enterprise. She early developed a national railway policy and after opening her first line in 1835 took advantage of her strategic economic position to carry the exports of her more tardy neighbours. A strong and uniform currency gave a firm basis to Belgium's economic progress.

Belgium moreover had long been an area of Europe which had taken advantage of her ports and position on major sea routes and had possessed a strong, though rarely united, middle class. After 1830 the rapid growth of towns and of a proletarian population was to bring the middle classes into closer alliance.

In France under the Bourbons economic policy was largely determined by the *haute bourgeoisie* that, as yet, unassailed victor class of the revolutionary and Napoleonic eras, soon to be victorious again in 1830. It was largely a financier and landowning class and thus government policy, particularly under Villèle was dominated by the needs of a strong currency and good government credit. British competition in manufactured goods with which France could not hope to compete, was met by a policy of protection which was to persist until Louis Napoleon's reign. Tariffs were raised against agricultural imports too, to satisfy the agricultural interests which, with finance, were paramount.

Such a policy led to foreign reprisals, damaging to agricultural exports and to nascent export industries, but the winegrowers and port authorities were in a minority and it was the bankers and the non-exporting agriculturalists who determined government policy. Government policy is, perhaps, a rather grand term for what amounted to 'minimum government' perpetuated to preserve the balanced budget. Only in canal building was the Bourbon era one of true economic progress.

'The bankers' revolution' which ushered in the Orleanist government tended to perpetuate these government attitudes: high tariffs, low taxation and non-interference were the governmental 'orders for the day' especially when the politics of the Orleanist government showed signs of fossilisation. Nonetheless it would be unfair to blame the Orleanist government entirely for the relative lack of economic dynamism in France before Louis Napoleon's Second Empire. The government of Louis Philippe, despite its *laissez-faire* orthodoxy, gave generous help to private industry and spent money on more canals, some roads and, above all, railways. The typical Orleanist attitude to finance and business can be seen in its railway policy. As in Belgium there was an overall plan but in France the construction was in private hands, heavily backed by government aid and with guarantees of a return on investment. Again it is financial and political considerations which govern policy, above all a realisation of how much the government depended on the banker class and it was among this class that the concessions were shared, not in a spirit of capitalist competition but in the co-operative spirit of a superior club.

For, in France, the capitalist ethic had not yet assumed great importance, as it had in Britain or Belgium and this is probably as much due to the tone of French society as to the political necessities of governments balancing on too narrow a franchise. In eighteenth century France a wealthy father had always felt the need to secure the future of his sons by obtaining for them a safe position, if possible in government; and it had been partly the closing of such avenues of advancement that had created middle class frustration before the

1789 revolution. In England a son who did not inherit, and even one who did, was obliged to make provision for himself and while there was certainly a market in government preferments it did not reach the proportions obtaining in France. In nineteenth century France the goal in life was security to a far greater degree than in England where 'speculate to accumulate' and 'self-help' were watchwords of a dynamic society. Capitalism in its early stages takes risks, and it competes. The ethos of French society did not encourage the taking of risks and combated competition. The great financiers did not compete for railway concessions, they shared them out. Even more damaging to the growth of a dynamic economy was the inferior social position of the man engaged in business. Something of this attitude can be seen in England but it never reached the proportions existing in France and although, as the novels of Disraeli clearly show, there was in England considerable antagonism between industrial and agricultural interests this was because the industrialists had reached a position of economic pre-eminence and political power whereas in France it seemed that they were never to be allowed to acquire such a prestigious standing. Moreover in France the businessman seemed eager to retain his inferior position. The family firm did not wish to take the risk of losing family security by expansion, even when such expansion was possible. Thus business attracted few people of talent and acquired neither social prestige nor economic dynamism.

Lack of credit facilities, too, militated against expansion of industry. John Law's failure in 1720 had frightened Frenchmen too much to allow them to set up a National Bank until Napoleon's reign, and even then the *Banque de France* made little credit available to private borrowers. Credit was obtainable only from the small private banking firms like the Rothschilds who felt no obligation to develop the means of making credit available for risky enterprises; they preferred to lend money to a government which guaranteed returns, just as in the eighteenth century wealthy middle class financiers preferred to loan money to a desperate government rather than to entrepreneurs.

It must also be remembered that the revolutionary and

PLATE 1A   *Joseph II wields a plough*

PLATE 1B   *William II, Emperor of Germany, 1797–1888*

'*Quid sum?*'   '*Je suis citoyen.*'   '*Je suis député*
                                          du Tiers.'

PLATE 2A   *The makers of the French Revolution:*
            Deputies of the Three Estates, 1789

PLATE 2B   *Massacre of the prisoners at the prison of St Germain*

PLATE 3 *Political cartoon satirising Napoleon's seizure of power, 18 Brumaire, 1799*

PLATE 5A   *The Second Republic, 1848: 'He's made his bed, now he must lie on it'—The King's bedroom, 24–25 February*

PLATE 5B   *Punch cartoon of Napoleon III: Leap Year— Liberty under the mistletoe* EMPEROR NAPOLEON *'Eh! No! Really I! What will my wife say?'*

PLATE 6A   *Goethe: Painting by Tischbein*

Romanticism in Europe

PLATE 6B   *Chopin: Painting by Delacroix*

PLATE 6C   *Marie Taglioni as La Sylphide: Lithograph by Lacauchie*

PLATE 7A   *A German bourgeois family in 1821 : Painting by Karl Begas*

Bourgeoisie and peasantry

PLATE 7B   *The Haymarket, St Petersburg, 1835*

PLATE 8A   *Serfs from the Don*

Russian serfdom

PLATE 8B   *Reading Alexander's manifesto freeing the serfs, 1861*

Napoleonic wars had diverted resources to unproductive outlets and enabled Britain to forge far ahead of France in industrial expansion. While this, on the one had, meant that France could borrow technology ready made, it also made it almost impossible for her to break into Britain's markets.

Above all perhaps it was the results of rural revolution in 1789 which prevented French industrial expansion. A peasantry tied to the land, deliberately reducing its families to keep partible inheritances to a reasonable size, and buying few consumer goods, kept back the advance of industry as surely as it preserved social stability.

Although this picture of a lack of any dynamism was undergoing some change by 1848, French economic progress was slower than in many other parts of Europe. Coal production, exports, railway building and large industrial enterprises lagged behind even the politically fragmented Germany. Steady growth there was, especially in a textile industry which found itself a luxury market in Europe with which Britain's cheap goods did not compete. The bourgeoisie began, on a small scale, in the 30s and 40s to invest in industry as well as land and *rentes*. The railway boom which began unsteadily in the 40s, (only 1500 miles were laid by 1848 and many of·those miles unprofitable) slowly brought into existence an association of new style capitalism, large scale organisations and bank finance which after 1848 was to be given greater governmental and private aid. As we shall see, from the railways was to spring France's belated industrial revolution, albeit even then hindered by France's social conservatism. All this was enough to continually add to the populations of Paris, Lyons, Marseilles and other major cities but probably not enough to absorb the number of people attracted to them by promise of better wages. Possibly the very slowness of expansion was itself a cause of political revolution. It was Louis Napoleon's reign which was to see the true burgeoning of French industry.

Germany also in 1848 was as yet merely on the threshold of the industrial expansion which was to make the German Empire the major economic force in Europe. In 1815, there was even less sign of this industrial miracle. Much of north-eastern Germany was still infertile despite the work of the

G

Hohenzollerns of the eighteenth century, and although Prussia was strategically placed on the Elbe and the Oder the Baltic was an economic backwater. The particularist pride of the new kings, grand dukes and princes did little to overcome the poor communications existing within the confederation or to speed the dismantling of customs barriers. The confederation itself was never planned as an active force in German affairs and obediently followed its calling.

Yet there did emerge during this period a development which profoundly influenced the economic history of Germany, the Zollverein. This originated not in any desire for unity but in economic and political conflict between the states, and the desire of Prussian bureaucracy for order.

Prussia in 1815 was still not a unified state. The Rhineland provinces were physically, as well as emotionally, separated from the traditional eastern territories of the Hohenzollerns. While much work was being done to build up the economy within the existing boundaries by such men as Von Motz, Beuth and Von Rother, some way of facilitating intercourse between the two territorial blocks was obviously necessary. The tariff law of 1818 facilitated such intercourse and soon smaller states completely surrounded by Prussian territory accepted the law also. This effective customs union, stimulated unions among other German states, notably those between Bavaria and Württemberg, and between Hanover, Brunswick, Saxony and smaller states in the Middle-German customs union. The latter is the best example of a purely political union since its main object was not economic but political — to prevent Prussia controlling communications between the interior and the North Sea. The failure of the Middle-German union led Hesse-Cassel to attach itself to the Prussian customs union, thus uniting Prussia's two territorial blocks. Other states quickly followed and at last Bavaria and Württemberg in 1834 joined Prussia, Hesse-Cassel and Hesse-Darmstadt in the Zollverein. Other states were soon to follow. Although this union was no part of a movement towards nationalism, and was brought about solely by the economic fears of individual states, which allowed no diminution of their rights in the Zollverein, it did have important effects. The financial advantages were early noticeable and although trade and industry developed only slowly, a useful basis had been created for expansion.

The Zollverein helps explain why Germany with its jealous rivalries should have been able to develop a railway system at all, and above all a system larger than that of France. By 1848, Germany had three thousand miles of track, France one thousand five hundred. The development in Germany however was patchy. Prussia, whose economic strength had been demonstrated by the success of her customs union, had half the German railway mileage in 1848. The effects of the railway on Germany were considerable. Germany's rivers flowed to the backwater of the Baltic, except for the Rhine whose estuary was controlled by Holland. Railways ended the total dependence on rivers, speeded the integration of the German people and made possible and profitable exploitation of her natural resources. Hence, although Germany was in 1848 still rural, backward and particularist, in the Zollverein and the developing railway system she had the prerequisites of industrial greatness established, and already where railway builders had passed, Ruritanian Germany had undergone a severe change.

The railway boom which preceded the great crash of the late 1840s suggests that the best pointer to the extent of economic change lies in the railway mileage in each country. On such a criterion Austria and Russia had hardly changed at all. In Russia the main channels of communication were the rivers, frozen in winter and too shallow in summer. Roads were still tracks and the first metalled road, from St Petersburg to Moscow was finished only a short while before 1848. The great period of railway building was not to get under way until the 1850s; before that time it was fitful and largely insignificant. Although Vienna could be reached by rail in 1848 there were less railways in the Austrian Empire in 1848 than in Prussia at the same time.

Nonetheless even in the more backward countries changes were occurring. The cities there, too, were expanding and industry was at last making headway. The machines that Joseph II had forbidden were welcomed into the Bohemian textile industries, and in a few places, in Vienna, Prague and St Petersburg a small class of entrepreneurs was making itself felt alongside a proletariat which, like that in Paris, found too little work to go round.

Although the speed of change was everywhere different there could be no doubt that all Europe was now seeing signs of development and was growing together into a more closely knit economic community. For centuries Europe had been similarly subject to the vagaries of the weather and of harvest failures which severely affected economies. Now they were even more drawn together by economic ties of credit and finance centred above all on the credit heart of Europe, Great Britain. Britain supplied money not only to her own entrepreneurs but to those of other countries and their governments. She led the way in railway expansion and the champion of that expansion was George Hudson, 'the Railway King'. When his Empire collapsed in 1847 all Europe staggered under a blow to which disastrous harvests only added. All Europe was being pulled into the same economic net, to suffer the same round of boom and slump. The troughs of economic depression were to bear a close relation to political disturbance in Europe; 1819, 1830 and 1848 were three such troughs.

CHAPTER SIXTEEN

Societies and Governments
1815-48

It is clear that Europe, while showing everywhere symptoms of change, was not undergoing transformation at a uniform pace. It is equally clear that everywhere it was the towns which were betraying signs of precocious development, often or nearly always out of keeping with the more leisurely progress in rural areas. Such disparity was bound to lead to friction between town and country, but more bitter now than in the eighteenth century and in many forms. There was often a straightforward antagonism between the aristocracy and gentry on the one side and the middle classes on the other because the development of towns seemed to pose a threat to not only the economic but also the political and social superiority of the landed classes. In Britain this struggle can be seen in the opposition to the repeal of the Corn Laws, and to administrative and police reforms after 1832, in Hungary in renewed opposition to the growth of towns and in Russia in the deliberately perpetuated ineffectiveness of town governments. But there was a further problem, for in many countries the systems of administration were based on a totally rural society, and whereas the peasantry in France in 1814 had formed three quarters of the population, by 1870 it formed barely a half. The growth of towns was outstripping the ability of administrative systems to cope. In France Napoleon's system was more successful than most in dealing with such problems but in England the delayed development caused severe breakdowns in public order and administration. Everywhere where towns were growing fast the technical, administrative and policing ability of the government was to lag behind social and economic change. This was dangerous in societies which were overwhelmingly rural but which had concentrations of population in certain small areas. Here the ethics of the whole society and its customs would be aristocratic, peasant and rural but the particular needs of the densely populated areas would be very different. While such a situation allowed governments to fall back on conservative forces in the event of revolutionary outbreaks it did make possible revolutionary outbreaks in the very areas where government itself was concentrated, as in Prague, Vienna, Paris and Berlin. London was not a major industrial centre in 1848 and therefore escaped the worst of the contagion.

Society was undergoing change before 1848, then, but in a way which made it difficult for governments to adapt themselves to it. Only after 1848 was the spread of industrialisation to acquire a momentum in certain countries which enabled governments to pursue a more forward policy, better suited to the new, rather than the old society.

French society even after 1850 was still aristocratic and oligarchic. The old aristocracy now tended to bury itself in the country while the Napoleonic and Orleanist aristocracy came to the fore. Once again the tendency of French society towards security manifested itself in the Orleanist aristocracy which though intended to be one of life peers only, became in fact hereditary like the rest. But it was the *haute bourgeoisie* which set the tone of French society after 1830 and against whose superiority and self-confidence the romantic movement battered itself. This *haute bourgeoisie*, of financiers, landed bourgeois or rich professional men, melted imperceptibly into the middle bourgeoisie where were to be found most of the industrialists, lawyers and civil servants. The petty bourgeoisie of shopkeepers, artisans, teachers and the rest had still to live down its revolutionary past and its links with the *sansculottes*, the proletariat into which they themselves merged.

It was among the middle bourgeoisie industrialists and the workers that movement in this apparently hierarchical society could be seen. As yet development was limited but it was present. Development was not seen in the class of skilled artisans nor in the domestic handicraft workers, both of which were declining in importance, though not yet as disastrously as their English counterparts. Real development was visible in the new factory workers, still not, except in the Alsace textile industry, working in large factories but nonetheless different from handicrafts workers. This class was growing in Paris, Lyons, Marseilles and other major cities where it lived in subhuman conditions, dependent on fitful charity and a wage which barely held its own with the cost of living in good times and never in bad harvest or slump times, when all the weekly wage, if there was one, would be spent on bread. Such people were a prey to political agitators in bad times like those immediately following the 1830 revolution, the period 1839 to 1841 and in 1847 and 1848. Then, too, they would be joined by the declining class of handicrafts workers and the artisans, in troubles which few governments really knew how to handle, least of all those of Louis Philippe which urged the starving to resign themselves to their fate and wait for the market to pick up. Laisser-faire was as much the doctrine of Guizot as it was of Peel.

Peasants, even in 1870, still formed the backbone of the social structure in France and their conservatism was both a rock on which a firm social order might stand resolute and an obstacle in the way of the ship of state's progress. In 1848 as in 1830 and 1780 they craved, above all, land and this craving perpetuated the system of subdividing property among heirs at a time when there was not enough available to give a reasonable standard of living to a growing population. Many peasants were share-croppers and as such loath to improve their methods, while peasant owners rarely had land, capital or credit for improvements. The peasant with a sizable amount of land was not admired but denigrated, because of the pressure on land from those with less or, as in many cases, none. The peasantry remained conservative, dissatisfied and, often, in debt, never a force for progress, rarely a reliable support for conservative government.

With such a large conservative force in the country and such a dangerous revolutionary force in the town any government which was not to stand absolutely still until it fell to revolution had to secure a wide basis of support for a programme of moderate reform. Louis Philippe's government was from its very beginning shackled to the interests of the very narrow class which had created the Orléans monarchy to protect its particular interests, the *haute bourgeoisie*.

Casimir Périer remarked in 1830 that 'not much has changed in France'. The Charter of 1814 was merely revised in a liberal sense and the franchise was extended to a total of only 170,000. The monarchy lost the right to initiate legislation and its suspending and dispensing powers. This was hardly a revolution, merely a change of dynasty, though the constitution was liberal and capable of further development. Nonetheless the situation of the government was not quite so secure. Louis Philippe had no real security because he had no 'principle of existence'; he had not been called to his throne by popular demand, nor did he have legitimism on his side. No change of dynasty could be a 'mere' change because with the change in dynasty must go a wholesale change in the personnel of government right into the heart of the country through the agency of the Prefects who must themselves be safe Orleanists. Moreover French government and politics had again demonstrated their inability to find the 'golden mean' which enabled English government to develop, not without difficulty but without revolution. That 'golden mean' while due in part to the principles of England's aristocracy, its advanced industrial state, its 'amateur' local government and the principle of the 'independent' civil servant, was chiefly the result of tradition and popular trust in the institutions of the country which France had not enjoyed since the eighteenth century and which Louis Philippe, a 'usurper' and king of a class rather than a nation, could not easily acquire. He played the role of a king but he had no qualifications or rights to be more than a president. His own character had been formed in an atmosphere of eighteenth century enlightenment which the young nineteenth century was rejecting as inadequate, and, a man of strong opinions, Louis Philippe was determined to rule as well as to reign. Thus from a position of weakness he pursued a policy of strength. He was 'the whole that transcends them (parties), which has an autonomous existence, which has its own demands. All this is personified in the Chief of State who. . .must be an arbiter and never lose control of diplomacy, the colonies or the Army'.

If his support was narrow, from a class point of view, it was made narrower by the fact that Orleanism as a political force was divided between the *'parti de résistance'* of which Guizot and Broglie were to be the chief exponents and the *parti de mouvement* of which Laffitte was chief representative but with which Lafayette was linked. Thiers roamed the battlefield alone. The *parti de mouvement* saw the constitution as a mere starting point in progress towards a wider franchise and a monarchy divorced from politics. It hardly appealed to Louis Philippe who was able to take advantage of the dangerous riots and insurrections which began very soon after the establishment of the régime in 1831, and which reached their climax in the fierce class warfare of Lyons in 1831 and 1834, to rid himself of the *parti de mouvement* whose anti-clericalist outbursts and whose revolutionary foreign policy were alarming to the King. He was able to portray their activities as giving encouragement to the rioting *sansculottes* in their dangerously 'socialist' demands. Better harvests and trading conditions then did the rest of the work. Never again did the King depend on the left. Casimir Périer of the *parti de résistance* restored the confidence of the government; Broglie, Molé and Guizot continued the 'résistance' tradition which not even Thiers' short ministry could upset. But although Louis Philippe might defeat the *parti de mouvement* he did not, and could not, defeat its principles. Effectively in 1831 the monarchy abandoned the idea of change and determined to rule with the backing of the wealthy élite, but such a system even during the comparatively slow economic and social change of Louis Philippe's reign was a basic miscalculation.

The defeat of the *parti de mouvement* added to those irreconcilably opposed to the régime. The Legitimists led by Berryer were embarrassing because they pointed out the King's lack of credentials and his apostasy in 1830, but they were no more than that, except in the rural areas where the aristocracy helped opposition candidates. The legitimist 'rising' organised by the Duchesse de Berry was a fiasco. The

Bonapartists were even less dangerous despite, or perhaps because of, Louis Napoleon's two attempted *coups d'état*. Apparently more dangerous was the left.

Republicanism was, by 1830, becoming a romantic word. The failure of legitimism made it more intellectually respectable than Orleanism while the first republic was far enough in the past for the younger generation of bourgeois intellectuals to treat the Terror as a mistake of their elders which they themselves would not repeat. But republicanism was not merely an idealistic rallying point, it was also a 'bread and butter' issue. While the republican impetus was no doubt sustained by war fever and the revolutionary traditions of *sansculottism* in secret societies like *Les Amis du Peuple* and the *Sociéte des Droits de l'Homme* it reached its apogee at times of great distress when insurrectionists movements in Lyons and Paris, and other cities, were endemic. At their climax in April 1834, over one hundred died in Paris alone.

As France went through the difficult stages of industrialisation irreconcilables of the left, like Barbès, Blanqui, Buonarotti, a survivor of Babeuf's insurrection, and Cavaignac, kept alive the mystique of 1793 through periods of worker apathy, allied it to social romantic movements and fused it with industrial despair when the harvests failed.

Despite later assassination attempts on the king, however, the republican movement had, for the time being, shot its bolt and the decrees of September 1835 tightening up the laws of libel and making it a criminal offence to declare a wish to change the dynasty or method of government were no longer so necessary. But they are important in another sense for they show how the Orleanists governments tackled symptons rather than causes of unrest. The rising of 1831 in Lyons had been a social protest against the refusal of employers or government to honour a minimum wages agreement. But such an agreement ran counter to the orthodox laissez-faire attitudes not only of the King but also of the narrow class on which his authority rested. Government activity, it was believed, could only make things worse, so Orleanist government is almost totally lacking in any reforms or attempts to control the effects of industrialisation on a helpless population. Nothing was done about conditions in mines or factories, except for a Factories Act which omitted to create an inspectorate, while government aid was given to railway financiers. The government felt safe in doing nothing because this was the way to national prosperity. Hardly any minister challenged this orthodoxy, certainly not Casimir-Périer or the Duc de Broglie. Thiers was too interested in foreign policy or opposition and Guizot put all his considerable talents into holding the *status quo* by techniques of parliamentary management worthy of the Duke of Newcastle, or at least Dundas. This only served to associate Orleanism with a corruption which enemies of Guizot, like Thiers, were able to make much of, thus damaging the régime without necessarily meaning to. But Guizot and Louis Philippe, who clung to his favourite minister like George III to Lord North, and for much the same reasons, could not see the arguments for an extension to the franchise or Place Acts which the opposition in parliament suggested, and even worse, they were afraid to move. 'Doctrinaires', like Guizot believed that too great an extension to the francise would mean an end to those freedoms in which they believed. Like the 'Adullamites' in Britain they wished to see the sovereignty of the people limited by the liberty of the individual — a doctrine admirable in itself but not when the individuals are limited to the haute bourgeoisie. Thus the 'liberalism' of Louis Philippe's régime slowly ossified since the King was reluctant to make any changes in the franchise. Seeing itself defending liberty from the evils of democracy and absolutism the plight of the régime reflected the plight of many individual and sincere liberals in the mid-nineteenth century; afraid to go forward they either stood still and hoped that the bogey would go away or jumped backwards into the arms of reaction. Social reform was 'socialism' and electoral reform was 'democracy' and both were shunned. Many young people, in despair, turned to millennial ideologies, others pretended that politics did not exist. No-one seemed to know in which direction it was really safe to move.

In the Hapsburg dominions the problems were different but rather more intractable. Essentially they all concerned nationalism, the most dangerous force possible in a multi-

racial Empire, where a 'patriot' to the Emperor meant 'a
Patriot for Me', as the only unifying force. In the Hapsburg
Empire the type of nationalism varied as often as the
language of its people. In Northern Italy nationalism affected
the town dwellers, who were influenced by it in a quite
different way from the Magyars, who had found a new
weapon with which to fight for class interest against the
reforming or centralising tendencies of the Germanic
monarchy. Nowhere in the Hapsburg dominion had nationalism yet penetrated seriously to the peasants. Such a development was not to occur until after the Austro-Prussian war.
Nonetheless national feeling was a growing force and its
impact on Austrian government was felt with misgiving. For
Metternich saw in all change disorder, in nationalism only
destruction and he knew that the monarchy under Francis
was paralysed by the Emperor's sloth, while under his successor Ferdinand by actual idiocy:

> I became. . .the representative of something that should
> have been in existence but in fact was not.

In his attempts to meet the threat of nationalism, which he
was only partially convinced could successfully be challenged, he tried two remedies; both failed. Economic
amelioration encouraged the growth of those classes most
attracted by nationalism, and attempts to foster the historic
and traditional forces in Bohemia and Hungary — language,
history, folk-lore — merely fostered the nationalism of the
present which found succour and inspiration in the past.
Metternich's failures encouraged his enemies, particularly the
bureaucrat Kolovrat, and the 'liberal' Archduke John, to
seize the initiative from Metternich on the death of Emperor
Francis I in 1835.

The new triumvirate gave even greater encouragement to
provincialism: Ferdinand was crowned King of Bohemia, the
Bohemian nobility paraded Czech patriotism, the Diets were
encouraged. But while this may have been in part a charade it
gave an opportunity to liberals and nationalists. In Bohemia,
Palacky, the Czech leader saw the advantages of the Diets as
possible mouthpieces for new ideas.

Bohemian nationalism was a growing force and one to which the vacillating and nervous government in Vienna had a rather equivocal attitude. It saw obvious dangers in it and yet felt that it might be useful in the face of growing Magyar nationalism which had taken a more intransigent turn under Louis Kossuth, the representative of the gentry who saw new dangers in the Vienna government's patronage of alien minorities in Hungary. Kossuth replaced the conservative aristocrat Szechenyi as leader of Magyar patriotism, which henceforth took an increasingly uncompromising road, demanding liberty before prosperity where Szechenyi had always argued that prosperity was the prerequisite of change. The illiberal liberalism of Kossuth was largely a class movement to preserve the political and economic independence of the Magyar gentry. As such it could not be a Hungarian national movement since it threatened the Croatian and Transylvanian minorities and it would only temporarily be able to appeal to the Slav peasantry, as yet aware only of social grievances rather than national aspirations. The peasantry was finally freed from the personal servitude of serfdom in 1836, but not yet from many of the burdens that had gone with it, particularly the Robot. This marked no diminution in the power of the gentry and at the Diet of 1844 Magyar replaced German, the language of Viennese bureaucracy, and Slav, the language of the peasants, as the official language of Hungary.

Thus although the court might see Magyar 'nationalism' as a counter to Bohemian 'nationalism' and vice-versa it was a counter-weight which made for instability and a negative policy. It had never been in the dynasty's interest to encourage the uniqueness of Hungary which had been such a problem since the eighteenth century. The only thing that could be said for it was that it awakened Croatian nationalism which could, if necessary, be used against the Magyars. But this was a sterile way to run an Empire when Prussia was gaining strength in the West.

Revolution would not, in our case, mean a forest fire. If the Hungarian revolts. . .we should immediately set the Bohemian against him, for they hate each other; and after him the Pole, or the German or the Italian.

The fact that this was precisely how the Hapsburgs survived 1848 and proved the necessity of the dynasty to their subject peoples does not make the system more palatable. It was small wonder that in the growing cities and at University meetings people were looking to a new Germany, incorporating Austria and Bohemia, but giving Hungary and Italy their freedom. For some, progress meant the dissolution of the Hapsburg state.

For indeed it could hardly be said that the Empire's government was capable of doing much but drift with the tide. It had contemplated resisting Magyar demands in 1844 but had not dared rouse the peasants. It failed, in 1847 at the last Hungarian Diet, to accept taxation, land and peasant reforms which Joseph II had fought for unsuccessfully because it distrusted the motives of Kossuth who had persuaded the gentry to pass them. Faced by the popular, dynamic, demagogue Kossuth it merely awaited events in an attitude of suppliant prayer.

The society of the Austrian Empire was slow to change for it was far from major industrial centres. While the city of Vienna suffered from the same malaise as Berlin or Paris, it was among the peasantry that real social unrest could be seen in the opposition to the robot or labour service, which despite Joseph II, was a feature of their lives.

Yet even Metternich could still be sanguine about the future:

Our country, or rather our countries, are the most peaceful because they enjoy, without having suffered any previous revolution, most of those benefits which undoubtedly arise from the action of empires overthrown by political strife.

The one area of the Hapsburg Empire about which he was never hopeful and which gave him most trouble was Italy. Although 'no country is less well fitted than Italy to be handed out to popular government' and although the Italian 'makes a lot of noise, but he does not take action' Metternich's spy system belied his confidence. He feared the 'see-saw' gymnastics, and juggling' of the Piedmontese and the machinations of Mazzini's 'Young Italy' which originated in 1831, and above all he feared the apparent liberalism of Pio Nono's reforms in 1846.

Piedmont, despite the extreme caution of its ruler, Charles Albert, was again in the nationalist van. It was here that despite opposition to railways and banks real economic progress was being made, in cities like Turin where industries were being founded and ports like Genoa, the centre of Italian trade. Northern Italy generally was in all respects becoming more intransigent as it flexed its economic muscles and sought literary inspiration in its historical past. The younger generation was like its counterparts, France, Austria and Germany, less willing to compromise.

If Italy was one part of Hapsburg sphere of influence which consumed a great part of his energies Germany was another. Münchengratz and the Six Articles had driven liberal and nationalist movements underground but the accession of Frederick-William IV to the Prussian throne in 1840 had revived these movements, and in a way which Metternich could hardly approve. Frederick-William was thought to be liberal, though in fact he was merely erratic, but at least he compared favourably with Ferdinand of Austria, and the hiatus caused by the failure of leadership in Austria allowed Prussia to seem to progressive thought the ideal leader of the new Germany, while it also underlined the ineffectiveness of the Frankfurt sham. To this impression Frederick-William's restoration of the deposed university professors gave apparent credence. The Schleswig-Holstein question, concerning the two predominantly Germanic duchies ruled by the Danish king, gave added strength to national feeling while the Zollverein seemed to suggest that Prussia was the state most able to take a nationalist initiative. The liberal national movement gained impetus with the publication of the new newspaper, the 'Deutsche Zeitung', and the beginnings of a National Liberal Party.

Germany therefore seemed to be on the threshold of a liberal union. There was a sizable professional middle class and a growing class of entrepreneurs like Krupp and

Camphausen in major towns, particularly in the Rhineland-Westphalia lands of Prussia and in Saxony. The Zollverein had achieved a vigour all its own and railways were forcing people to think in less narrowly particularist terms. But success was to elude the men of 1848 and it is not difficult to see why.

Progress there certainly was in the 1840s but towns outside certain growth areas remained small, and the middle class was essentially professional or intellectual, men of ideas rather than action. There were still small states almost untouched by the nineteenth century. Besides this class there was the aristocracy, still with considerable power, especially in Prussia where pressure from the Junkers in 1847 showed itself stronger than the influence of the more industrialised and liberal western provinces of the Hohenzollerns. The peasantry remained conservative save where, in the west, there was a hunger for land which gave that class an air of radicalism. There remained only the urban working classes and here there was a possibly explosive situation. For where, as in Berlin and Silesia, the handicraft workers existed they were being driven into poverty by the competition of British factories while the factories of Germany were still far too few, too scattered and too small to absorb them or the growing drift from the countryside. Nonetheless the factory worker of Berlin or Rhineland-Westphalia was an increasingly familiar figure. Slums, child labour, long hours and the cycle of slump and prosperity made their lot a wretched one and their protests when times were bad ever louder.

Frederick-William was no liberal champion and certainly not an apostle of nationalism. His early liberal moves quickly turned to repression when Rhineland liberals became too pressing in their demands for a liberal constitution. The revolutionism of Berlin workers and the pressure of conservatives at court lined up behind the heir to the throne brought him back to conservatism. His constitutionalism was merely a medieval sham. In 1847 he called a United Diet of Prussia, in effect an assembly of representatives of the almost defunct provincial Diets, its main task being to give loan sanction for the construction of a railway to East Prussia whose Junkers viewed with alarm the economic strength of the western provinces and their middle class elements. The Diet was dissolved having achieved nothing, since it began to demand regular meetings and a right to consent to taxation before it would give the necessary loan sanction. In the opposition to Junker demands from the Rhinelanders and the townspeople of eastern Prussia there can be seen the development of conflict between aristocracy and third estate, land and industry but there is no sign in 1847 that the third estate is the stronger element.

Outside Prussia developments were slow. The Confederation, though seen by many as unsatisfactory was not seriously challenged, nor was the existing social order except in Bavaria and Baden and it is fitting that the state which saw one of the few real attempts to establish enlightened despotism should have developed in the 1840s not only a strong liberal movement, but a radical social revolutionary movement under Hecker and Struve, and that it should have been in the Baden assembly that in February 1848 the first open call for a German national parliament should have been made.

Although Russia remained a most important element in European diplomacy she was still very much cut off from cultural and political developments in Europe. Alexander I had flirted with a dynastic liberalism but this had had very few roots in Russia's own infertile soil and under Nicholas I constitutional changes of any kind were hardly to be looked for. Essentially soldierly in outlook he was completely an autocrat. Reforms took the form of codification of laws or of attempts to control the nobility and gentry more closely and in this way Nicholas can be seen as an eighteenth rather than a nineteenth century figure. It was in this sense that he took an interest in conditions in the estate factories of landowners and restricted the hours that children might work but that there could be organic changes in society or political life was beyond his understanding.

If Nicholas had had any leanings towards liberalism these would have been quickly corrected by the Polish nationalist uprising in 1830. Censorship was so strict that many writers left the country altogether. Gogol was perhaps the greatest loss. His play *The Government Inspector* pokes merciless fun at Russian officialdom, and although Nicholas I personally gave permission for its presentation Gogol still felt that the weight of censorship was too great to be born:

> All are against me. Old and respectable officials shout that nothing must be sacred for me if I dare to speak of civil servants in such a fashion: the police are against one, the merchants are against me, the writers are against me. . .As soon as the slightest wisp of truth appears everyone is against you — not only individuals but whole social groups.

Despite the great difficulties inherent in any attempt to discuss reform in Russia during this period, two schools of thought arose with very different answers to Russia's peculiar problem both of which reflected the dualism of Russia's cultural outlook present at least since Peter the Great opened his window on Europe, and visible as late as the time of Stalin and Trotsky. The westernisers felt that only by opening herself to Western influences could Russia build anew. Peter Chaadaev put the problem and the solution:

> Not a single useful thought had grown in the sterile soil of our fatherland. . .We have to speak Europe's language.

But there was little comfort for them in a sterile Russia and many of the westernising leaders left Russia for the west. The Slavophils also saw that Russian society was unique and also saw that it needed reform but they believed that Russia's salvation could only be worked out against a purely Russian, or Slav background and one based on the cultural traditions of the orthodox church and the village community, or 'mir'. The Slavophils found little comfort in the Tsar's rule either, its intense centralisation seemed to them alien to tradition.

Thus in Russia as in the other major European centres there were people at odds with the government, small groups certainly but capable of growth and sudden stimulation if governments remained static, sterile and afraid. The philosophical opposition to government in Russia was unique and hardly to be transferred to people west of the Elbe fed on different traditions. But everywhere there was growing dissatisfaction and everywhere philosophies of change were warring with each other for the control of the minds of the dissatisfied peoples.

CHAPTER SEVENTEEN

Diplomacy 1830-48

The 1830 revolutions did not in themselves materially alter the nature of international relations after 1830. Although the creation of an independent liberal Belgium in the thirties did seem to add weight to the idea that Europe was dividing into liberal and reactionary camps no such simple process was occurring. Certainly France for a time was obliged to depend on British friendship in view of the hostility of the Eastern powers but such dependence did not last long and French manoeuvres in the Near East were to show how ideological differences between Russia and Britain, were as nothing compared with their common suspicion of France and Mehemet Ali. The 'liberal monarchies' of Spain and Portugal lacked any real attributes of liberalism and were soon to decline again into inefficient despotism. The truth is that no country can pursue a policy dictated by a philosophy or ideology all the time. To Palmerston liberalism as an element of foreign policy was accorded a place well below the simple pursuit of British interests. If Austria came nearer than others to diplomatic and ideological purity that was perhaps only because she was too weak to take any positive actions.

The Belgian revolt was the first cause of diplomatic activity. It soon became obvious that the Belgians were not willing to accept any settlement which left them under the rule of the King of Holland, though it was a solution along these lines which suggested itself to Russia and Prussia under the accepted leadership of Metternich. The eastern powers were, however, afraid to take military action for fear of inciting retaliation by the French, whose government of the *parti de mouvement* was eager to advance both revolutionary standards and French boundaries. Palmerston feared the same possibility; it became British policy to keep both sides from taking military action and thus to secure Belgian independence.

Louis Philippe's own unwillingness to go to war prepared the way for a conference of the five Powers in London. This conference agreed to create an independent Belgian state, but the Belgians were angered by the frontier arrangements which excluded the rich areas of Luxembourg, Maastricht and Dutch Limberg from the new kingdom. Possibly in retaliation the Belgians elected a younger son of the French monarch as their new king, an arrangement which Louis Philippe foolishly accepted, thereby creating a new diplomatic crisis.

This was resolved by Louis Philippe withdrawing his permission for his son's election after Palmerstonian pressure, but further resentment between the two nations was built up by the election of George IV's widower son-in-law, Leopold, as a Belgian king who might be expected to have close relations with the British government. When in August the Dutch invaded Belgium and the French came as requested by Leopold to her aid, it seemed as though all the work of the London conference was to be destroyed, especially when, after the Dutch defeat, Talleyrand for France spoke of acquiring some Belgian territory and the Prussians began to make significantly warlike noises. Fortunately Louis Philippe could see the dangers and although final arrangements for the frontier were not settled until 1839 there was no further danger of war.

The Belgian crisis was in its way a Palmerston triumph, but his attitude to France was bound to lead to friction with Louis Philippe as later with Louis Napoleon. Palmerston had learnt the lesson of post-Vienna diplomacy, that Britain required an ally in Europe for her opinion to be effectively pressed; France, with a liberal constitution and a monarch regarded as a traitor by his fellow rulers, seemed the ideal partner. Partners however are usually equals, but France could never be Britain's equal for Britain feared new outbreaks of French revolutionary chauvinism with its conse-

quent threat to the Vienna settlement in Italy, Germany and
Belgium. Louis Philippe faced with domestic pressures could
certainly not afford to be seen simply as a lackey of perfidi-
ous Albion, and he felt, with some justification, that France
had a right to independent activity in certain diplomatic
spheres. Perhaps an alliance between a foreign minister wedded
to the Vienna settlement as his diplomatic touchstone and a
king who had, not only in France, but also in Belgium, upset
two of the decisions of Vienna, was an impossibility.

Meanwhile in the Near East another crisis, destined to
destroy the Anglo-French entente, was entering its first stage.
The Near East was an area of particular significance to Britain
for on its stability seemed to depend lines of communication
with India. The continuing decline of Turkey and the
ambitions of Mehemet Ali endangered the peace of the area
because Russia's historic advance to the straits, Constantinople and the Mediterranean was helped by it. Russia's
advance threatened Austria's communications and trade with
the outside world through the Danube, and even French
interest in the Levant was being re-awakened. In the crisis
occasioned by the Greek revolt Britain had found herself
aligned with Russia against Turkey so it was clear that in the
Near East no simple rift between reactionaries and liberals
could be counted upon.

Mehemet Ali, Pasha of Egypt, was anxious to create an
Empire for himself and, he hoped, for his heirs. Nominally he
was the vassal of the Sultan, Mahmud II, but when the Porte
rewarded Mehemet Ali's services in the Greek revolt with the
gift of Crete instead of the coveted Syria, the Egyptian
quickly invaded and overran his heart's desire and advanced
into Asia Minor defeating the Turks at Konieh (1831). The
Ottoman Empire seemed to be on the point of total collapse.

The response of the allies was surprising. Palmerston paid
very little attention to the events in Asia Minor, perhaps
more concerned with the Iberian peninsula and the Belgian
question, and although the British ambassador to the Porte,
Stratford Canning, held out the hope of British assistance this
was refused by the British government. However, Britain
could not wish to see the collapse of the Turks and might
have been expected to work with Austria who feared that the

result of such a collapse could only be Russian aggrandisement. But Austria was committed to Russia over the Belgian
and Iberian questions and alienated from Britain by
Palmerston's apparent encouragement of France. France
herself, though by tradition and desire for self assertion, not
averse to Mehemet Ali's success, could not at this critical
juncture in European affairs afford to alienate Great Britain.
So while France, Britain and Austria remained inactive or
estranged Russia seized the initiative. Nicholas I did not wish
to see a weak Ottoman Empire replaced by a strong Egyptian
one and he was persuaded that the Egyptian attack was 'a
result of the spirit of insurrection which has now seized
Europe, and especially France'.

It transpired therefore that when neither France nor
Britain responded to Metternich's appeal for a forced mediation Turkey sought refuge from the sphinx in the hug of the
Russian bear. Russia occupied both shores of the Bosphorus at
the beginning of 1833. The other powers now realised their
error and imposed a settlement whereby Mehemet Ali
received the Pashaliks of Egypt, Crete, Damascus, Tripoli and
Syria, but for his lifetime only. However in July a far more
serious event took place when the treaty of Unkiar Skelessi
was signed between Russia and the Porte. In the event of war
Russia could demand that Turkey close the straits to all
foreign warships. Shortly afterwards Russia and Austria
regularised their relations at Münchengrätz agreeing to
collaborate in central Europe and in the maintenance of
Turkish integrity. Thus Great Britain particularly, and to a
lesser extent France, had been totally outmanoevred.
Palmerston, whose fault in part this was, determined to reverse
the terms of Unkiar Skelessi while France began to look with
an increasingly favourable eye on the doughty, if shifty,
Mehemet Ali and his warrior son Ibrahim Pasha.

While this drama was in progress comic opera was being
performed in Spain and Portugal. In Portugal the throne of
the rightful queen, Maria, had been usurped by her uncle Don
Miguel while in Spain in 1833 Queen Isabella, unfortunately
too young and too plain to be a real heroine, found her
succession threatened by her wicked uncle, Don Carlos.
Liberal opinion, such as it was, in both countries supported

the queens, whose wicked uncles were thoroughly autocratic. Both France and Britain had given considerable, if unofficial, help to the Queens since 1831 but Britain remained highly suspicious of French motives, perhaps justifiably in view of the later Spanish marriages dispute. Hence when Talleyrand proposed that France and Britain should form a military alliance to help the Queens, Palmerston would only agree if it was extended by the addition of the liberal governments of Spain and Portugal. The main purpose of the Quadruple Alliance was to defeat the uncles without allowing France to act by herself, and if Palmerston really believed that the Alliance would 'serve as a powerful counterpoise to the Holy Alliance in the East' he was greatly deceiving himself, and it is probable that the statement was made only in the light of the meeting of the eastern powers at Münchengrätz. The Alliance succeeded in securing the thrones of Maria and Isabella but not in making them liberal, except in outward form.

The Alliance and the *Entente* were unable to withstand another Near East crisis. France's increased interest in the Mediterranean was not confined to Spain, but extended also to Algeria in the thirties and increasingly to the Levant where a potentially explosive situation continued to exist. Mahmud II, though discouraged by Russia and Great Britain, wished for revenge on Mehemet Ali. Palmerston's opposition to the Turko-Egyptian war was not the result of any respect for Mehemet Ali; 'I look upon his boasted civilisation of Egypt as the arrantest humbug' he wrote, but he was eager to see Turkey pursue a policy of solid reform which Mahmud was too impatient to realise, Russia was satisfied with Unkiar Skelessi and Austria after Münchengrätz wished only for peace and vigilance against liberalism.

Unfortunately, although most powers sought only peace, French public opinion supported Egyptian expansion, and French commercial interests echoed these sentiments. At the same time relations between Russia and Britain worsened considerably because of British fears for India occasioned by Russian activities in Circassia. Already one serious incident had been caused by the Russophobe David Urquart, who ran the Russian blockade of the Circassian coast in his ship, the

Vixen, in 1836. The third element of instability in this situation was Mehemet Ali himself who had still not secured hereditary possession of Egypt and Syria.

In May 1838 he announced his intention of declaring his independence but was forced to withdraw by the powers. Mahmud however took the opportunity to invade Syria where at Nizib in June 1839 he suffered a severe defeat. The Sultan's death brought to the throne an ineffectual teenager, so inspiring to his warriors that the entire Turkish fleet crossed over to the victor, who was able to demand terms amounting to the destruction of the Empire in Asia Minor. Britain France and Austria now concerted action to arrange a Vienna conference of the five powers. This situation halted the Egyptian advance for Ibrahim refused to advance to the straits, preferring to wait and see. In effect this ended the military threat but the powers were in no position to comprehend this.

Although the powers at first appeared united they were far from being so. Britain wished to force Mehemet Ali back into Egypt, but France, though not wishing to see the Pasha independent of the Sultan, wished him to keep Syria. This aroused British suspicion, for French technicians had for some time been helping to reform the Egyptian forces as British technicians had been helping with the Turkish forces, and the French consul at Basra, though no doubt without official support, has been trying to interfere with overland routes through Mesopotamia. Palmerston began to see the ghost of Napoleon in Egypt.

Russia meanwhile was not eager to see a Five Power settlement of the affair but at the same time was in no financial position to make war. Even more weighty considerations encouraged Nicholas in his actions however, for he saw an opportunity to break the Anglo-French entente, the cracks in which widened as Palmerston's determination to coerce Mehemet Ali strengthened.

Russia made approaches to Britain and by the beginning of 1839 the two powers were agreed that the Pasha must be confined to Egypt. This agreement came at a strategic moment, for the new Thiers government in France had now embarked on a policy of wholehearted support for Mehemet

Ali which could result in either complete success or complete humiliation, but which must in any case destroy the Franco-British understanding. Thiers' government would accept no compromises put forward by Austria or Great Britain and insisted that the French protégé receive all Syria in hereditary possession (1840).

Such an unreasonable attitude allowed the other powers to impose their own terms and obliged Britain to bind herself more closely to Russia. 'England is a widow.' On the other hand Russia was now willing to detach Britain from France by the promise of a settlement of the straits question as Palmerston had always wanted.

In July 1840 the Four Powers (without France) issued an ultimatum to Mehemet Ali, who foolishly counted on French military support, which the government of Louis Philippe now realised they were in no position to give. A combined allied naval and military operation near Beirut coupled with a revolt of Lebanese Christians drove Ibrahim from Syria after his defeat at Junieh.

In the settlement which followed Mehemet Ali was given hereditary but not entirely independent possession of Egypt. At the Straits Convention of 1841 Russia gave up the privileged position given her by the Treaty of Unkiar Skelessi, while the Sultan agreed to maintain the older system forbidding the entry of foreign warships into the straits while the Porte was at peace.

France's immediate reaction to the Four Power agreement of July 1840 had been one of patriotic fury. Thiers reminded France that 'even when alone she had been mistress of Europe' and his government began making military preparations. There was as much bluff and bluster as real danger in the situation however; Louis Philippe's anger soon abated. Thiers was obliged to resign and France took part in the final peace arrangements and the Straits Convention.

As the decade of the forties opened the Anglo-French entente was in disarray. Although Palmerston had succeeded brilliantly in securing Russian co-operation, Nicholas I had been more than prepared to meet him half way. Now that the eastern question was settled for a while what possible reason was there for Anglo-Russian friendship. Despite appearances,

Britain was isolated. Nicholas nursed his new found friendship with Britain, even going so far as to visit England to meet Lord Aberdeen, Peel's foreign secretary, in 1844. Here a verbal agreement was made which was to be of considerable importance in the misunderstandings which culminated in the Crimean War. But although Nicholas might be pleased, Britain knew that the alliance was one sided. Russia was of no great use to Britain but Britain was useful to Russia because an Anglo-Russian entente could keep Britain and France apart.

Peel and Aberdeen were aware of this danger and in the very year that Nicholas visited England Anglo-French relations took a significant turn for the better. Aberdeen was more polite than Palmerston and did not attempt to make the French ministers feel inferior while Louis Philippe and Victoria got along 'famously'. The honeymoon was however too short. The French annexation of Tahiti and expansionist aims in North Africa had already been sources of friction but it was to be the return of Palmerston, the issue of Spain and the domestic pressures on Louis Philippe which were to lead to the final breakdown.

The question of the marriage of Queen Isabella of Spain had arisen as early as 1840. The French government had put forward a French prince for the ten-year-old Queen but the British were strongly opposed to any such match and countered with a spare Saxe-Coburg. Both governments wished to avoid any rift and it seemed that a compromise might have been reached when Peel's government fell. The arrangement was vague but it involved a possible marriage of the Queen to a cousin and her sister to a French prince. In 1846 Palmerston inadvertently gave the impression that he was eagerly pressing the Coburg candidature whereupon the French decided to be greatly offended. Louis Philippe, backed by public opinion, arranged the betrothal of Isabella to her cousin, the supposedly impotent Duke of Cadiz, while her sister was betrothed to Louis Philippe's son, the Duke of Montpensier. In the ensuing fury the entente dissolved in mutual recrimination.

Whatever had been the intentions of the French government in Spain their interest had sparked off immediate

British fears, reminiscent of Palmerston's reaction to Talley-rand's proposals of military alliance against the 'wicked uncles'. The Entente was not strong enough to withstand Britain's fears for her interests in the Mediterranean area, occasioned by the needs of an independent French policy. A similar pattern was to emerge in the entente with Louis Napoleon. Whatever the reasons for the Entente's failure, 1846 saw Britain totally isolated and France moving towards friendship with Austria. Russia's hopes of binding Britain to her interests had considerably increased but Palmerston had had no part in the verbal agreement with Nicholas I, a fact which the Tsar tended to overlook.

Despite the affair of the Spanish marriages international affairs after the eastern crisis were more stable than for many years. The eastern powers seemed to have checked internal dangers and were agreed on matters of international affairs; there were no outstanding problems facing the diplomats and while this state of affairs continued neither Britain nor France would feel their isolation keenly. In 1848, however, Europe's apparently healthy body endured serious convulsions.

CHAPTER EIGHTEEN

Revolutionary Movements

In the years between the revolutions of 1830 and 1848, many people felt that Europe was rushing to her destruction, if not to democracy which was generally felt to be the same thing. Some, like Guizot, stood on the cliff top immovably awaiting the tidal wave, others like De Tocqueville studied American democracy to discover how to make the best of a very bad job. Perhaps they were all too alarmed. If they had reflected that the smaller a movement is the louder must it shout they might have panicked less easily; or if they had looked at Europe they might have seen that, while everywhere there was unrest, hope and fear, there was no coherence. French revolutionaries were interested in social and political issues, they were the vanguard of the proletarian revolution, but revolution in Germany and Italy meant chiefly the creation of the nation state and the achievement of constitutionalism, while in Austria's territories and those of Turkey in the Balkans aspirations were merely national. The appearance of unity was given by the optimism and generous feelings of the idealists and the fears of those people who might suffer from any change and who rightly feared a revolutionary chain reaction.

Paris was the traditional home of revolutionary causes and the likely starting point of revolution. To it looked all young idealists; 'I entered it with reverence', wrote Alexander Herzen, an exiled Russian 'westerniser'. Paris was the home of the new social theorists with their theoretical roots in the works of the Comte de Saint Simon and Charles Fourier but with their emotional roots in the tradition of 1793 and the Babeuf plot. Although St Simon's theories of progress through the application of technology to social problems and his utopian ideal of a society guided by an élite of entrepreneur engineers had little direct appeal to the workers many of his ideas filtered through other people's minds and came to have a profound effect on the development of socialism and Marxism.

Fourier's plans for small communities — phalanxes or *phalanstères* — of exactly 1620 people, spread equally around the countryside, rather than crowded in cities and governed through the collaboration of capital labour and inventions was equally too rarefied for immediate proletarian consumption. But in its revulsion against the effects of competitive capitalism and its message of co-operation it had wide effects. The workers of the French cities wanted immediate remedies for immediate problems and it was men who offered such solutions who won mass support. Louis Blanc's doctrine of the co-operative resembled Robert Owen's ideas in England but with a more violently revolutionary tradition of direct action. Direct action was also the watchword of Auguste Blanqui who demanded the abolition of private property and who was never happier than when on the barricades. His attempt with Barbès to organise an armed rising in 1839 landed him in prison. He was the true heir of Babeuf.

Pierre-Joseph Proudhoun rejected political action and advocated purely economic action by the workers, though where the dividing line might be it is difficult to say. He saw no benefit in the workers gaining all power since this would be a new tyranny, therefore he advocated a more equitable sharing of property and power in order to achieve a balanced society.

Unfortunately all of these theories were badly flawed, or insufficiently thought out. It was left to Marx to work out a more complete and practical scheme of revolution, ruthless where his predecessors had been too genteel. But Marx's arrival in Paris was delayed until 1843; before that he had had a varied career in Germany. He had edited the *Rheinische Zeitung* in Cologne until 1843 when his criticisms of Prussian government and the ruling classes had obliged him to leave.

He was not particularly popular in Paris among the socialists who found him too unwilling to accept criticism. His theories owed something to St Simon, but even more to Hegel. Marx believed that he had discovered the laws of historical change which were leading mankind to an absolute — the classless, stateless world — by a process of dialectical materialism. All societies consisted of exploiters and exploited; the former controlled production and distribution whose nature in itself controlled the other aspects of life — religion, culture, thought and law. But each society contained within itself the seeds of its own destruction; thus feudalism gave way to capitalism as capitalism would itself give way to socialism, through the growth of a vast and ever poorer working class and the diminution of the capitalist class by competition. By claiming to have discovered the laws of economic change upon which every other aspect of society depended and by 'proving' his thesis in a cogent, and not altogether fanciful, treatment of history Marx gave an inevitability to the workers' victory.

The *Communist Manifesto* was not to appear until 1848, *Das Kapital* was even later and Marxism was to play little part in the revolutions of 1848 even in France, but already in the German refugee 'League of the Just', later 'the Communist League', there were the seeds of a movement which in two decades after 1848 was to sweep away the utopian romanticism of Owen, the Chartists, Saint Simon, Fourier, Blanc and others and replace it with the scientific inevitability of dialectical materialism, and the harsh creed of total class war.

In Germany, the working class movement was too embryonic for social questions to play a large part in the discontented atmosphere of the forties. Marx and Engels were German certainly but their revolutionary ideas were based on experiences of Manchester rather than Mannheim. Further discontent was still absorbed in nationalism and liberalism and the dead hand of Austrian domination was the enemy, not capitalism. German nationalism was not a united movement: Prussia was not trusted particularly in the catholic south and the whole problem of the nature of the government of a united Germany and the place, if any, of Austria's empire, were too vexed for a coherent and practical national movement ever to develop. Thus nationalism tended to wallow in a romanticism which the universities, the home of radicalism in Germany, furthered, and while there was a widespread belief among intelligent people that a constitutional liberal regime was required few thought in practical terms of how to achieve it.

The past was the inspiration and France the scapegoat. The hatred of France in Germany partly explains the inability of Marx and the French socialists to agree on common policy or doctrine. The German revolutionary movement tended to be too intellectual, too reactionary and romantic. In the harsh world of practical nineteenth century politics it was even less capable than French socialism of meeting the challenge of *Real-politik*.

Italy's movement, too, tended to be philosophical and literary, finding expression in Verdi's operas and Mazoni's historical novels. As in Germany there was an Austrian presence; as in Germany particularism of rival states. As in Germany, too, there was discussion of the need for constitutional government but accompanied by an unpractical romaticism like that of Mazzini. The other Italian movements were more practical; Gioberti looked to the church for leadership, D'Azeglio to Piedmont, but neither had any real concept of how to achieve their ends.

It has already been pointed out how in eastern Europe reaction to Hapsburg control initially took the form of a new interest in local language, culture and history. In Hungary the revolutionary movements could hardly have differed more from those in Western Europe. Here both major movements were aristocratic whether led by Szechenyi or Kossuth. Even in Russia the forces of change still argued about the cultural rather than the political differences which separated them. The world of revolutionaries on the eve of 1848 was still, in many ways, a world of political innocents. The revolutions of 1848 were to alter this world more drastically than at first appeared.

In 1830, a rehearsal of the opera *William Tell* was in progress on the stage of the *Opéra*. The rehearsal was proceeding normally until in the trio in Act Two, William Tell cried 'Ou l'indépendence, ou la mort', a slogan at once taken up by singers, violinists and stage hands alike as they rushed out to help man the barricades against Charles X. The artistic and political movements were not always so closely, or picturesquely, allied.

Initially after the restoration romantic writers were supporters of conservative forces. In Great Britain Walter Scott, Wordsworth, Southey and Coleridge and in France Châteaubriand in his *Génie du Christianisme* are typical of the conservatism of the Romantic artist. Goethe himself in Germany stood aloof from liberalism, Novalis and Schlegel opposed it. Thus in the first years of Restoration Europe liberals shunned romantics and in France supported classical learning as opposed to the new individualism.

Romanticism turned to the past, to folk tales like William Tell with its obvious nationalist message, to the world of fairies, the balletic land of Sylphides and Wilis, the epic work of Delacroix. The romantic ballerina of La Sylphide evokes perhaps more than any other figure the spirit of the romantic movement, she and the Bohemian poet, the swooning heroine and the tortured hero. Romanticism was part of the individualist revolt and could not for long align itself with reactionary forces. Even the conservative romantics of Germany, by delving into the past history of its peoples encouraged nationalist sentiments.

The generation of romantic artists and writers who took the stage after the 1820's had far more in common with liberalism and democracy than with reaction, and for that reason could still not entirely win the approval of solid citizens even though romanticism's victory over classicism was by then complete. Victor Hugo, Lamartine, Balzac, Shelley, Keats and Byron, Delacroix, Pushkin, Berlioz, Chopin, Taglioni, Perrot and Carlotta Grisi were the new artists to be lionised. Many of these artists, except in the world of the lyric theatre, showed an interest in politics and social questions, but it was an interest inspired by romantic passion rather than by realism or knowledge; George Sand wrote romantic socialist novels, Byron 'died for Greece'. Victor Hugo wrote,

Le poëte aujourd'hui doit marcher devant les peuples

H

comme une lumière et leur montrer le chemin.

And he saw romanticism as 'nothing more than liberalism in literature'.

But as in political life 1848 was to see an end to romantic utopianism, so in the world of the arts a similar process was to occur and was already visible in the pre-revolutionary Europe. There was the beginning of a new mood of realism far from the world of Wilis and Delacroix's great canvases. Stendhal urged that imagination should bow to the 'iron laws of reality' and in England Dickens, and even Disraeli, brought a new realism to novels.

Thus as 1848 approached romantic self-expression in itself was being increasingly questioned and in France was soon to be actively resisted. In those arts which did not sense the new mood there was decline. Self-expression became self-indulgence, technique became an end in itself whether the technique of the pianist or the ballerina. Théophile Gautier, describing an Italian dancer, Caterina Beretta in 1858, said she had

a body developed by the violent gymnastics of dance exercises, possessing perhaps more strength than grace.

The idealised version of the thirties was already in decline. It was time for new directions.

Part Four :
The Disintegration
of Viennese Europe

CHAPTER NINETEEN

The 1848 Revolutions

'Le 24 février a été fait sans idée' *Proudhon*
1848 was the turning point at which history
failed to turn' *G. M. Trevelyan*

No one expected revolution in 1848. Surprise was, in part, the element which caused monarchs to give way so rapidly to revolutionary demands; surprise and the belief in a European-wide radical conspiracy which did not in fact exist. Even Marx, who was developing ideas of the inevitability of revolution, was himself taken aback by this series of outbreaks. Hardly any revolutionary leader was ready.

The revolutions were as unco-ordinated and as dissimilar as they were spontaneous and unexpected. It is clear that Europe in 1847 was not an economic unit enjoying equally rapid social, economic or political progress and therefore it would be foolish to expect the revolutions to bear a common stamp. There was considerable dissatisfaction with the *status quo* in all countries in at least certain sections of the community, but this dissatisfaction varied widely. The English Chartists' complaints were not those of the Magyar gentry, nor were the French worker's complaints those of the Italian liberal nationalist, or the nationalist professor of an ancient German university.

There were, of course, factors common to all these revolutions. It has already been shown how large cities throughout Europe were facing problems caused by a floating population only fitfully able to find work, and often hurt by the introduction of new technical processes. Such people were often the shock troops of revolutions in countries where the subsequent events bore no relation to their demands or needs. These European working classes were particularly severely hit

in 1848 by the poor harvests of 1846 and 1847 which sent
the price of staple foods soaring at a time when the minutest
variation could ruin the precarious family economy. Typhus
and cholera soon attacked wasted bodies and the misery of
life was further increased by the great slump which followed
the collapse of the railway boom in England and France and
Belgium. The consequent severe curtailment of capital avail-
ability brought economic dislocation. Thousands of men
throughout Europe depended on the unco-ordinated efforts
of charities. Cities were full of hopeless and angry men; those
who could not join the swollen emigration to America and
the colonies sought their salvation in revolution when it was
offered to them.

This common factor in the revolutions is important, but
working class grievances are only in some few cases what the
revolutions were about; in the most industrialised nation,
Britain, the factory workers were relatively quiet in 1848 and
it was the out-workers who plotted revolution. Socialism was
everywhere a tiny movement. It would be as misleading to
see the working classes as the most important factor in the
revolutionary situation as it would to offer the same place to
the students, another common denominator of the initial
outbreaks. Perhaps the most important class in Central European revolutions was the disaffected peasantry which was
increasingly ground between the millstones of robot and
shrinking holdings. The revolutions were connected, but not
by ideology, despite what the upper classes thought; they
were connected as a time fuse, each revolution detonating the
next. It was the speed of the process which gave to monarchs
and observers the feeling that it was all a great conspiracy.

It is fitting that the flame which ignited Europe should
have been applied by the Milan tobacco riots of January. The
citizens of Milan had boycotted the Austrian tobacco monopoly and, possibly as a result of the irritability which giving
up the habit provokes, a series of incidents occurred,
involving the citizens and Radetzky's troops. It was soon
obvious that this was only the beginning: First Sicily then
Naples were unwillingly offered full independence and a
constitution on the lines of that of 1812. In Piedmont on
February 8th Charles Albert, on a tightrope between the

demands of his citizens for reform and fear of Metternich's intervention, promised a constitution in order to forestall mob violence. The Grand Duke of Tuscany offered a constitution almost immediately and in March this was proclaimed in Rome, though not by the apparently liberal Pius IX, *Pio Nono.*

By March however an event of even greater significance had taken place — the abdication of Louis Philippe, an occurrence so shattering to the morale of Europe's crowned heads that only the fall of Metternich himself could possibly shock them more; and that event was to follow on March 15th.

The elections of 1846 had given Guizot a parliamentary majority of 100: even so politicians had seen trouble imminent in the stubborn refusal of king and minister to make concessions to change. Revolutionary activity in industrial areas had increased with the busy attention of Louis Blanc, Proudhon and others. The year 1846 had seen the first 'socialist' histories of the French revolution by Blanc and Michelet. Even among Guizot's own followers, especially the young, there was unrest; Louis Philippe's eldest son felt it. Nevertheless the result of the February revolt was out of all proportion to the cause, despite the harvest failures, slump and rapid inflation.

Unable to hold public meetings, opposition leaders had taken to holding banquets. Unfortunately these had been quickly taken over by demagogues, and after over sixty of these events had taken place the government's patience was exhausted; it banned a projected Paris banquet for February. Although most sponsors accepted the ban a few announced that they would defy it, and on February 22nd students and workers clashed with police. Louis Philippe was not initially worried by this but when the National Guard was summoned the response was somewhat half-hearted. The King's most solid support was gone. A day later a few National Guardsmen fraternised with rioters though Guizot had already been dismissed; it seems likely that conservatives stayed home, convinced all was well. That same evening troops and crowd clashed, and sixteen people were killed. Molé's chances of forming a government were spoiled. Thiers urged the King to be firm and Marshal Bugeaud was appointed to subdue the city by force. But the King dreaded the shedding of blood and when, as he reviewed the troops and National Guard, he was greeted by shouts of *à bas le système* from one group of Guards, his will to fight was gone. Neither he nor Thiers would order Bugeaud to take effective action and Bugeaud himself felt unable to do so. The revolution was won by default. The thought of the blood which must be spilt to retain his Crown destroyed Louis Philippe's confidence and will to succeed. Rejecting Thiers' advice to invest the city from St Cloud he fled to England.

Once again Paris had dictated to France; before the provinces knew what was happening the monarchy had fallen and a Republic been proclaimed. But the provinces could not be ignored for ever, and, although few people mourned the loss of the Orleanists, the Republic would have to prove itself to the provinces if it was to survive. Outside the few great towns, provincial France was essentially conservative; more than half the population were peasants. If the revolutionaries were radical they should also be democratic but, not for the first time, an extension of the suffrage implied conservative government, and it remained to be seen whether revolutionaries would accept the consequences of their own doctrines.

In contrast with 1830 the 1848 revolution had been to a far greater extent a revolution of the barricades, and the provisional government of February 1848 lacked a sense of unity or a clearly pre-eminent leader. Its membership was essentially bourgeois, though it did contain in Albert one representative of the Paris proletariat. It was not the kind of bourgeois government of 1830; Lamartine its most eminent figure, was a democrat and all its members accepted universal manhood suffrage as the most important feature of the new order. Nor was the government unaware of the plight of the workers, for the effects of the depression were only too visible, and no government, in an immediate post-revolutionary situation, could afford to ignore the revolutionaries' front line fighters. Thus the government agreed to set up commissions, directed by the socialist revolutionary Louis Blanc, to examine and recommend satisfactory schemes for social reform or experiment. They also agreed to the creation of the National Workshops, intended by Blanc to be workers co-operatives, the first stage in the proletariat's seizure of France's industrial life.

But this was as far as the concord within the provisional government extended. Essentially the struggle which broke out was between those for whom the revolution was political (the moderates) and those for whom it was the first stage in a social and economic regeneration, predominantly socialist in character. In turn this developed into a struggle between those who wished the revolution to be French, and those who wished to impose the revolutionary will of Paris on the conservative provinces.

The first draft of the provisional government had laid down that

> neither the people of Paris nor the provisional government pretend to substitute their opinion for the opinion of the citizens. . .

thus far at least were the revolutionaries aware of one bitter legacy of the first revolution.

But even when this was being proclaimed, the echoes of 1793 were reverberating. On February 25th a mass of workers organised by the radical clubs had demanded *la droit de travail,* and on the following day the National Workshops were declared to be government policy. A few days later another mob, with assistance from Louis Blanc, persuaded the government to create the Workers Commissions under Blanc and Albert. Yet the success of such commissions was limited and few employers took notice of their decrees limiting working hours. For already the moderates were showing signs of resistance; although on March 17th the radicals under Blanqui managed to persuade the government to put off the general election for a fortnight in order to convert the country to socialism, Lamartine was not prepared to accept a 'demand for the implicit obedience of the government to the dictatorship of the mob', and in April the National Guard paraded with cries of *à bas les communistes.* The election was not to be put off again.

The weakness of the radicals, opposed as they were by half

Paris and most of France, became apparent in the career of the National Workshops. In no wise did they resemble Blanc's original concept. Instead of agencies of social and economic regeneration they became, to the government which administered them, agencies of relief, government charity organisations. Socialist impotency was only too obvious also in the moderate foreign policy pursued by Lamartine.

As in 1791 revolutionary fervour expressed itself in a desire to march over frontiers, bringing death to tyrants and relief to the suffering masses; but to such a concept Lamartine gave only lip service; he was not prepared to run the risk of an anti-French coalition, and he knew only too well that the call for war was the call only of a few, who saw in a war situation the chance to put off the election and establish a revolutionary dictatorship, inspired by the memory of Robespierre.

The failure of the socialists was evidenced in the results of the election. The Assembly which met on May 4th was overwhelmingly conservative, only a ninth of the seats going to radicals; even in Paris the extreme left did badly. An Executive Commission of five was appointed by the Assembly to name the ministers; it was inimical to radical pretensions and reflected the hostility of France to Paris, which was such a feature of the 1848 revolution. 'For the first time', wrote De Tocqueville, 'Paris inspired universal hatred as well as universal terror'. Peasants feared for their property just as much as the landowners and bourgeoisie; and in 1848 railways and telegraphs had given the countryside the ability to come to the aid of the Assembly if it was attacked by the city.

In this atmosphere Lamartine's attempts to salvage something for the workers in assuring the radical, Ledru Rollin, a place on the commission and in finding an alternative to the National Workshops, so hated by tax payers and property owners, were doomed to failure, especially after the incident of May 15th when a mob invaded the Assembly and declared it dissolved. On that occasion the National Guard saved the Assembly but it was obvious that a further trial of strength was coming. When the Assembly decreed the abolition of the Workshops, (the camps of discontented workmen levelling the *Champ de Mars*) fighting broke out. The 'June days', three days of civil war in Paris, followed. The workers were defeated, not just by the troops of Cavaignac and the National Guard, but also, morally at least, by the stream of people from the provinces who set out to Paris to destroy the *sansculotte* bogey.

Many of the reforms of the revolution were quickly swept away and the Assembly turned its attention to the task of constructing a constitution. In September their labours bore fruit in a compromise. Universal male suffrage was retained; there was to be a single chamber legislature and a President chosen for four years, also by universal male suffrage. It was necessary therefore to choose this new President whose powers were carefully limited, but whose relationship with the chamber was imperfectly defined. The candidates were Ledru-Rollin, a left wing candidate, Cavaignac, the bourgeoisie's hero of the 'June days', Lamartine, the rather tarnished hero of the revolution, Raspail and Louis-Napoleon, known only by his foolish attempts to unseat Louis Philippe and his book *Des Idées Napoléonennes*. He was backed by politicians, above all by Thiers, who saw in him a weak executive who could prepare the way for an Orleanist restoration.

In the December elections Louis Napoleon won 5,500,000 votes, the other four candidates won less than 2,000,000 votes between them. In the following April a royalist majority of 400 legitimists and Orleanists was returned to the chamber with 200 radicals and a mere handful of moderate republicans. Thus revolution destroyed moderation and suggested the possibility of a further struggle.

Many features of the French Revolution were to be repeated in Europe; the early success of the revolutionaries and the decisive participation of the workers; the reaction of the provinces, propertied classes and conservative peasants to a 'socialist' threat, the isolation of the moderate. Throughout Europe conservatism was to demonstrate its continued strength.

The Paris revolution precipitated a series of similar revolts throughout Europe; the ease with which the French mon-

archy had fallen gave to enemies of the *status quo* a feeling
that their plans would meet the inevitable success, a feeling
which the monarchies shared. In the Hapsburg lands the monarchy was perhaps least well equipped to deal with revolts in
its ramshackle patrimony. Although the towns and cities of
the Empire were small (with the exception of Vienna whose
population had outstripped the progress of industry), there
were three revolutionary classes within the Empire, the
students, the small urban proletariat and the peasantry. The
latter were anxious to be rid of the Robot, but they possessed no other revolutionary aims and had no sense of
national identity.

Yet it was the cities which sparked off the peasant revolts.
Already in the last Diet of Hungary in 1847 reforms of taxation, land ownership and serfdom had been proposed under
Kossuth's aegis, accepted by the nobility but rejected by
Vienna. Now, in February, under the impetus of Paris, radical
Magyar students in Budapest demanded a democratic constitution, the abolition of the robot and equal rights for all
nationalities. Such a series of demands threatened the
position of the gentry but rather than retreat immediately
into reaction they followed Kossuth. He was to them the
embodiment of the Magyar nation but he was also a sensible
politician who saw that if the gentry were to survive as a class
they must outbid the students for peasant support. Kossuth
requested that students' demands should be granted and with
them the nomination of a Hungarian government and
national elections. On March 16th Kossuth nominated a
government headed by Louis Batthyány with himself as
Minister of Finances. Déak was to be Minister of Justice and
Szchechenyi Minister of public works. In April, after futile
resistance, the Emperor consented to the formation of this
government and to the establishment of a representative
parliament, tax reform, peasant ownership, a national militia
and the unification of Transylvania and Croatia with
Hungary. But, although Hungary now had a separate army,
budget and foreign policy the results of revolution were not
as extreme as those demanded by the students. Kossuth
preserved Magyar hegemony by restricting representation in
Parliament.

Concessions by Vienna were unavoidable. Prague's intellectuals had quickly followed Budapest's lead, demanding the usual liberal freedoms; the abolition of the Robot, the equality of indigenous languages with German, and a common government for Bohemia, Silesia and Moravia. Metternich tried to calm the situation by calling an Estates General of all Diets to rally the privileged classes, but the privileged had lost heart and wished to sacrifice Metternich on the altar of revolution. He certainly could not survive the Vienna revolution of March 13th, which gave power to a 'student committee'.

Further disasters followed. News of Metternich's flight on March 15th led to a revolt in Milan which forced the army to retreat from Lombardy. Venice revolted, the princes of Parma and Modena fled, allowing the Piedmontese army to take over; and on March 26th Charles Albert, rather against his will, declared war on the beleaguered Empire. In Vienna there was fresh violence. The city was taken over by a Committee of Public Safety and after promising to call a constitutional assembly to create a constitution for an Empire which appeared to be disintegrating, the court fled to Innsbrück (May). The position of the monarchy appeared desperate; yet in fact it was stronger than at first might appear. The revolutionaries of Budapest, Bohemia and Vienna were not seeking the same solutions to the Empire's problems; everywhere there were minority races, fearful for their future; above all, the army was intact and already in Italy under Radetzky preparing to ignore Ferdinand's concessions to Italian nationalism. The way back to power was tortuous, but there was a way.

Germany experienced a series of revolts in quick succession. Liberal reforms were given to the citizens of Baden, Saxony, Hanover, Württemberg, Bavaria and the Hesses by their frightened rulers. In Prussia political strife was already visible. In 1847 Frederick-William IV had called a United Diet, partly on the insistence of the Junkers of East Prussia who needed loan sanction for the *Ostbahn*, the railway to East Prussia. The Diet had immediately tried to establish regular meetings and the principle of no taxation without consent, and had been dissolved. It was hardly the best time for the country to be hit by an economic collapse. Workers of Berlin, like their counterparts in Vienna, could find little enough work in normal times as handicraft industries suffered from British competition, but in the continent-wide collapse of 1848 they became desperate. The barricades which appeared in Berlin in March 1848 were as much the result of unemployment as of revolutionary philosophy, but the workers' demands were quickly backed by radical elements who wished to add weight to their liberal demands. Frederick-William did not resist; the army was withdrawn from Berlin; a bourgeois Civil Guard was formed; a constitution was promised; a National Assembly was to meet in May and representatives were allowed to go to the new centre of German aspirations at Frankfurt.

The collapse of Austria and Prussia allowed the liberals free rein in the early months of 1848, but the collapse was only apparent. Frederick-William still had an intact and loyal army, officered by an intact and loyal Junker caste; it only needed him to recover his nerve and the Emperor to recover his ascendancy for the whole edifice, which the liberals were building, to come tumbling down. In truth the revolution in 1848 had been too easy and the speed with which the revolution was accomplished encouraged the facile optimism of the well-meaning, kind-hearted philospher-revolutionaries who were now turning their feet, and directing their gaze to Frankfurt.

The National Assembly at Frankfort grew out of two bodies. The first was a meeting of academics at Heidelberg. This gathering on hearing news of the revolution, constituted itself as a *Vor-Parlement*, summoned a Constituent Assembly, and laid down rules for its election. The second organisation was the Federal Diet which invited states to send new and more liberal representatives, who devised their own plan for a National Assembly and then amalgamated with the *Vor-Parlement*.

When the National Assembly met, it was the result of differing modes of election but though some members had been elected by universal suffrage it included only one peasant and not a single artisan or working man among its predominantly academic and upper middle class membership. In short since neither the urban nor rural poor were represented the delegates chiefly represented themselves, for although their viewpoints ranged over the full political spectrum, they were mainly cautious, peaceful men of moderately philosophical opinion. They were not inexperienced in government or political life, many were the civil servants of the princes of the German confederation, nor were they unaware of the virtues of expediency and compromise, but they were called on to deal with huge problems incapable of peaceful solution. The main problem facing them was the nature of the new German nation; whether it was to be *Kleindeutschland,* excluding the Hapsburg Empire and thus likely to be dominated by Prussia, or *Grossdeutschland*, in which case the role of the Empire's subject races would have to be carefully worked out.

The Frankfort parliamentarians found themselves faced with other problems. Although they appointed Archduke John of Austria as Regent in August, and although he formed a government, none of its ministers were recognised abroad. Besides this there were no soldiers and no means of obliging people to obey the Assembly's laws or collect its taxes, especially as the Princes's governments were everywhere left completely intact. The men of 1848 were not united. In general the Frankfort representatives resembled the moderates in France, in that they saw political reforms as an end in themselves. Thus they offered no progran.mes of social reform for the peasants or the small working class, and yet the peasants especially were in a position to make or break the revolution being by far the largest class. Above all, however, the future of the revolution in Germany depended on events in Austria and Prussia.

In the spring of 1848, there appeared to be nothing else for the Hapsburg court to do but to accept the decentralisation of the Empire, the control of its constituent parts by the 'master races', Germans, Magyars, Italians and Poles (in Galicia), an Austrian participation in the Frankfort Parliament. In late March, however, Prague's demand for a separate government for Bohemia with Moravia and Silesia shocked Germans everywhere, for Bohemia had had no autonomous history for two hundred years, and Silesia and Moravia were seen as even more specifically German. The Czechs and Slovaks had not hitherto been accorded the accolade of 'master-race' and had automatically been included in the future German nation; now Slavism was flowering and Germany seemed in danger of losing Bohemia's industrial wealth.

The Bohemian leader Palacky suggested the formation of a federation of free peoples under Hapsburg rule, 'Austro-Slavism', as the answer to the future organisation of the Hapsburg patrimony. Such a solution could not permanently recommend itself to the Hapsburgs but it was a useful counter to both the radicalism of Vienna and the conservatism of the Magyars, who feared national feeling among their own Slav subject peoples, and among the Croatians. The court covertly encouraged Croatian independence from Hungary at the same time as it accepted the March laws which had declared Hungary indivisible.

In June, a Slav Congress at Prague shook itself free of Palacky's control and issued a clarion call to all Slav peoples. The Congress broke up amid riots which, though of little significance in themselves, allowed the general in command of Imperial forces in Prague, Windischgrätz, to assert control and effectively defeat the Prague radicals.

The defeat of the radicals in Prague pleased Austro-Slav moderates who now looked forward to the Constituent Assembly of the Empire in which they could pursue their aims. Austrian revolutionaries, moderates and radicals, were grateful to Windischgrätz for defeating not merely the radicals but for defeating Austro-Slavism entirely and therefore permitting the union of Bohemia with the other German states at Frankfort. What neither realised was that Windischgrätz's action, the assertion of Imperial force over revolutionary force, had sounded the death knell of liberal hopes throughout the Empire.

Bohemia was not the only area in which Imperial hopes were reviving. When the Austrian army-had been told to retreat from Italy in March Radetzky had ignored the imperial command, receiving, for this act of insubordination, not dismissal but reinforcements. Charles Albert proved himself a brave man but a poor general and he was hampered by the wilting support of Pio Nono and the Neopolitan section of his army. After the fall of the Austrian stronghold of Peschiera in May the King was increasingly distracted by political events at home and was unable to raise enough troops to meet the reinforcements reaching Radetzky. After Custoza (July 25th) Charles Albert requested an armistice.

The Hungarians, or more accurately the Magyars, were also facing difficulties. Batthyany's government was finding Kossuth's extremism in his dealings with the minorities difficult to bear, and its position was not helped by grave doubts among civil servants, many of them Germans, as to whom to obey, since the relationship of Hungary to Vienna was ill-defined. Moreover, true to its age-old practice, the court at Innsbrück was actively encouraging Croatian, Serb and Rumanian minorities to demand autonomy from Budapest. It was not to be expected that after the victories of Windischgrätz and Radetzky the court would be willing to leave Hungary alone for long. Hungary's attempts to stifle Croatian autonomy gave the dynasty an admirable weapon which it would not hesitate to use.

On the eve of the Constituent Assembly the dynasty was stronger than it had any right to expect and was showing itself indispensable to its peoples; the Slavs needed it to protect them against German and Magyar nationalism; the German moderates wanted to preserve their position as the 'master-race' of the Empire against the Slav threat, and feared and exaggerated the radicalism which was manifesting itself in Vienna and in parts of Germany. Such needs were, of course, contradictory but they were nonetheless useful to the Hapsburgs who had already found in Italy one way of rallying the German peoples of the Empire to their cause and were about to find in Hungary a second. The Hapsburgs were allowed to keep control of the army because of the Italian threat and because each race of the Empire felt the need of Hapsburg protection against another race. Never was the ramshackle nature of the Empire better displayed; never was the need for the Empire and the Hapsburgs better demonstrated than in 1848.

The Assembly, which met in July, was a moderate body.

One of its most important works was the Emancipation of
the Peasants; the Robot was abolished and security of tenure
assured. This had important effects; the peasants had aided
the revolution by widespread refusal to perform their labour
services, now they were satisfied and those peasants who
stayed on the land lapsed into conservatism. Emancipation
eventually encouraged a drift to the towns. There nationalism
was to be fostered and was to filter back to the countryside,
creating a movement disastrous to the stability of the
Empire. But this was still in the future; the conservatism of
the peasantry, the isolation of Hapsburg lands from the main
centres of trade, capital and industry delayed industrial
expansion for many years yet. Nonetheless the crucial step
had been taken.

That was all in the future when in September the
Assembly came to discuss the question of the national debt,
and, above all, of Hungary's part in it. Emancipation already
promised to destroy the economic position of the Hungarian
gentry and Kossuth therefore fiercely resisted any
compromise which Déak might wish to reach with Vienna.
Kossuth's opposition prompted the Hapsburg government to
present a governor to Croatia, Jellaçic, who on September
11th marched on Budapest. Kossuth appealed to the
Assembly but the Slav members had no love for Magyars, and
Germans failed to see why Hungarians should want to be
independent in a liberal Empire and were opposed to the
break-up of an Empire in which they were treated as the
most important race. Only the radicals and the Poles who
were eager to see Poland reborn and therefore wanted to see
the Empire dismembered, supported Kossuth.

Radicals feared a Hapsburg victory for they saw it as the
prelude to a re-establishment of absolutism; Magyar victory
would hasten the union with Frankfort. When the Hungarian
position seemed desperate a revolution again broke out in
Vienna but was quickly put down, but not before it had
frightened the moderates into supporting the Hapsburgs more
fervently than would otherwise have been the case.

The Hungarian war of Independence broke out in earnest
when Ferdinand in a last act of supreme cynicism before his
abdication (December) nominated Jellaçic as Batthyany's

successor. Kossuth rallied all classes in support of Hungarian independence but few officers of the Imperial army would serve.

The war against Kossuth's Hungary foreshadowed the end of the revolution and the liberal Empire. The Constituent Assembly was moved to Moravia. The constitution which it prepared was pointless long before the work began. After Hungarian defeat (February 1849) the Assembly was dissolved (March 4) and an Imperial consitution introduced. A single parliament for the whole Empire was to sit at Vienna and the government was to be responsible to it. The Empire itself was to be centralised, each ethnic division becoming a mere province, and each province a mere amalgam of administrative units. Thus the response of the Hapsburg monarchy to revolution was a return to the worn-out answer of centralisation. When Russia joined Austria the Hungarian revolt was snuffed out. Kossuth fled and the last Hungarian troops surrendered to the hated Haynau in August. Fierce reprisals followed.

In Italy the aftermath of Custoza was despair and radical action; 'The war of Kings is over, the war of peoples begins.' The papal constitution of 1848 soon broke down beneath the weight of warring faction and the murder of Pellegrino Rossi, the moderate chief minister, paved the way for an extremely democratic constitution, which the Pope accepted only a week before he fled the 'eternal city'.

In Tuscany, Leghorn and Piedmont radical governments were set up. The attempts of these Piedmontest radicals to secure French help and to punish the defeated generals divided the country, encouraging Austria to demand humiliating terms in the face of which the Italians could offer only factional squabble. For the moment, except in Piedmont, where the democrats' call for war was resisted, the radicals ruled supreme. In Rome the Republic was proclaimed; in Florence the Grand Duke was forced to flee; Even in Piedmont under the radical Prime Minister, Gioberti, the drift to the left and to war accelerated. His dismissal made the King's attempts to maintain peace more difficult. Faced with radical pressures and Austrian intransigence Charles Albert attempted to cut his way out of trouble by declaring war. Within six days the Novara campaign ended in disaster and the King's abdication.

But by the beginning of 1850 the most famous story of the Italian revolution had already been played out. The Pope's flight and his subsequent call to the Catholic powers led to a conference in which the future of Rome was the main consideration. This was attended in March 1849 by Austria, France, Spain and Naples. As the only country which sought anything other than the utter surrender of the republicans, France took the initiative, but although their legionaires were sent to occupy Civitavecchia, the French had no intention of suppressing the republican government. Yet if France merely sought to establish a compromise, the other powers had no such laudable intention. As the armies of Austria, Spain and Naples also approached, Rome revolted. The flight was a glorious one but France eventually took the city of Rome; Garibaldi's redshirts, evading the Neapolitan army, disappeared into the hills.

Venice's resistance under Manin soon collapsed; Sicily was already defeated; Novara completed the tale of woe. The 'war of the people' was also over. How much of a war of the people it had been it is difficult to estimate; a war of the towns it had been, but the peasantry had in most places shown its customary apathy, its support, as in Tuscany, for the legitimate ruler and, above all, its support for the church. The failure of the war of the peoples cleared the air at least. Radical republicanism had suffered a severe blow; it had divided the Italians when they most needed unity. Garibaldi now doubted, he told Mazzini, whether a united Italian republic was yet a possibility, and from 1849 Garibaldi increasingly saw Piedmont and France as likely saviours of Italy and the monarchy as Italy's best leader. The age of Mazzinian revolts was, if not quite over, approaching its end. The monarchy of Piedmont was respected for defeat at Novara and for Victor Emmanuel's staunch constitutionalism in the face of Austrian pressure.

Only two clouds lay on the horizon; the French presence in Rome, and the now irreparable breach between Italian liberalism and the church.

The Hapsburg recovery was naturally bound to have a

major effect on the future of the Frankfort parliament. Throughout 1848 that unfortunate body worked away at the constitution of the new German state, discussing 'fundamental rights' and other windy concepts while the real future of Germany was being settled by armies and conservative statesmen in Austria and Prussia.

While the philosopher revolutionaries talked they failed to grasp the opportunity offered by the discontent of the peasantry, especially of the Rhineland, where the continued existence of feudal dues, the dwindling size of peasant holdings, and harvest failure had created the explosive situation which had helped to make 1848 possible. To these peasants the Frankfort liberals had offered little; the fear of offending the sacred right of property prohibited any final solution of the peasants' problems and it was left chiefly to the landowners themselves to make their peace with their tenants. Although the peasants got less than they had hoped for they found that they could expect little from the liberals. In such ways did the men of 1848 ignore the fundamental role of force in revolution. Only temporarily in 1848 did they hold the initiative in this important respect. They let it fall.

The draft constitution eventually allowed for an hereditary Emperor, a Reichstag of two houses, one representing the states and one the nation, a ministry responsible to the Reichstag and control of foreign affairs, taxation and the army. But it was control of troops that Frankfort altogether lacked. The Schleswig-Holstein affair of 1848 was to show the effects of such a situation. Schleswig and Holstein were duchies in the Confederation, whose Duke happened to be Frederick VIII of Denmark. In 1848 the Danish King promulgated a constitution detaching Holstein from the Confederation, placing the duchies more firmly under the Crown in order that they might descend to his female heirs. The duchies protested to the Confederation and the male heir to the duchies, Christian August of Augustenberg obtained recognition from Prussia. Although the Danes retreated from their position somewhat, the force of German nationalism was such that in April the *Vorparlament* called on Prussia to drive the Danes from the duchies. Prussia's liberal ministers quickly responded, but pressure from Russia and Britain forced a Prussian withdrawal. Significantly, although the Frankfort liberals looked on Prussia's action as a betrayal there was nothing that they, without an army of their own, could do.

Meanwhile in Prussia itself, conservative forces regained their nerve; nobles and landowners, especially of the East, resenting the strength of the liberals of the Rhineland provinces, and fearful for their future in a liberal Prussia and a liberal Germany, met frequently to league against the Assembly at Berlin. Bismarck was among the contributors to its newspaper, *Kreuz-Zeitung,* which advocated, not a return to absolutism, but 'constitutionalism'. In October and November a conservative cabinet was sworn in, the Assembly was moved to Brandenburg and dissolved. General Wrangel occupied Berlin, dissolving the National Guard. Two constitutions followed in rapid succession, the second dividing the electorate, according to the amount of tax it paid, into three classes. By this system the wealthier voters dominated the elections.

Thus, when, in March 1849, the Frankfort Assembly came to choose between a *Klein-* or a *Gross-deutschland* it was choosing whether Prussian or Austrian authoritarianism should govern Germany, and it was depending for its very existence on the rivalry of Austria and Prussia. When Frederick-William was offered the crown he refused to take if 'from the gutter'. He would accept it only from sovereign princes, not a sovereign people and, besides, he genuinely believed that a Hapsburg had a historic right to the Imperial German crown. Austria withdrew from Frankfort, Bavaria, Württemberg and Hanover refused recognition to the constitution and even Prussia and Saxony withdrew.

The final humiliation came when the Assembly at Frankfort was forced to call on Prussia to put down radical revolts. Moderates throughout Germany had long been alarmed by the radicalism of certain elements in parts of Germany particularly in the Rhineland and in Berlin. Marx had hastened home to Germany in 1848 to prepare for the revolution and setting up the newspaper 'Neue Rheinische Zeitung'. Such activities alarmed the solid bourgeoisie who assumed too readily a 'communist' or 'socialist' conspiracy which never existed. It is almost impossible to find any significant signs of socialism. However it was the case that radical elements were certainly vocal in their opposition to the preservation of the monarchs, and to the offer of an Imperial crown to a Hohenzollern who had in 1848 'betrayed' the revolution. Such radicals used violent language and in September 1849 there were riots in west German towns and in Frankfort itself. Prussian arms now guaranteed the existence of the German nation. The revolution was over; even before September many moderates had gone home dispirited, or fearful of radicalism, and only too glad to leave the future to Austria or Prussia.

Although neither Spain nor Portugal suffered from revolutions in 1848 the troubles in the rest of Europe nevertheless made their impact. Spain, in particular, suffered from a series of city revolts, but both countries were going through a period of intense instability which produced regular revolutions. In both countries the situation was essentially the same.

Neither Spain nor Portugal possessed a sufficiently well organised or large bourgeoisie to carry the burden of representative government until well after the turn of the century. While both countries possessed liberal movements, particularly in the cities, strong enough to cause revolution, especially in the light of palace intrigues, the overwhelming majority of the people still clung to a life of servitude, to church and landowner. The result in both countries, though more acutely in Spain, was a constant swing between revolution and reaction which undermined parliamentary institutions and the crown, and increasingly concentrated power in the hands of the army, or 'a strong man'. Given the public morality of the politicians and, in the case of Spain, of the Regent, Maria Christina and the Queen, anarchy was perhaps inevitable.

By 1836 the threats to the Queens of Portugal and Spain from their wicked uncles were nearly over, though the Carlist movement in Spain was to cause much trouble yet, particularly in alliance with the regionalism of the Basque country, Catalonia and Valencia. In both countries good government was now required.

For a number of reasons, however, this was to prove well nigh impossible. Isabella's Spain fell under the sway of Espartero, the man most responsible for the defeat of Don Carlos. His rule became increasingly military, especially after the quarrel with the Vatican in 1841, and his last two years (1841 and 1842) were troubled by revolts in the Basque country and Catalonia. Revolution brought about his downfall but afforded no respite, in so far as his successor was the thirteen-year-old Queen herself, now again under the influence of her immoral mother Maria Christina. It made no real difference that thirteen was an early age for a monarch to be given rule over a nominally constitutional state, for never in her life did Isabella reach an age of discretion. She ushered in an era of rule by generals and favourites, particularly Narvaez, under whom popular sovereignty was further restricted.

The regional and city risings of 1848 had little immediate effect except to strengthen the reactionaries at the palace. Narvaez's temporary overthrow, since it was not by popular action, did not prevent a Concordat with Rome. This made Roman Catholicism the exclusive religion of Spain, giving it control of education and censorship as well as a state endowment as compensation for Mendizabal's confiscation (albeit never fully executed) of church property in the more liberal days of the Carlist wars. Spain's revolution came in 1854 when the Queen reacted to a liberal petition for reform by banishing the liberal opposition leaders. This, together with public disgust at the Queen's immorality, led to a revolution in most major cities. Once again the country returned to constitutionalism: once again it would swing back to reaction, for even in 1855 the liberals were frightened by the revolutionary nature of their own constitution and did not implement it.

The trouble was that parliamentary government struck no roots in the soil of Spain; the real manoeuverings went on in the royal palace to which all politicians found that they had to gravitate. Parliamentary institutions were undermined by royal hostility, popular incomprehension and increasing liberal disillusion. No amount of tinkering with different kinds of legislatures could aid this situation.

Portugal had at least two monarchs who tried their best, and thus Portugal better avoided the contagion of 1848. In this part of the Iberian peninsula the problems were similar but there were at least three constitutional doctrines which had their adherents. The first, the Miguelists, is hardly constitutional at all since it looked to absolutism, but the other two were more important. The constitution of 1822, forced on the unwilling John VI, was the more revolutionary of the two in that it proposed a unicameral legislature and did not allow the monarch a veto; the constitution of 1826 given by Pedro of Brazil when his daughter Maria II ascended the throne was bicameral and gave the crown a veto. The charter of 1826 was the guiding light for Maria throughout her effective reign — from 1834 when she was fifteen. Although forced to revoke it in favour of the constitution of 1822, by the Septembrist revolt of 1836, she remained a Chartist (Portuguese-style) at heart. Portugal too declined into dictatorship under Cabral, who in 1842 crushed the Septembrists and ruled for four years by manipulated elections, which drove the opposition to extremes, even to a temporary alliance of Miguelists and Septembrists. Cabral's rule was not without benefits in terms of public works and economic improvements but the national debt's unhappy expansion drove him to initiate tax reforms which caused his downfall in the 'Mana da Fonte' rebellion of 1846, a series of unco-ordinated but effective revolts.

As in Spain liberal revolt had no permanent effect, for although Maria conceded what almost amounted to universal suffrage she soon found another strong man in Saldanha. When civil war broke out between him and the Septembrists the presence of a British fleet saved the toppling throne. Maria died in 1853 after a conscientious effort to establish limited constitutionalism on the politically barren soil of Portugal.

Even in Scandinavia the effects of 1848 caused thrones to rock on their pedestals. Charles XIV (Bernadotte) ruling from 1818–44 had proved himself a capable but conservative monarch, in the Bonapartist mould. Although he inspired much personal affection, there was anger at his repeated failure, often against ministerial advice, to accept reform of a governmental system, still largely based on the Napoleonic model and philosophy.

His successor Oscar I (1844—59) saw during his reign the acceleration of the economic changes and liberal tendencies visible in the old king's last years. 1848 promoted dissatisfaction with the speed of change, for little had been done since Charles XIV had given ministers greater responsibility in 1841. Such was the unrest that the government put forward a conservative-liberal scheme of its own which was however not acceptable to the majority in the *Riksdag*. Real progress had to await Oscar's successor, but even so the constitution was interpreted in an increasingly liberal way in the period of liberal ascendancy.

In Germany and the Austrian Empire the revolutions had been in part doomed by the close connection between liberalism and nationalism, whose incompatibility 1848 had proven. Germans in Austria or at Frankfort could only conceive of Bohemia as part of Germany and were shocked and dismayed by the rise of Slav national feeling. Thus the Hapsburgs were able to defeat the Prague radicals when they began to take up the cause of Slav and Polish minorities everywhere. Yet Germany's revolt was as much a national as a liberal revolt. When the Poles revolted in 1848 the Germans were again faced with a dilemma. The cause of Polish nationalism had been an emotional one since 1795, but in 1848 only extreme radicals were prepared to accept the consequences of Polish nationalism — the loss of the Polish territories of the Hapsburgs and the Hohenzollerns, just as only the radicals welcomed the Hungarian insurrection and the collapse of the Hapsburg Empire entirely. Moderates tended to see Poland, as Bohemia, as a legitimate area of German control.

When faced by such problems moderates sought solutions which depended for success on the dynasties; so moderate German and moderate Bohemians sought Hapsburg guarantees. Radicals, alone, were willing to talk in terms of the Republics and the dissolution of both Empires. Here again they fell foul of the moderates, who, following the French pattern, associated republicanism with socialism. The outbreaks of September 1849 served to prove the point. Moderates everywhere in Europe, whether they were the moderate republicans of Paris, the learned men of Frankfort, or the moderate Austro-Slavists like Palacky, found themselves caught between a reaction and republicanism associated with mass involvement in politics and attacks on property. In such a situation moderates generally sought safety with conservative forces; only a few, like Lamartine, attempted to follow a middle way.

Revolutions everywhere were certainly defeated by the strength of the conservative forces. Peasants were either loyal to the old régime throughout, as in France, the Iberian Peninsula and Italy, or after concessions, as in the Hapsburg Empire and in Germany. In no country did the powers lose control of the army, indeed there was rarely any attempt to wrest control of it from them, either because a section of the revolutionaries felt they needed its protection, or because of the disastrous miscalculation, made especially in Frankfort that once the political heaven was achieved, all else would be given free. Most moderates were too nice; there was not enough viciousness about the revolutionaries. A revolution must be bloody; if an enemy is left intact he is in a position to counter-attack, a lesson never learned by the moderates, and grasped too late by the radicals, who were numerically insignificant.

In 1849 Europe seemed to regain the *status quo*. Territorially indeed this was a fact, nationalism providing no other alternative. German liberalism could not solve the problem of German nationalism because this involved a question, that of Austria's place in a German nation, which could only be solved by the collapse of Austria, or by war between Austria and Prussia. It could certainly not be settled by intellectuals possessed of no troops and no taxes. European liberalism could not solve the problem of Polish nationalism because Russia was involved, as well as Prussia and Austria; Italian independence could now be achieved only with help from an outside power. Politically little had changed; true, Prussia and Austria had parliaments but Austria's was soon to disappear and Prussia's, though more meaningful, was far removed from what had been hoped for. At Frankfort there was now a meaningless rump. There is a real sense therefore in which 1848 was 'the turning point at which history failed to turn' but the 1848 revolution did have effects of singular importance.

If the 1848 revolutions had been borne in optimism they died in pessimism. The lessons of 1848 to the nationalists and liberals were only too plain; German and Italian nationalism must be achieved by diplomacy and force of arms. Liberal governments must be worked for where possible, in conjunction with the established powers and not in such a way as would lead to socialism or radicalism. Radicalism, it was felt, had weakened the revolution of Italy and Germany. This did not mean that liberalism was dead but it did mean that liberals would be circumspect. They believed that the lesson of 1848 was that democratic ideals lead to socialism or republicanism and they came to associate even social reform with socialism; again, this was not entirely new, but 1848 seemed to make it more self-evident. In fact, of course, socialism played but a tiny part in any revolution outside France, and even there it never achieved power; in the one place where democratic elections were held they produced a conservative government. In 1848, however, the conservative tendencies of the middle classes increased and tempted them to leave major questions, particularly nationalism, to their masters.

The revolution was therefore a turning point in the relationship between the monarchies and bourgeoisie in Europe. Nor were the monarchs themselves unaffected by this. Frederick-William did preserve a constitution of sorts which gave the middle classes a voice and himself a source of opposition. Franz-Josef could not rule without at least the appearance of a constitution; Victor-Emmanuel strenuously resisted Austrian pressure to alter the constitution. Louis-Napoleon did not return to the Orleanist reliance on a narrow haute-bourgeoisie, but extended the francise and sought support among rising industrialists among others; governments also had learnt lessons in 1848 and in only a few cases, as in Rome or Naples, was the reaction complete.

The romantic age was ending; 'But the Italians of today', wrote Garibaldi, 'think of the belly not of the soul'.

Realpolitik replaced liberal romanticism as the weapon of nationalists; the bourgeoisie re-ordered its relations with governments or turned to making money through capitalist enterprise; even artists abandoned romanticism for a new realism. The age of evolutionary thought was dawning in Europe; Marxism and Darwinism were to make romantic solutions to complex problems seem altogether too simple. Science was fast becoming the new God; science and realism. Delacroix's romantic inspiration gave place to Courbet's accurate detail. Ranke's exhortation to historians was to find *wie es eigentlich gewesen*. Radicals accused of being socialists in 1848, when very few were, turned to socialism as a practical and revolutionary answer or, like Garibaldi, sought co-operation with the existing powers; Marx, who, with Engels, had published his *Manifesto* in 1847 now absorbed the lessons of 1848 and prepared *Das Kapital* (1867) a theoretical and practical work of revolutionary propaganda. In many ways 1848 was a turning point. As the romantic fog began to lift, problems were seen in the harsh light of reality. It was the age of Bismarck.

The great question of the day will be decided not by speeches and the resolution of majorities, that was the mistake of 1848 and 1849, but by blood and iron.

CHAPTER TWENTY

Economic and Social Development 1848-70

Whatever might have been its meagre political results 1848 did mark an important stage in the development of European industrialisation. Europe had lagged behind Britain in this field for several reasons, but above all because Europe possessed a vast peasant class which was closely tied to the land, in whose philosophy Adam Smith had not appeared and which, in many cases, dwelt far from the fingers of railway tracks, then spreading across Europe. Above all, in Britain the old institutional framework of feudal ties, social dominance by a landowning nobility interested only in its rents, had been far earlier mitigated by the demise of the peasantry and the rise of a commercial and financial middle class which had begun the industrial revolution independently of state intervention. Convenient distances, the early collapse of guild organisation and the use of land as a commercial asset, gave Britain a head start.

In Europe the industrial revolution, while borrowing much from Britain, could not follow the same pattern. In Britain, re-organisation of industries began before the machine transformed the landscape; in Europe too it was not the introduction of British technology which created an industrial revolution but the transformation of society. This transformation was the sum of many events and trends which had been noticeable since 1780; the French Revolution; Napoleonic occupation of Germany and Italy; the impact of Britain's capital and know-how; changes in the relationships of autocrat and peasant; railways, and the revolutions of

1848 were all part of the background which made Europe's industrial revolution follow a unique course.

It is perhaps well to talk in terms of Europe, rather than of France, Germany and Russia. because, as raw materials and communications, so industrial expansion cut across national boundaries. Nonetheless national boundaries were important; not only because nationalism and liberalism were so interwoven with the fabric of a rising bourgeois society, which was concerned with economic progress, but also because the traditions of each country put a particular stamp on the industrial society each created. We have already seen how the social results of the peasant revolution in France affected the progress of industry in France; each country will have its own individual revolution as well as being part of the general movement of industrialisation.

The European movement distinquishes itself most clearly from the British in the fact that it took place in a still predominantly traditional and agrarian society. German industrialisation did not disturb the Junkers; the French peasant is still perhaps the 'typical' representative of his nation. Whereas in England the countryside became involved with the town, accepting the same market-based economic philosophy, and whereas the town became the place to which the country came to buy the products of the cities, in Europe the small market town, the peasant economy, the subsistence economy, lasted throughout our period with its attitudes largely unchanged. It might be a conservative enclave in a dynamic economy, as in Germany, or of even more importance, as in France. This phenomenon meant also that artisan industry lasted longer, guild organisations survived more vigorously than in England (in Germany the spirit survived the abolition of 1862) and that there was always a conservative opposition to radical industrial change, or industrial control of government. In this way Europe avoided the era of the 'robber baron' which disfigured contemporary American economic life.

In Britain the industrial revolution was the work of independent men working with their own or borrowed capital. The family firm was still the norm in 1870. In Europe, lack of the private capital, which British merchants had acquired in eighteenth century exploitation of Empire, dictated greater state participation, and in Europe it was to be the railways which were to 'stimulate industry by forcing governments to expend money, make money more readily available, and make investments profitable for foreign, above all British, capital. After the scares of 1847—8 British capital was soon again oiling the wheels of Europe's railway boom, just as Irish navvies were building the viaducts and mining the cuttings. In the early 50s Thomas Brassey was building railways in Italy, France, Norway and Austria. Railway-building encouraged governments to make the creation of joint-stock companies easier (as in Prussia in 1843) and credit companies grew in Germany, Austria and France to promote the creation of joint stock companies.

Railways were therefore everywhere in Europe, as opposed to Britain, the necessary precursor of industrial revolution on any significant scale. They created advanced financial and business methods, and stimulated iron industries, coal mines and engineering. Thus while in Britain it was in textiles that industrial change first bore fruit, in many parts of Europe industrialisation first affected heavy industries, and these heavy industries, needing heavy capitalisation, soon found it unprofitable to compete with too many neighbours, as well as too expensive to remain in the hands of families, unless they were the Krupps. In Europe, as in America therefore, late industrialisation implied the 'corporation' and the 'trust'.

It must not be assumed that this expansion was everywhere even or everywhere of the same kind (France's industrial revolution is very different from that of Britain) but the years between the revolution of 1848 and the economic crisis of 1873 saw a quarter century of optimistic expansion, as railways linked Berlin, Munich, Stettin, Cologne and Mannheim with Basle, Prague, Vienna, Amsterdam and Paris and as steel production soared (in Germany from twelve million tons in 1860 to twenty-five million in 1870). Areas where raw materials were found were linked with manu-facturing centres, those with ports, ports with distribution centres. Everywhere, almost, the phenomenon was visible, but everywhere history, custom and tradition gave an individual slant.

France's industrial progress had been hindered by a number of factors, particularly the effects of the French Revolution, and by 1848, though the railway boom had begun and changes were visible in her textile industries, credit facilities were still poor and the small private banks uninterested in lending capital at risk. Nonetheless the financier bourgeoisie was waking up, and under Louis-Napoleon industrialists were given some social and political prominence for the first time; the Paris Bourse was busier than ever before. As the weight of public finance was thrown behind the railway expansion and vast public works like Baron Haussmann's rebuilding of Paris began, new financial institutions and methods were developed. *Crédit Mobilier* which advanced loans to private joint stock companies and *Crédit Foncier* which advanced loans for land development were two results of Louis Napoleon's energy. The property owning classes found ever more lucrative schemes and organisations in which to put money which they had formerly thought safer sewn into their mattresses.

In 1863 joint stock companies were freed from governmental control; in 1867 limited liability companies had complete freedom; *Crédit Lyonnais* provided a system of deposit banking. Rail mileage increased sixfold; new coal fields, as at Lens, were opened and the use of steam power quintupled, suggesting a rapid expansion of the factory system, hitherto very much an exception. New shipping companies, *Messageries Maritimes* and *La Compagnie Générale Maritime* contributed to the trebling of French trade under the second Empire.

In 1860 a real attempt to get away from the protectionist mentality which fear of Britain's superiority had induced, was made in the Chevalier-Cobden Treaty, though in the 1870s Europe, including France, slumped back into protectionism. France was developing away from the family firm mentality, from the wish to remain small which had been hampering her progress; and in the declining numbers of her peasants and the swelling size of Marseilles, Lyons, Rouen and other major centres as well as Paris there was hope, misplaced perhaps, that her population growth would revive strongly.

I

France however was not going forward at a truly rapid pace. Her agriculture remained backward, her peasants stubborn. Over many areas of industry older forms of organisation than those now encouraged by machinery, credit and railways still held sway; capital was still lacking and not even *Crédit Lyonnais* could provide the average Frenchman with the credit facilities his contemporaries across the channel would consider adequate. Many industrialists still liked the idea of retiring in their old age to live on *rentes*. The peasant population held back internal demand and abroad Germany's progress was far more spectacular. Only in the last quarter of the nineteenth century would France join the ranks of modern industrial nations, and even then with problems and characteristics all her own.

Against Germany in 1870 France's efforts seem almost puny; but forty years before it would have been difficult to imagine that Germany could ever become industrialised. Even in 1870 her development was extremely uneven and the power of the landed aristocracy, the old artisan industries and the peasants very strong; in many localities life had hardly changed at all. Despite the serf emancipation in East Prussia and the influence of Napoleon's reforms in the western parts of Germany, which provided a latent work force and the legal freedom which expanding industry needed, Germany's industrial explosion was delayed. Not even the agrarian crisis of the thirties and forties in the west German provinces, which precipitated the largely successful peasant risings of 1848 provided an impetus for anyone to take advantage of a surplus population. But 1848 itself did have important effects. In west Germany the conservatives granted concessions which freed the peasants from those legal and other burdens which had replaced the earlier feudal obligations. The completion of the emancipation of the peasant in the west at last allowed some of the agrarian conditions which had precipitated the English industrial revolution to appear in Germany. Above all the market economy entered German agriculture and a supply of labour freed from any contractual obligations to a landlord became available for work in the towns.

The Zollverein stimulated development by widening

markets, making possible free movement of trade, breaking-down particularism and encouraging the vast expansion of the railway system. At the same time the conservative political framework of Germany emerged intact from 1848 and was accepted by a middle class which turned its energies from politics to finance and industry. The railways encouraged the expansion of other industries; by 1870 German output of pig-iron outstripped that of France whereas in 1850 she had produced only two-thirds as much. The textile industry quickly adopted British machines and technical know-how though the handicraft industry survived in remoter areas. But it was in the heavy and chemical industries that Germany really forged ahead, not, as in England, with the slow accretion of capital by family firms but with joint stock companies of a vast size, aided by bank finance. German industry from the beginning had to buy large quantities of expensive materials and equipment and thus the large concern, closely tied to financial institutions, was the norm.

Much of the industrial strength lay in Prussia. There Von Motz had laid the foundations by master-minding the Zollverein. Beuth deliberately borrowed the best technical ideas from abroad and through the *Technical Commission, Technical Institute* and the *Association for the Promotion of Technical Knowledge* he broadcast his ideas. He was also Director of the Berlin Technical Institute, presiding over the beginnings of Germany's superiority in technical education which Britain, to her cost in the latter part of the century, was to ignore. In Prussia too Van Rother, Head of Prussia's Overseas Trading Company (*Seehandlung*) and the Bank of Prussia, facilitated credit and sought outlets for Prussia's trad-itional and new manufactures.

Thus it was not by accident alone that Prussia achieved industrial as well as political hegemony in Germany. But deposits of coal, iron, lignite, and potash in Silesia and the grudgingly acquired Rhineland provinces, certainly aided Prussia's progress. It was this strength that enabled Prussia to defeat the economic threat from Austria. Karl Lüdwig Brück, Austrian Minister of Commerce from 1848, planned to create a Pan-German Union to unite Empire, Zollverein, Tax Union and other German states, which Austria would dominate. The industrialists of Bohemia, which was then undergoing a revolution similar to that of Prussia, opposed the idea through fear of Prussian competition. But it was Prussia's own opposition which effectively destroyed the scheme. Prussia admitted Hanover to the Zollverein on favourable terms; such an accession of strength stifled doubts among other members and the Austrian plans fell through. There was no point in quitting such an obvious going concern. The Zollverein was strengthened by the Austro-Prussian war and was merged into the German Empire of 1870.

Thus Germany developed, under the shadow of the Hohenzollern monarchy whose special relationship with Junkerdom events of 1848 had left intact. As a result, the vast industrial expansion took place in a Germany still politically controlled by conservative monarchies, and their conservative aristocracies and bureaucracies. The great industrial concerns did not therefore produce a middle class eager above all else for the liberal reforms of which they had been cheated in 1848. The middle class of 1848 was a professional class and Germany did not produce a large class of self-made men running their family firm, independent-minded and politically active, as in England. After 1848 all the energies of the middle classes were absorbed in building Germany's industrial greatness. A modern industrial state co-existed with an eighteenth century political organisation, an industrial proletariat with a conservative peasantry, and factories with domestic handicrafts. The old order was not perpetuated simply by the tacit understanding between crown, bourgeoisie and aristocracy but also by the traditional docility of the first generation of peasants to move into the towns. Coexistence between two orders did not imply liking, however, and some historians see the seeds of Nazism in the conservative fears and prejudices of the German peasant.

Elsewhere in Europe, industrialisation tended to be rather more delayed, except in Belgium and other north-west European states like Denmark and Holland, where agricultural conditions similar to those in Britain predominated. Here too a large middle class, used to investment techniques, predominated over a weak aristocracy. In eastern and southern Europe however conditions were very different.

In Russia it took the Crimean War to underline Russia's internal weakness and the technological gap that was opening between her and her rivals. The intractable climate, vast distances, low yield soils, poor communications and the distances from centres of world trade helped to perpetuate this backwardness. Above all however, it was the social structure which prevented any progress. The village community (*mir*) was tenacious, the powers of the nobility and gentry almost untouched since the eighteenth century and a middle class with mobile property practically non-existent. But it was not a desire to industrialise Russia that made Alexander II begin the reforms which culminated in the emancipation of the peasants. Rather it was a wish to reform from above in order to forestall a revolution from below. The story of the emancipation is told later but it did have important economic consequences though not immediate ones.

There could be no immediate consequences. The peasant gained only a small proportion of the land he used to work and thus was in no position to provide part of a consumer society for industry. He was still tied to the land by the need to redeem his land through the agency of the *mir*. Thus little in Russia was altered by emancipation. The economic effects lay in the results of the slow undermining of the *mir* and the increasing differentiation of the roles of the peasant. In the 1860s the state took a further hand; it constructed railways and encouraged an influx of foreign capital. By 1870 Russia had changed little and the intelligentsia still saw Russia's future to lie in the regeneration of the peasantry.

That peasantry did not, even before emancipation, entirely neglect industry. In those areas where serfs were liable for *obrok* (cash payments) rather than *barschina* (labour services) some earned their livings as artisans producing articles as different as candles and jewels. Occasionally such an artisan serf would show true skill as an entrepreneur and build up a business employing several other serfs. Such businesses flourished in both the eighteenth and nineteenth centuries. Perhaps the most famous was that of Sauva Morosov who in 1797 set up a silk ribbon workshop; by 1900 Morosov's enterprise, carried on by his son, employed twenty-two thousand workers.

Before emancipation however such industries were subject to the whim of the entrepreneur's master, whose serfs had no individual property rights of their own. Emancipation may have helped to alleviate the evils resulting from such situations, but the economic and social weaknesses of Tsarist Russia made it imperative that the motive power for industrial expansion on any significant scale would have to come from two sources, government and foreign investment.

Government activity on any significant scale came with the activities of Count Sergei Witte between 1892–1903. Before that Russia relied on foreign-born entrepreneurs of genius like the German born, English trained, Ludwig Knoop whose efforts in the 1840s spread spinning machines throughout Russia, giving the Empire the fifth largest number of spindles in the world by 1860. But looms followed more slowly.

The iron industry in the Ukraine owed much to the Welshman, John Hughes, whose 'New Russia Company' was created with government help, specifically to manufacture rails for the expansion of Russia's transport system. Much of the railway system itself was the work of foreign entrepreneurs, and in the seventies it was to be Swedes who were to open up the oil wells of Baku. As in the eighteenth century Peter the Great and Catherine the Great borrowed the skills of men of western Europe for Russia's army and navy so in the nineteenth new skills were borrowed for the industrial leap forward.

The Austrian Empire was only shaken out of its lethargy by defeat in 1866. Before that, isolation from trade routes had, as in Russia, perpetuated conservatism, a conservatism which the creation of a landed peasantry by emancipation did little to undermine. The soldiers who after 1848 were so important to Franz Josef's government opposed railways on the curious grounds of military security. The defence-mindedness of her generals thus helped to perpetuate backwardness.

Nonetheless not even the Hapsburg patrimony could escape the fever. In Hungary the Great Magyar patriot and feudal entrepreneur Count Istvan Szechenyi promoted industrial advance. He helped found the Hungarian Commercial Bank of Pest (1841), linked Buda and Pest by a new suspension bridge, ran a steamship service, sponsored the Budapest-Vienna railway and created the Pest Steam Flow Mill Company (1842). Such expansion could only quicken once Hungary began to recover from her defeats of 1849 and assumed a place of equality in the Dual Monarchy of 1867.

Russia and the Austrian Empire suffered from their isolated position. Italy's southern provinces had the same weakness; even the Po valley with its developing industry and its good transport facilities was outside the main centres of international trade. Napoleon's rule, though providing a legal framework friendly to economic liberalism, had a bad effect on the peninsula's economic progress and accentuated its geographical weaknesses, the effects of a technically backward agriculture, and political fragmentation. Unification brought single tariff, legal and currency systems but it could not easily eradicate the sectional strife between north and south with its geographical, social and agricultural problems and its background of centuries of neglect, indifference, waste and despair.

For similar reasons, especially agrarian backwardness and social conservatism, industrial expansion was minimal in Spain and Portugal in 1870. In fact nowhere in Europe was progress as rapid as in Britain, Belgium, Germany and France. Modern industrial centres were developing in northern Italy, and in the area round Vienna, in Bohemia, in central Russia and in Switzerland which was already finding a special niche for itself in the production of high quality goods for export. The scale was still small in 1870, but once a society consciously or unconsciously took the decision to industrialise it could not go back; Europe was irrevocably called to accomplish an economic and social revolution more profound than anything imagined by the good, honest professors of Frankfort.

The people of Europe were, however slowly, changing. The industrial revolution gave new opportunities to individuals to express their inventive, financial or entrepreneurial talents. In Britain Stephenson, Wilkinson and Roebuck were the first of a new race of men who would by 1900 be as remote as the great military conquerors, so rapid was industrialisation and so soon the end of the period of individual enterprise, which made the whole process possible. In Europe, though the process of industrialisation is different, the type is still visible.

Wenier Siemens is the type of the inventor turned entrepreneur in the fast developing world of metallurgy, communication by electrical means and electricity itself in the invention and promotion of the dynamo. Alfred Krupp is the self-made man; from owner of a small iron works employing seven men in 1826 he rose with the help of Prussia's militarist government and the railway boom, to be the sole controller of a vast industrial concern employing seven thousand men. For this expanding world financial expertise of a high order was necessary from men like the Péreire brothers, Emile and Isaac, Saint-Simonian founders of the *Crédit Mobilier*. Such expertise replaced the conservative rentier world of the Rothschilds who were themselves forced to break out of the clubland atmosphere of family banking and enter the riskier and more highly developed financial world demanded by large and sophisticated industrial concerns.

Industrialisation created, and was created by, a new aristocracy, and this aristocracy needed its own new proletariat. Though, as we have seen, the rise of an industrial proletariat was in many places slow, in some areas non-existent, the urban worker was an important addition to the European social scene. Germany's urban population increased at a faster rate than that of the country at large. In France, too, though less spectacularly the towns were growing and filling with the new masses. As these people increased in numbers so they developed a self-awareness, in part created by the disciplined world of the factory, (though it must be remembered that in 1870 more workers were employed in workshops or their own homes than in large factories) partly by memories of the traditional customary un-competitive world of the peasantry, and partly by traditions of artisan organisation through guilds. This self-awareness was frightening to the established orders, especially after 1848, and it manifested itself increasingly in the philosophies of socialism.

The temptation to define socialism in glib terms as though it was Marxism is too easy just as it is facile to use the language of class warfare. The modern world where both capitalism and socialism are fast losing their meaning thinks more in terms of 'greedy' capitalists and 'virtuous' workers than did the people of the mid-nineteenth century. The sham, sentimental socialism of professional bourgeois misfits must be discarded. Recent studies have shown that histories which see the social consequences of the English industrial revolution in terms of simple class warfare are inaccurate political polemics; when it is appreciated that Luddites smashed machinery to order, for financial reward, and that employers often encouraged machine breakers and protected them faith in a glib approach to Europe's economic revolution should be shattered. This does not mean, of course, that the conditions and status of the workers were not often appalling, or that the poverty which so horrifies us in the underdevloped world today was not once present in Europe, but it does mean that we should expect regional differences in the responses of the workers to the 'Condition of Europe' and also that we should not too easily assume the presence of simple class conflicts, from the Marx and Engels text books.

Marxism had had little effect on the revolutions of 1848; the Manifesto was published in 1848 but made hardly any impact outside London in the year of revolutions. The Cologne trial of German communist leaders caused Marx and Engels to flee to England.

Socialism in Germany, when it revived in the early 1860s was not strictly Marxist at all. Ferdinand Lassalle, leader of the Düsseldorf workers in 1848, founded the 'General German Working Men's Association' in 1862, but though Lassalle proclaimed Marxist principles, his programme looked back to theories more akin to Chartism's political and constitutional ideas, than Marx's social revolution. Certainly Marx and Engels viewed Lassalle with suspicion and criticised his plans for co-operative factories on the grounds that these were more likely to preserve the powers of the bourgeoisie than hasten the proletarian revolution. Similarly they found the emphasis on universal suffrage too constitutional for their revolutionary tastes. Above all, perhaps, they feared Lassalle's association with Bismarck. Lassalle was killed in a duel in 1864, while his active following was probably less than five thousand. By his death Marxist ideas were enabled to penetrate German proletarian thinking, and before 1870 socialism in the developing Empire was to be divided between supporters of Marx led by Wilhelm Liebknecht and followers of Lassalle.

The weakness of the proletarian movement was accentuated by the suspicion of artisans in workshops for their 'comrades' in factories, and by the strength of Germany's conservative forces, a conservatism which tended to influence what was still only a first generation proletariat. The change from agrarian to industrial country was at once so swift and so incomplete that the paternalism of the agrarian aristocracy and the relative quiescence and conservatism of the rural proletariat were inherited by their urban cousins. Similarly the paternalism and authoritarianism of the governments of Germany, particularly Prussia, before 1870 carried over into the period of industrialisation, and there was no ideological reason why such governments should not themselves take over part of the socialist programme and impose it by state action — hence Bismarck's discussions with Lassalle. Although there might be some alarm expressed by conservatives at the growing socialist strength there was certainly no immediate danger to the established order in 1870.

In France socialism tended to have a sharper cutting edge and to provoke more vigorous response in the context of class warfare, largely as a result of the tremors of successive revolutions, the Jacobin tradition and the fatal French failing of reducing all disputes to logical arguments. The 'workers' were perhaps more isolated than in Germany; industry tended to be localised and the dead weight of peasant conservatism and provincial torpor more acutely felt by a people suffering appalling conditions. Perhaps for this reason by 1870 the French branch of the Marxist First International (1864) was the largest in Europe at the very moment at which Louis Napoleon was attempting to alleviate the social and economic ills from which the proletariat suffered; ills perpetuated by the very slowness of France's progress from workshop to factory-based economy.

French socialists were divided; but while they might not know what they were for they were increasingly sure of what they were against. In Louis Napoleon's reign while Blanquist Anarchists, red republicans and Marxist socialists bickered, Marx's materialism was slowly emerging as the dominant doctrine and submerging, though never entirely, the romanticism of French radicalism.

As in Britain in the early years of her industrialisation so in Germany and France, trade unionism was hampered by governments which favoured the employers. Only in 1868 did French workers gain partial recognition of the right to strike following years of industrial strife and court prosecutions, especially in the textile industry. In Germany too the sixties saw industrial organisation by the workers recovering from the setback of 1848. Friendly societies and social clubs grew in strength, disguising their basically trade union activities. With the north German Industrial Code (1869) legalising workers combinations, trade unionism came of age, and associated itself increasingly with the Marxist Social Democratic party and drawing that party increasingly into constitutional activity. Socialist trade unions won the support of the majority of workers, but catholic and other trade unions were not unimportant. At the time of the Franco-Prussian war, therefore, the workers in the more advanced industrial countries, were not only aware of their existence as a burgeoning class but were already organising themselves to win better conditions and greater political involvement in the societies they were helping to create. Perhaps most interesting of all they were channelling their efforts into legal and constitutional organisations, and, even where Marxism was the dominant ideology, taking the road of social democracy. This positive advance was not yet necessarily inevitable — anarchism and syndicalism still lay in the future — but it was a significant departure.

The rise of the workers was not however simply a matter of self-help. In Germany philanthropically-minded members of the middle class began the first retail co-operative societies in the eighteen sixties following the creation of co-operative banks a decade earlier by F. H. Sebulze-Delitzsh, in an attempt to encourage the middle class virtues of thrift. In France the co-operatives, tarred with the brush of Louis Blanc's co-operative workshops were not such a success.

State action was bound to be the force behind most efforts to alleviate distress. In Britain where the industrial revolution came earliest, government activity was likewise more advanced than in other countries. In France a law prohibiting children below the age of eight from working in factories had been passed in 1841, and ten years later further protection was extended to children. Prussia's first similar law was passed in 1839. Louis Napoleon's France and Bismarck's Prussia accelerated this process under increasing working class pressure. But until 1870 the prevailing philosophy was that of laissez-faire. This doctrine could be cruel in that it tended to assume too easily that distress was a fact of life which could not be altered and which therefore must be endured. No doubt it perpetuated poverty and allowed the greedier employers to take advantage of their workers, but it also allowed great industries to rise and give unemployment to a population, growing independently of the means to employ it. No doubt the lack of government activity enabled employers to cut wages in times of economic crisis, but it must be remembered that employers suffered too from slumps, particularly the owners of small firms, and often sympathised with the plight of the men they employed. The ogre capitalist, if he ever existed, is a figure of the late nineteenth century; in the years before 1870 the most common employer, despite the great industrial complexes already developing, was the small entrepreneur, perhaps living in close proximity to his employees. In most places the class struggle must have been remarkably muted.

This was the developing new world to which governments after 1848 were being forced to adapt, however conservative they may have wished to be. A developing skilled middle class, no longer simply professional men or *rentiers*, but a class whose functions the industrial revolution was multiplying as fast as it was multiplying those of the proletariat. But beyond these two expanding classes the old order still existed, declining perhaps, but of great importance and political economic and social weight. How were governments to survive the challenges of peasant conservatism and worker socialism in the same society? Would governments develop quickly enough the techniques of dealing with the unruliness of fast expanding towns and the social and economic problems they created; would they absorb the energies of a vigorous new growth, or would they try to preserve the political hegemony for the old order? Whatever happened the old order which survived 1848 was not going to remain untouched by the awakening giant in 1870.

CHAPTER TWENTY ONE

New Departures
in Government

In 1850 liberalism sat triumphantly enthroned only in Great Britain and Belgium. 'The beacon light of an ordered freedom' was wholeheartedly hated in Europe's capitals from St Petersburg to Naples. Only in Paris was there apparent hope for the future. There 'the would-be liberal' sat 'discontented in the Tuileries under the protection of priests and bayonets', at least according to G. M. Trevelyan, the last of the great Whig historians. But though liberalism was in purdah, the governments of Europe were not entirely impervious to the forces of change. No government could ignore 1848, even less the upsurge of commercial and industrial activity which characterised the years 1850 to 1870.

In Great Britain the era of laissez-faire, if it had ever existed in a pure form at all, was beginning to be challenged by 1860. Even before then the Public Health Board, though short-lived, proclaimed an era of the more active government which would be necessitated by the new politics, foreshadowed in the parliamentary reform agitation of the 'sixties. In England the unnaturally prolonged period of aristocratic government with middle class participation was coming to a peaceful end.

The forces of change were felt even more strongly in that country across the channel which had never achieved, in the nineteenth century, the *juste milieu* in politics which makes for sound and safe government. In Louis Napoleon, however, France had found a ruler who at least felt the currents of change even if he did not entirely succeed in harnessing them.

'Today', he wrote in his book *L'Exinction du Pauperisme*, 'the reign of castes is over, one can govern only with the masses; they must therefore be organised so that they can formulate their wishes and disciplined so that they may be directed and enlightened concerning their interests.'

This may well resemble fascism but at least there was an awareness of the importance of the masses in politics. 'St Simon on horseback' never forgot this; sometimes in his later years the thought haunted him.

How great France could be if she were permitted to attend to her real business, and reform her institutions instead of being incessantly troubled either by demagogue ideas or by Monarchist hallucination.

Napoleon therefore saw himself as the strong guardian angel under whose wings Frenchmen would come together for protection, and warring factions be stilled. Louis-Napoleon was to prove a great healer, even if, perhaps, chiefly by accident. He had dreams rather than specific plans.

His dreams could not become a reality within the confines of the constitution of 1848, whose chief feature was the inadequacy of the powers given to the executive. The election of 1849 forced Louis-Napoleon to work with the conservative forces in order to oppose the strong 'red' contingent in the Assembly. He secured conservative support by helping to destroy the Roman republic and by accepting the Falloux Law which gave the church greater control over education. Louis however chafed under this conservative policy. He did not wish to be associated with clerical pretensions and after the death of Louis Philippe in 1850 he feared a monarchist front. He was depressed by the need to restrict the franchise in 1850 after the 'red scare' and was faced with the prospect of ceasing to be President before he had accomplished anything.

His *coup d'état* of 1851 was well prepared but it was only carried out after his failure to achieve a revision of the constitution by legitimate means. Some barricades were raised against him but his half brother, the Duc de Morny, Minister of the Interior, was ready and although there were twenty-seven thousand arrests and nine thousand deportations a plebiscite supported his action by a vote of seven and a half million to half a million.

The revision of the constitution in December 1851 guaranteed a term of ten years to the president who could nominate his successor. The legislature consisted of two bodies: a Senate nominated by the President and with the power to modify the constitution and a legislative body with only two hundred and sixty (as opposed to its predecessor's seven hundred and fifty) members elected by a revised universal suffrage. It was to sit for a mere three months in the year, might discuss bills but could not question ministers or debate the presidential address. The power of the executive was further enhanced by the greatly increased importance bestowed on the Prefects. The army was to be given greater prestige, the number of police increased significantly. A year later Louis Napoleon became Napoleon III. A plebiscite endorsed his action with a ninety-seven per cent majority.

Possessed of real power at last, Louis-Napoleon could rule as he wished. He appealed to the mass of people, tired of faction, of red scares and reaction, and bored with politicians. He wished also to put an end to that situation whereby any government, Republican, Legitimist or Orleanist automatically created for itself, in the politicians and civil servants it displaced, a vested interest in its overthrow. He did not therefore base his new regime on a Bonapartist party, though such a thing existed, but on men of position, Bonapartist or not, who would attract support in the localities. Persigny, the Minister of the Interior in 1852, working with the Prefects, therefore supplied a government list of candidates which was not narrow or doctrinaire. Such a procedure enhanced the government 'ticket' and it greatly enhanced the standing of the Prefect, who under the Empire assumed a role of major importance, not only as the government's eyes and ears, but as its election manager, and as the social leader of the local community in place of the old legitimist aristocracy. This in turn convinced many that Napoleon was genuinely anxious to rescue politics from control by oligarchy and it won him much gratitude and support.

Louis-Napoleon's personal part in these transactions may have been limited but his name came to mean success in elections, except perhaps in the major towns, where Bonapartism made very little headway. The government, through the Prefects, made full use of all the agents at its disposal; the Mayors, teachers, clergymen and postmasters were all at the government's service. Judicious promises of money for local improvements, of a railway spur, or a new road could accomplish much. Only in 1860 did this system seem to be breaking down, for reasons which are not at all clear.

Nor was Louis-Napoleon's Legislative Assembly packed with Bonapartists. Prefects would allow many shades of opinion to achieve official status. Legitimists, Orleanists and Republicans were present in the early assemblies and independents were a numerous body. Bonapartism was so vague that its devotees could be found right across the political spectrum. One notable feature of the *Corps Législatif* under Louis-Napoleon was the increased number of businessmen and industrialists. The legislature was not therefore a flock of sheep following the shepherd; it remained to be seen whether it would accept for ever its lowly position.

The regime was of course in many ways a sham. It gave the impression of representative government, yet the legislature was largely powerless. Opposition was possible but press controls, the restriction of the right to hold public meetings, the police and the penal colonies were signs that opposition could be difficult or dangerous. Yet Louis-Napoleon had begun to do something important. True, he had won over few republicans; true his working class and lower middle class support in elections was small; but he had begun to win over Orleanists and legitimists, he had largely destroyed the factional bitterness without making a revolutionary change in the nature or location of political power. The plebiscite is, of course, a favourite trick of authoritarian regimes which wish to give the impression of popular will without having to suffer from its consequences. But there is no reason to suppose that the plebiscites of the Empire gave a very false idea of the support for the regime, and they, with the univer-

sal suffrage, did give the mass of people some say, however
slight, in decision-making, in a way which did not threaten
either demagoguery or reactionary monarchism. The regime
also provided a period of stability which gave to France
economic expansion unparalleled·in his history, expansion
which owed not a little to Louis-Napoleon's own encouragement. Even Palmerston was of the opinion in 1858
that Louis-Napoleon could 'do much more for the prosperity
of France than the Roman Emperor did for the Roman
Empire'.

The establishment of Louis-Napoleon's authoritarian
regime required a *coup d'état*, repression and the loss of
several lives; the re-establishment of Hapsburg rule also
required repression. In Hungary alone thirteen generals were
hanged, Batthyany was executed and under the Austrian
patriot, Bach, a bureaucratic police state was established and
Germanisation accelerated. But Bach was by nature radical,
though not nationalist, and neither he nor Schwarzenberg,
Metternich's successor, intended that Austria should return
to the situation obtaining in 1848. Reforms did come, even
in Hungary; the feudal privileges of the gentry and aristocracy were abolished, Hungary was united with the other
provinces in a customs union, and although landowners were
soon in difficulty, the first important steps had been taken
on a road which would lead to a developing agriculture, and
industry run on capitalist lines. Absolutism was able slowly to
relax.

The decision to avoid a return to pre-revolutionary conditions in Hungary, or anywhere, was part of a determined
sometimes frantic, search for a new system of government in
the Austrian Empire which would avoid the pitfalls of
capitulation to provincialism, separation, nationalism and
aristocratic privilege, or of provoking such forces by careless
centralisation. The task was probably impossible but it had to
be attempted.

Bach had been appointed during the liberal period when
optimism was the preponderant emotion of Bohemian and
German nationalists. While Bach hoped to centralise, to
impose his 'system' on Austria, he wished to do so under the
guarantees of an Imperial liberal constitution. Such a solution

was beyond the capacity of Franz-Josef to comprehend; duty, discipline and the Hapsburg's sacred role in Eastern Europe were the bounds of his blinkered vision. He was more open to the pleas of the conservatives and to Bach's rival Kübeck. Even the limited constitution was abandoned and replaced by a nominated Reichsrat presided over by Kübeck (1851). Although Bach continued as minister his liberalism was effectively circumscribed. Other liberals, Brück and Schmerling left the government and even the Reichsrat was ineffective. Bach continued in office to perfect his system; for the first time the Empire had a single administrative organisation and a tariff-free internal market and formed a single unit for law and taxation.

On the surface, the Hapsburgs had recouped their position, but in reality their nerve was shaken and the financial crash of 1857, not of immense significance in itself, set the Empire's raw nerves on edge. The result was an attempted *douce violence*. In Lombardy the Archduke Maximilian relaxed the penal laws and censorship, in Hungary the retreat from absolutism accelerated and moderate nationalist leaders found life easier. But although Cavour at one time feared that Italians might come to accept Austrian rule in Lombardy, the relaxation of absolutism was without real purpose or effect. Hungarians continued their resistance to incorporation, the capitalist classes of the Empire re-opened demands for a constitution under which they could effectively oppose the cost of the army and the consequent slow development of railways and industry, while in Italy Austria's concessions were soon understood to signify a fatal weakness. A disastrous ten years was dawning for the Hapsburg Empire. Despite the reforms which 1848 had procured for the subjects of Franz-Josef the work of the Imperial government had been essentially negative. Bach had seen centralisation as part of a concerted effort to find a viable system of government under a proper constitution for the whole Empire. But for the traditionalists, of whom Franz-Josef, despite his youth was the most traditional, centralisation was purely negative; it was, like the vast army, a means of combating nationalist and liberal feeling, of keeping it within bounds. Centralisation was an approach to the problem of the

Empire's rival nationalisms, different indeed from the 'divide and rule' solution employed during the revolution; but without a constitution it was no less negative. A constitution promised immense problems, particularly in relation to Hungary, but any other answer was bound to lead to disaster.

It was not of course in the Empire alone that the Hapsburgs had been severely shaken. Germany too had broken away and had tried to establish a rival German Empire of which Prussia should be the head. Not only did Austria feel bound, therefore, to re-establish her hegemony in Germany but she felt that it was necessary to teach Prussia a lesson. Frederick-William had, it was true, refused the crown 'from the gutter' but the revolution had not been without its effects in Berlin also. Frederick-William was not averse to an Imperial crown, only to a 'democratic' Imperial crown, and there was an even more positive side to his attitude. If Prussia's monarchy could obtain leadership of Germany it might be able to resist the creation of a liberal nationalist Germany which would destroy the powers of the Hohenzollern monarchy. Equally, however, something of Frederick-William's old nationalist leanings remained and he was emotionally sympathetic to nationalist aspirations. Such were the motives of the Prussian king when, in May 1849, under the influence of his foreign minister von Radowitz, he invited to Berlin representatives of the German states to discuss the future organisations of Germany. Austria was to be placated by the signing of a treaty with the 'new' Germany. But by May 1849 the Empire was recovering its poise and withdrew from the meeting on the first day. The princes of Germany soon saw that Austria, to whom many still held a sentimental loyalty stronger than their fear of Prussia, would never accept the creation of any German organisation which excluded herself. Even Saxony and Hanover, who had given initial approval, withdrew when it was decided to hold elections in January 1850 for a lower house to meet at Erfurt in March. By that time Frederick-William, too, had lost his nerve.

Schwarzenberg, despite the absence of Prussia and her allies, was able to reconstitute the German Confederation in May. Prussia could have outfaced Austria but the continuing problem of Schleswig-Holstein provoked the hostility of the

Tsar who wished to see a full return to the *status quo* in Europe and who looked to Austria as its sheet anchor. A dispute arose between the Diet and the Duke of Hesse-Cassel as a result of which the Duke called on the assistance of the Frankfort Diet. When the Federal Diet's troops occupied part of the Duchy, Prussian troops occupied another part in order to protect two military roads running through the duchy, over which Prussia held sole rights of passage. In this trial of strength Prussia gave way, and at Olmütz in 1851 rejoined the Federal Diet.

Prussia had suffered a grievous setback but Austro-Prussian rivalry was not dead and Prussia was by no means defeated. The Prussian economy was strong and successfully resisted Austria's economic onslaught under Bruck (see p.245). Austria's political strength was only apparent and after 1857 was visibly tottering. Austria's negative policies were too much, even for the princes of the Confederation, and Protestants throughout Germany, not to mention most lay catholics, were disgusted by the Empire's Concordat with Rome in 1855. Above all, Prussia's constitution, though not perfect, was more in tune with the desire for progress in moderation which was the prevailing sentiment of informed, and particularly middle class, opinion after 1849.

Frederick-William's brief flirtation with nationalism had alarmed the Junkers of the *Kreuz-Zeitung* party (p.232). They could not understand how Junker power could survive in a united Germany. Consequently they approved of the *Punktation of Olmütz* and took their stand on a policy of resistance to liberalism or nationalism of any kind. Such a view was by no means unanimously held. Hollweg's moderate conservative party saw Olmütz as a betrayal engineered by Russia. Their views were shared by the Prince of Prussia, who in 1858 became Regent and in 1861 King, but not by Bismarck who was already a rising hope of the conservatives and who wished to promote an alliance with Russia, not, like the Kreuz-Zeitung party, in order to re-establish the Holy Alliance, but in order to defeat Austria. For the moment, however, conservative liberals held the stage and Bismarck, to his annoyance, was despatched as Ambassador to St Petersburg. (1858).

Piedmont had survived the wreck of liberal hopes with the help of England and France and the courage of her King, Victor Emmanuel, who, even after Novara, refused to alter the new (1849) constitution. This had established a two chamber parliament consisting of a Senate and a Chamber of Deputies, elected on a narrow franchise. The weakness of Piedmont's political life was caused by the war between the conservative right and the democratic left which wished to pursue an aggressive foreign policy and an anti-clerical domestic policy. After Novara it was, in part, quietened but anti-clericalism was generally strong enough to permit moderate support for the abolition of church courts in 1850 (Siccardi laws). Stability was to be looked for in a moderate centre government. In the great Cavour moderation found a worthy champion. Minister of Agriculture, Commerce and Marine in d'Azeglio's government of 1850 he became leader of a coalition government of the centre in 1852.

Cavour spent the first years of his premiership in providing for the economic prosperity and administrative efficiency which alone could guarantee the success of a government of the centre. The government encouraged rail and road construction and vastly improved docks facilities. He took steps to end the stifling effects of monastic control of so much of the land by suppressing over three hundred monasteries and by redistributing clerical incomes. 'Josephism' characterised the new official attitude to the church. Piedmont began to develop a national secular education system, demanded greater control over the election of bishops and restricted the powers of the church over censorship. He signed Free Trade Treaties with Britain, France, Belgium, Holland and the Zollverein. Typical of the post-revolutionary realist, he would not tolerate nationalism by conspiracy. The activities of Mazzini annoyed him. He would not accept grandiose plans for the unification of all Italy. Like Charles-Albert he foresaw in the near future only the unification of Italy north of the Papal lands. Progress by slow, properly thought-out, well prepared stages was his method.

Cavour's major works were in the diplomatic field but by his efforts at home, aided by the strategic position of Piedmont's ports and the fertility of its soil, Piedmont established itself, like Prussia in Germany, as the pre-eminent Italian state, by virtue of its constitutional and economic strength. Naples relapsed into primitive barbarism, Sicily into conspiracy and despair, the Papacy into blind reaction.

Pio Nono (Pius IX) had for two years (1846 to 1848) enjoyed a reputation as a liberal. Vincenzo Gioberti had seriously suggested that he should head the looked-for Italian Federation, but the defeat of the Roman republic had changed all that. While it is just possible that the Pope could have come to some compromise with moderates, it was unlikely that he would find anything in common with anti-clerical radicals. The history of the Roman republic made *Pio Nono* more determined than ever to resist the new heresies and the liberals, even moderates, more determinedly anti-clerical than the history of Italy from 1780 had already made them. In liberalism Pio Nono saw an over-optimistic and wicked reliance on man's own capabilities, with which attitude the modern world might sympathise, but he failed to see that mankind was coming of age, at least in the more advanced parts of Europe. The encyclical of 1864, *Quanta Cura* and the *Syllabus Errorum*, anathematised socialism, communism, liberty of press and religion, the separation of church and state, rationalism and liberalism.

Only in the decaying world of the Hapsburgs did he find sympathy. The Concordat of 1855, giving back to the church an independence and a control over education unheard of since the days of Maria Theresa, was an agreement between powers who not only saw the disintegration of their power in Italy, but also between powers who believed they had most to fear from the revolt against renewed authority. Both sought a similar answer in centralisation. In Austria, the Bach system was imposed, in Rome the process, which was to lead to the doctrine of papal infallibility and almost it seemed to papal canonisation, was under way. The papacy had more success than Austria which was not saved by centralisation. For although Pio Nono, like his predecessors, saw his temporal power as absolutely necessary for spiritual and political control of the church, the promotion of loyalty to the Pope as a semi-divine person, was, in fact, to make temporal power unnecessary. While 'mankind would no longer endure clerical authority' as a 'great Roman Catholic lady' once told Disraeli, it was to find that it still loved a Pope.

Nicholas I's iron rule in Russia had made expressions of liberal feeling almost impossible and although the spirit of *Decembrism* was not dead it could find few outlets. Nicholas had tried to destroy Polish nationality and had lent his troops to Franz-Josef to quell the Hungarian revolution. The powers of the gentry, the continuing strength of serfdom in Russia, the difficulties of communication in a country where railway mileage was derisory and only one metalled road of any length existed, combined to prevent the real economic progress which would have allowed liberalism to find a firm basis for growth. As it was, liberalism was the expression of a few intellectuals inspired by noble sentiments, alien to the vast majority of the people. While song, dance and literature have always been dear to Russians the intellectual's political power has been minimal. Russia is ruled through the belly and heart, not the brain.

The year 1848 itself had very little influence on Russia and when Nicholas was succeeded in 1855 by Alexander II few people looked for change from this young conservative disciplinarian who had so wholeheartedly supported his father's repressive policies. However Alexander was not a mere conservative like Franz-Josef; he was a well meaning man prepared to accept change if its necessity could really be proved. While he was not exactly open-minded on major questions, he could be persuaded by the logic of events.

Ever since 1767 it had been known that serfdom was the root of Russian ills. Nicholas himself had grasped the problem, and had taken steps to define the rights of the serfs to protect them from the claims of the gentry, but the costly and disastrous Crimean War made it more obvious. The serf was a very inefficient soldier, since he was rebellious.

In 1855, therefore, Alexander did what Catherine had done: he encouraged free discussion. Travel abroad was permitted, the universities were freed from minute scrutiny by secret police, and censorship of the press was temporarily withheld. The results of discussion were disappointing, for the liberals failed to seize the opportunity of forwarding constructive proposals. Reform would have to be undertaken by the Tsar. Russia alone of all European countries still seemed to have faith in the reforming autocrat.

From 1850 to 1860 Alexander pondered and prepared his solution; or rather solutions, for it became obvious that the vastness of Russia, the different qualities of the soil, the variation in the density of population would render a single approach untenable. Throughout this gestation period the Tsar was plagued by the obstructiveness and obscurantism of the gentry, whose economic, political and social position was threatened, not only by serf reform itself, but by the administrative and economic reform that would have to follow any measure which so fundamentally affected the powers of the class which had formed the backbone of the administration for over a century. Nevertheless the gentry were consulted at all stages, not only by Alexander but also his servants Rostovtsev and Milyutin.

In March 1861, the Emancipation Proclamation was issued. It was a compromise measure. While the serfs were entirely emancipated from the gentry and retained half of the cultivated land, they did not themselves become owners. The land was now owned by the *mir,* the village community, which distributed it to the peasant families assuming to itself the responsibility for tax collection. Yet peasants could lease land, or work it as labourers. In over-populated areas leasing land was particularly necessary as peasants found they had less land to cultivate after emancipation. The land given to the *mir* had to be paid for over forty-nine years; meanwhile the state would compensate the gentry.

In general, the proclamation was welcomed, though the serfs had expected far more and particularly resented not owning their own land. In many cases the results were disastrous; overpopulation led to a situation in which the *mir* was parcelling out land in amounts too small for subsistence and many peasants became dependent to a dangerous degree on their old masters for wages. The process of emancipation was slow and many peasants were still outside the scheme twenty years later. Nonetheless 1861 was a year of supreme importance in Russian history; it was the beginning of a revolution.

The Europe of 1860 despite the reaction of 1849 was not at all the Europe of 1848. Every country had in some way adapted its policies or its institutions to meet the challenge of a new age. But in 1860 it was not simply Europe's political, economic and social systems which were undergoing change. Borders which since 1815 had remained stable were in the process of undergoing major revision. Europe's 'Diplomatic Revolution' was having more profound effects than had been the case with the revolts of 1848.

CHAPTER TWENTY TWO

Diplomatic Revolution: Crimean War and Italian Unification

If no government could reconstruct its own political system as it had existed in 1847 it was equally true that no international system could be revived. Too many weaknesses had been highlighted, too many leaders toppled, too many rivalries unearthed and in the new harsh light of reality sentimental and emotional attachments had dissolved.

The chief architect of the Holy Alliance and the system, Prince Metternich, was an exile in England; the motive power of the reactionary alliance was itself dead. Alone among the three eastern monarchs Tsar Nicholas remained loyal to the concept of a holy war against change, and for this reason he aided the young Emperor of Austria in his suppression of the Hungarian revolt. But of all three eastern potentates the Tsar was the only one who had not been severely shaken by the revolts of 1848; in 1850 he simply saw the triumph of reaction, a return to the *status quo*, a vindication of the principles of the Holy Alliance. Frederick-William IV and Franz-Josef, for all their blindness to much that was changing in Europe, knew that there had been no return to the *status quo*.

In Germany, a rivalry between Prussia and Austria had been awakened which Olmütz could not entirely smother. German nationalism was not dead, but it was divided between forces, either catholic southern and agrarian, looking to Austria as Germany's natural leader, or protestant northern and increasingly urban, finding fulfilment in the prosperity, unity and apparent stability of Prussia. In such circumstances neither Prussia nor Austria could remain indifferent to pressures which urged them to be enemies. Once opened, moreover, the question of nationalism and its leadership could not easily be closed.

Under Brück, Austria momentarily dreamed of a pan-German Empire centred on the Danube; under Radowitz Prussia envisaged a Germany controlled by Berlin separate from but allied to Austria's Empire. Olmütz evaporated the dreams but not the rivalry. Austria and Prussia retreated to Confederation. But while Austria's retreat was irrevocable because of the multi-racial nature of her Empire, Prussia's retreat need be only temporary. Despite her Polish subjects, Prussia had shown herself to be more 'German' than Austria. The lesson was not lost, though the conclusions were not yet to be drawn. The Holy Alliance, based, albeit in distorted fashion, on the principles of the 1815 settlement, was doomed. Austria and Prussia had, by attempting to control German nationalism in 1848 and 1849, significantly abandoned those principles. Only the appearance of adherence remained in 1850. Russia was resuscitating a ghost.

The old-alliance system was a phantom in more ways than this. The basis of the old alliance had been Austria's role as the guardian of order in Germany and Italy. Despite Olmütz and Novara few intelligent observers really believed that Austria's grip was firm. Where once Nicholas had been Metternich's pupil he was now Franz Josef's guardian. Russian troops had been needed to secure Austrian control of Hungary, and the Empire had been saved only by allowing subject races and master races to tear each other apart in a way which left bitter and festering tensions. The Empire had been fatally weakened; so much many appreciated. The Hapsburgs were still needed for the control of Eastern Europe but it was no longer the case that they could be the best guarantee of the stability of Germany and the Italian peninsula.

In short the post-revolutionary world was still revolutionary. Neither liberalism nor nationalism were dead. Frederick William, the future William I, Bach, Schwarzenberg, Cavour, Napoleon III were all in their own way working now towards ends not dissimilar from those of the moderate revolution-

aries. Yet they did so in a manner which was not revolutionary. In Prussia and France moderate men were, on the whole,
not averse to playing along with the monarchs. The revolution against the Vienna settlement was proceeding under
the guise of order.

France's Prince-President (later Emperor) was himself a
living embodiment of the truth that the 1815 settlement was
breaking down. Louis-Napoleon, as a Bonaparte, was
debarred from the throne of France by the Vienna settlement
but no-one lifted a finger against him. Napoleon was determined that France should no longer be made to pay for the
ultimate failure of his uncle. The Vienna Settlement was an
insult to France; every move France made in Spain, Italy or
Germany or the Near East was viewed by Europe as a resurgence of France's martial spirit, and to be resisted. If
Europe's alliances, or Europe's map could be redrawn, France
would cease to be the 'naughty boy' of Europe. The
'dreamer' was further convinced that, as Napoleon's heir, he
ought to support the legitimate aspiration of German and
Italian nationalists, particularly if territorial arrangements
could be made on the side. That apart, he was sincerely convinced that he ought to play the role of friend to nationalism,
which he believed Napoleon I had encouraged, then
neglected. In Piedmont, Cavour, for his part, was convinced
that Italian nationalism needed French arms.

Napoleon was eager to pursue a 'forward' policy but to
maintain at the same time the *entente* with Britain. Unfortunately Palmerston made the latter aim impossible; stubborn
and of little imagination, *'Pam'* failed to comprehend the
strength of German nationalism and under-estimated the
power of Prussia. He mistook the intentions of France (which
he mistakenly saw as the major danger to stability in Europe)
and failed to see that the 1815 settlement had been fatally
undermined by the effects of the 1848 revolts.

In the eighteenth century Kaunitz accomplished a diplomatic revolution because he saw that events had made the
existing alliance system anachronistic; in the nineteenth
century Bismarck was to show a similar singular foresight
with even more dramatic results.

The Eastern Question was to precipitate the first stage of

the great diplomatic revolution of the nineteenth century. The question of Turkey's future had always seemed to Russia one which to some extent lay outside the competence of the Holy Alliance and, indeed, since 1815 disputes arising in that sphere had usually been solved by the concerted efforts of both Russia and Great Britain.

In 1844, Nicholas I had come to a verbal agreement with Peel's Conservative government to the effect that the two powers would co-operate if the Ottoman Empire reached the point of collapse. In the meantime they agreed to maintain the Porte's integrity. Such an agreement meant little, for it could not bind the succeeding British government, while Russia's views as to when the Empire was on the point of collapse need in no wise coincide with those of Britain. Neither of these limitations was made at all clear to the Tsar, who believed that 'Gentlemen's Agreements' were made to be kept. Little of real moment arose to test the arrangement before 1850. Palmerston approved of Russia's part in suppressing the Hungarian revolt, though not the bestiality of Haynau, and did not, any more than Austria, object to the suppression of the Wallachian revolt in 1848. True, the flight of Polish and Hungarian revolutionaries to Turkey in 1849 had led to an awkward situation, when Russia and Austria demanded their extradition, and Britain and France supported the Porte's refusal, but although British and French fleets violated the Straits Convention 1841, no real harm had been done and the crisis had quickly passed.

The genesis of the Near East crisis lay in the conflicting claims of France and Russia in regard to the Holy places. Louis Napoleon, eager for catholic support in France, sought to obtain it cheaply by supporting the rights of the Roman church, which despite concessions made to it by treaty in 1740, had fallen into disuse because of the greater strength of the Russian-backed Orthodox church after Kuchuk Kainardji (1774). The Sultan found himself assailed from both sides, and in 1852 granted the Latin church right of entry to the Church of the Nativity.

Sadly the result was not 'Peace on earth to men of good-will'. The Russian answer to Louis-Napoleon's victory was the Menshikov mission to Constantinople bearing (to the

hapless Sultan) the gifts of alliance or the blight of a sever-
ance of diplomatic relations (1853). Menshikov met resistance however, not only from the Porte, but also from
England and France; at least from Stratford Canning who as
British Ambassador took it upon himself to answer for his
superiors. Menshikov returned to Russia in May, having cut
the diplomatic ties which contributed so little to mutual trust
and understanding. A Russo-Turkish war seemed imminent.
In June, British and French fleets moved to Besika Bay.

Anglo-Russian relations were at a low ebb even before the
Menshikov mission. Conversations between the Tsar and the
British ambassador to St Petersburg convinced Britain that
the Tsar was comtemplating the dismemberment of Turkey.
Nicholas's belief that the Ottoman Empire was on the point
of collapse was increased by a brief Austro-Turkish alter-
cation over Montenegro in which Austria had won all her
points. This was doubly dangerous, for it convinced the Tsar
that Turkey would always give in to strong pressure and that
Austria, Russia's protégé, would if necessary go to war
against Turkey in the event of a Russo-Turkish war.

Nothing could possibly have been further from the truth.
Few European leaders, least of all Franz-Josef, wanted to go
to war. In Britain, Aberdeen's coalition government drifted
on the ground swell of an increasingly anti-Russian public
opinion. For British people the war fever assumed something
of the nature of a crusade against tyranny. The government
failed to negotiate, and until June 1853, omitted to make
clear to Russia the exact nature of the British position.

The ideological nature of the opposition to Russia might
have been expected to arouse support for the Tsar from
Prussia and Austria. But Prussia did not feel involved in the
eastern crisis and certainly was not prepared to incur the
enmity of Austria or Russia. Austria was so beholden to the
Tsar for past services that help might well have been expected
from that quarter — and indeed was. But Austria's military
weakness was too palpable, and her economic stability
precarious. Austria could not wish to see even her friend
Russia control the Danube basin, and feared for Moldavia and
Wallachia should war break out. On the other hand Austria
did not wish to see Russia defeated by France and Turkey for

several reasons; France was a threat to Italian stability; Russian weakness might be dangerous for Austria's internal health and Turkish strength would hinder Austria's own expansionist plans. Faced by this dilemma Austria frantically sought peace; war offered the possibilities of defeat, revolution, or, at best, diplomatic isolation and its concomitant the loss of Italy. When war did break out, Austria's dilemma became acutely embarrassing.

Only two leaders saw the advantages of war. Louis-Napoleon was eager for prestige, but more than that he looked for an opportunity to show his friendship to British interests and in any negotiation he could expect to make useful changes in the European power structure and the frontiers which protected it. Cavour also saw advantages in war. Piedmont could offer little military help, but a token force would earn the gratitude of England and, more particularly, France. Nor was Cavour unaware of the acute embarrassments which Austria would suffer in the event of conflict.

In July, Russia occupied the Danubian principalities of Moldavia and Wallachia. Austria's reaction was immediate but not violent. The Austrian minister Buol called a meeting of non-belligerent powers (Britain, France, Prussia) which despatched the 'Vienna Note' suggesting a compromise in the matter of the rights of the Orthodox church. Russia accepted, but Turkey, egged on by Stratford de Redcliffe (Stratford Canning) refused conciliation, and in September decided to go to war.

In desperation Austria again proposed peace talks, but this time British suspicions and Turkish intransigence prevented success. War broke out between Russia and Turkey in October. Again (December) the four powers agreed to mediate, but the British cabinet was unable to agree on terms and the 'massacre' of a Turkish squadron at Sinope in November had the same effect on British policy as Navarino in 1827. In January 1854 an Anglo-French fleet entered the Black Sea; in March war was formally declared.

The month preceding the war had seen attempts to secure four-power agreement on the demands to be put to Russia; chiefly Russian evacuation of the principalities and recognition of the integrity of the Ottoman Empire. Austria, however, was too feeble to accede to anything definite, contenting herself with a meaningless defensive agreement with Prussia. Only in June did Austria take the step of demanding Russian evacuation. In addition Turkey gave Austria sovereign rights in the principalities until the achievement of peace, a move which Austria saw as the first step towards annexation. To the surprise of all concerned Russia, probably over-estimating Austrian strength of will and military might, evacuated the principalities, effectively ending any real justification for the war's continuance.

The war did continue, but the theatre of operations shifted to the Crimea in September. The struggle itself is too well-known to merit discussion; it is the diplomatic manoeverings of Austria which require attention. Once war broke out, Austria was in a very awkward position. Pressed by Britain and France to join the alliance Austria hesitated, fearing not only the effects of war on her internal situation but also aware of how exposed the Empire was to military action by Russia. Russia's evacuation of Moldavia and Wallachia and the remoteness of the Crimea made an alliance even less welcome, but at the same time Russia's hostility could not now be ignored. Austria was obliged to progress sideways, negotiating with France for an alliance, and, at the same time, trying to secure a general peace.

Austrian peace proposals were rejected by Russia in August, but in November, under pressure from Frederick William who now feared involvement in war, Russia accepted the four points negotiated with the other powers by Austria in August. The points demanded renunciation by Russia of any rights in the principalities, a revision of the Straits Convention, free navigation on the Danube and a renunciation by the Russians of their claim to protect the Orthodox Christian subjects of the Sultan. Unfortunately by November Britain had extended Austria's points and demanded the withdrawal of all naval vessels from the Black Sea and the destruction of the naval base at Sebastopol.

France was in general less extreme than Britain, and it was the intransigence of Britain and Russia which destroyed the attempts made by Austria and France to secure peace at the Vienna conference in spring 1855. From this point Anglo-

K

French rivalry increased. Louis-Napoleon's enthusiasm for the war had declined even before war had broken out, for France's motives in opposing Russia were concerned with enhancing the French position in Europe rather than in saving the Ottoman Empire. Now the Emperor was alarmed by the casualty figures from the front, and when Britain rejected a French suggestion that a condition of peace should be the creation of an independent Poland, Anglo-French relations reached their nadir. The only other result of the abortive peace negotiations was the adherence of Piedmont to the Anglo-French alliance.

France and Austria were not alone in their eagerness for peace. The new Tsar of Russia, Alexander II, who came to the throne in March 1855, was appalled by the waste of the war and by the social effects of its continuation. When Austria and France, without British participation, defined their peace terms, and when Austria presented them to Russia in the form of an ultimatum in November, Russia felt obliged to accept them, more particularly because Prussia urged her to do so. Britain accepted the terms in December; Turkey was not consulted.

The ultimatum formed the basis for the negotiations which opened in February 1856. It defined the peace terms as the acceptance by Russia of the neutralisation of the Black Sea and the cession of part of southern Bessarabia, held by Russia, to Moldavia. The peace conference itself was a diplomatic triumph for Napoleon III. It was held in Paris, but more than that, Napoleon's friendship was eagerly sought and his word much heeded. It was, for example, Napoleon III who prevented Britain from making extreme demands on Russia. It was he, with England, who obliged Austria to give up the Danubian principalities, or accept the loss of Italy.

The Treaty of Paris laid down that the Sultan should, in return for guarantees of the territorial integrity of his Empire, guarantee fair treatment for his christian subjects; Moldavia and Wallachia achieved separate semi-independent status, guaranteed by the powers. But most important the Black Sea was made a neutral zone.

Such an arrangement could not last. The 'Black Sea clauses' were too humiliating to Russia, and as a result of this treaty Russia sought a revision of treaties and of the balance of power. Almost alone Austria and England now remained committed to the preservation of the *status quo*. Austria's plight was pitiful. Franz-Josef had to face the enmity of Russia as well as the opportunism of France. Britain was of no military use to him and Prussia could not be trusted for her leaders were only too well aware that Russian enmity was more dangerous than the feeble hatred of Austria. Austrian weakness was manifest, and both Louis-Napoleon and Cavour were eager to prey on the body.

The position of Moldavia and Wallachia itself was by no means stable. The inhabitants were increasingly national-istic; their position, surrounded by Austrian, Russian and Turkish troops, encouraged them to be so. They would not long accept either their false division and weak Turkish suzerainty or Austrian and Russian annexation. Rumania was conceived in 1856.

Turkish integrity could not be guaranteed by a piece of paper. The Empire's continued decline encouraged Slav and Serb revolt in the Balkans and the Sultans did not keep their promise to treat their Christian subjects well. At most the Peace of Paris enabled the powers to take a short respite on the road to the creation of a new European settlement, so that the long-term results of the Crimean war were far more important than the treaty which ended it. Austria was isolated; France and England were estranged; Russia was seeking revenge; Prussia was no man's enemy; Piedmont was France's friend. The Europe of 1815 was in dissolution.

It must not be imagined that the Treaty of Paris satisfied Louis-Napoleon. He had failed to secure an independent Poland and although Piedmont, much against the will of Austria and England, had been present at the treaty no positive steps had been taken towards Italian unity. Russia too was dissatisfied and, despite France's Polish escapade, it was not surprising that the two powers should make common cause, temporarily at least. Russia was flattered by France's deliberate moderation in Paris. The steady deterioration in the good relations between France and England accelerated after the Orsini bomb plot of 1858 and it was hardly likely that Palmerston should accept Napoleon's assurances about

France's naval rebuilding programme at their face value. France entered on a 'revolutionary' phase in her foreign policy which temporarily recommended itself to Russia. Both set themselves up as champions of Rumanian nationalism though for rather different ends. It was Napoleon who encouraged the peoples of Moldavia and Wallachia to unite in 1859 under a hospodar Alexander Cuza who in 1861 became a short-lived Prince of Rumania, though nominally still a vassal of Turkey. Such a policy hardly pleased the Austrians, who had been disappointed by the pressure put upon them in 1856 to give up Moldavia and Wallachia unless they would give up Italy. The British government was equally incensed, for it saw that a united Rumania would weaken Turkey and could only see in such a situation a strengthening of Russian power Any alteration in the arrangements made by the Peace of Paris threatened the Black Sea clauses, the main British achievement of the war. Russia was only too delighted to help sever the ties which bound England and France together and to weaken the provisions of the Paris peace treaty.

Of all foreign lands, however, it was Italy for which Napoleon entertained a special care and affection. His family's destiny, his own romantic nationalism, the desire for prestige and territory all drove him in the same direction. Since Austria would not exchange Italy for Moldavia and Wallachia she must be obliged to give it up. Louis-Napoleon's ambition did not extend south of the Papacy's northern borders. How could they when French troops were protecting the Pope in Rome?

Napoleon's own predilections were probably for a federated Italian state presided over by the Pope, but such an arrangement was hardly likely to recommend itself to the Italians or to Cavour with whom Napoleon was in frequent contact after 1855. Cavour bided his time, not willing to offend the man on whom Italian hopes really depended. The Orsini bomb plot was the catalyst which forced Napoleon into action. An attack on his life by an Italian patriot might be expected to give the Emperor jaundiced views about the troublesome peninsula, but, in marked contrast, it actually emboldened the Emperor to take effective action, especially under the impetus supplied by economic recession and unsatisfactory election results in 1857.

Serious negotiations opened in May 1858, culminating in formal agreement in January 1859 after a meeting between the Emperor and Cavour at Plombières. France was to supply an army of 200,000 men to supplement Piedmont's army of 100,000. Cavour was to engineer a war with Austria and after its completion Italy would become a federated state consisting of a kingdom of Upper Italy containing Piedmont with the addition of Lombardy, Venetia and the Papal state of the Romagna; a central kingdom of Tuscany and some of the Papal states; the Papacy itself; and the kingdom of the Two Sicilies. France would receive Nice and Savoy and Napoleon III would marry his unprepossessing cousin, Prince Napoleon, to the unfortunate Clothilde, daughter of Victor Emmanuel. The wedding took place and Piedmont began to make the first warlike sounds.

Napoleon was not entirely happy about going to war without other allies and negotiated an arrangement with Russia, by which Russia would keep troops on Austria's borders in return for promises from the Emperor and Cavour of support for a revision of the Black Sea clauses. It was, however, a limited agreement, for Russia was not bound to prevent interference from Prussia. Napoleon felt this keenly and Cavour sensed his patron's determination wavering, under the onslaught of church, business and political circles. To Cavour's horror, Napoleon accepted Russia's plan for mediation between Austria and Piedmont and Cavour, and under British and French pressure, agreed to join Austria in a conference and to disarm as a preliminary. It is possible that Napoleon was merely trying to show how reasonable he was being, in order to forestall hostile action by other powers when the inevitable occurred. Luckily for Cavour, Austria prevented the conference by despatching an ultimatum to Piedmont, which Franz-Josef hoped would be rejected, thus forcing Cavour to go to war at the inopportune moment of partial demobilisation.

His hopes were realised, but before the end of June 1859 the Austrians had been twice defeated at Magenta and Solferino. They fell back on their stronger fortresses, the famous quadrilateral and prepared for the rest of a long

campaign. At this moment Louis Napoleon and Franz-Josef
met at Villafranca (July 11) and signed an armistice to which
Cavour was obliged to accede before he resigned the premiership in disgust and humiliation. The terms of the armistice
were embodied in the Treaty of Zürich; Lombardy was to be
ceded to Piedmont but Parma, Modena and Tuscany were to
be restored to their rulers, Venetia remaining under Austrian
control and a new Italian Confederation under the Pope was
to be created. France would acquire Nice and Savoy when
the Confederation came into being.

Louis-Napoleon had looked over his shoulder even before
he embarked on the Italian campaign; once the casualty
figures appeared and there appeared the prospect of a long
campaign fought by a French army which, despite victories,
was shown to be very deficient in organisation, tactics and
equipment, the Emperor's indecisiveness became acute. He
was alarmed by the reaction of church opinion to the war
and to the revolt in the Romagna which it provoked. At the
end of June Prussian troops were mobilised and the worst of
Napoleon's fears seemed about to be realised. Prussian
motives were mixed, and possibly even the Regent, William,
was not sure why mobilisation had occurred; perhaps it was
in order to offer armed mediation, perhaps to attack France,
perhaps even to take advantage of Austria's weakness as
Bismarck urged, perhaps merely to warn France not to
advance towards the Rhine. Whatever the reasons Prussian
arms drove Austria and France to seek a *rapprochement*.

'France', said Louis-Napoleon, 'would not with pleasure
see the rise on her flank of a great nation which might diminish her preponderance.' The Emperor was satisfied with the
arrangements made at Villafranca but to the rest of Europe,
and to Italy, his agreement with Franz-Josef was a betrayal.
It was more than that to Palmerston and Lord John Russell,
his foreign minister. Italy was left by Villafranca in a
thoroughly unsatisfactory position. Britain had always
wished to see Austrian power strong enough in Italy to form
an effective barrier to the French tendency to expansionism.
Now Italy formed no such barrier. Piedmont had received no
accession of strength sufficient to make her an effective sub-
stitute for Austria, or to resist Austrian demands for revenge.

It was admitted, however, that Austria had been shown to be too weak to resist French pressure. Palmerston and Russell took it upon themselves therefore to destroy the Villafranca agreement, to persuade Austria to depart entirely from Italy, and to set up a power in Italy strong enough to resist France. Overnight Britain became the main friend to Italian nationalism.

Britain was given her opportunity by the revolt in the Romagna and by the refusal of the peoples of Parma, Modena and Tuscany to accept the return of their former rulers. Piedmontese royal commissioners, sent by Cavour during the war, organised petitions in Parma and Modena for inclusion in Piedmont. Austria's hands were tied and those revolts were able to continue unhindered. Parma, Modena and the Romagna were organised into a unit under the name Emilia and with a volunteer army of which Garibaldi was second-in-command. Palmerston and Russell therefore put forward the suggestion that the people of the duchies should be allowed to vote whether to return to their old allegiances or attach themselves to Piedmont. The French Emperor, alarmed by British activities and afraid that as the central kingdom did not appear to be a possibility he might not win Savoy and Nice unless he encouraged the people of Parma and Modena to overthrow the Treaty of Zurich, offered to help Piedmont acquire Tuscany and Emilia in exchange for Savoy and Nice.

Cavour, sensing useful gains, returned as Prime Minister in January 1860, and by March had reluctantly agreed to surrender Savoy and Nice in return for plebiscites in the duchies of central Italy. In spring of 1860, Victor Emmanuel became King of all Northern Italy with the exception of Venetia, Savoy and Nice. Napoleon himself had achieved the worst of all worlds. Execrated in Rome for his willingness to sacrifice the Romagna, unpopular in Northern Italy for Villafranca and for failing to secure Venetia, and distrusted abroad for his seizure of Savoy and Nice he could not count on the friendship of Austria or Italy, Prussia or Russia, or worst of all, Britain which was shocked severely by the transactions over Savoy and Nice.

It was inconceivable that Italy's story should end there despite Napoleon's fervent hopes. For on the day that he came to an agreement with the Papal government to replace his troops in Rome by catholic volunteers, Garibaldi and 'the Thousand' landed in Sicily. Sicily had always been the most troublesome property of the Bourbons of Naples and in 1848 had briefly achieved its independence. The government was as brutal as it was inefficient and, as might be expected, the glorious deeds in the north of Italy sparked off a revolt in Palermo, the island's capital. The revolt was a curiously light-hearted affair, the work, in part, of bored young aristocratic romantics, but it gave Garibaldi his excuse. Garibaldi was the great hero of the radicals and republicans, but since the glorious days of 1848 he had appreciated that the House of Savoy was the best agent for the unification of Italy. Nonetheless when Garibaldi slipped away from Genoa with his thousand supporters Cavour was nervous. Garibaldi was known to be incensed by the loss of Nice, his birthplace. The Piedmontese Prime Minister was prepared to wait and see what success Garibaldi would have and then take steps accordingly. Besides, he needed radical support in Parliament.

Garibaldi's success was beyond all expectations. The Neapolitan army melted away, withdrew to Naples and allowed Palermo to fall. Nothing but the action of the great powers could now prevent Garibaldi from invading Naples. Cavour was not greatly alarmed by Garibaldi's republicanism but he feared the republicanism of his supporters and the 'mystique' of the Roman republic, and he guessed that Garibaldi intended to take Rome and try to crown Victor Emmanuel there. He was worried that too few diplomatic steps had been taken to prepare Europe for the fall of the Holy City or the Bourbons of Naples. Napoleon III, he knew, was alarmed by the prospect of a united Italy on his door-step, and the Emperor did propose that an Anglo-French fleet should prevent Garibaldi's passage across the straits of Messina.

Cavour, and Italy, were saved by Britain's refusal to accept France's suggestion and by Napoleon's unwillingness to take any independent initiative, despite his fears of Catholic opinion in France. But Italy was saved also by Garibaldi's good sense; he accepted that a radical or republican move-ment would be more likely to lead to foreign intervention

than the cry *'Viva Verdi!'* (Victor Emmanuele Re D'Italia)
which was sufficient to gain the mainland:

Thus when Cavour in his turn provoked insurrection in the
Papal States and occupied all but the eternal city itself and,
with the Piedmontese army, encountered the victorious redshirts he was not so much countering Garibaldi's supposed
republicanism as taking steps to calm the fickle Napoleon by
saving the city of Rome itself.

Early in 1861, the first parliament of a united Italy met at
Turin and proclaimed Victor Emmanuel King of Italy. Its
greatest architect, Cavour, lived only a little longer. His death
in June 1861 undoubtedly had serious effects on the future
of Italy. Without his moderating hand Italian liberalism and
constitutionalism lapsed slowly into disorder, Italian pride
overcame good sense and pushed the new and poor nation
into prestigious schemes beyond her economic strength. Perhaps worst of all, at least in the short term, Cavour's death
ended negotiations between Cavour and the Papacy which
would have permitted the embarrassed French to withdraw
from Rome. It was not until 1866 that French troops were
able to depart, and then not permanently.

The map of Europe had been significantly redrawn but the
process was not yet complete. The brief Franco-Russian
honeymoon was over; neither had anything of significance to
offer the other. Russia had to look to a more powerful ally;
Austria was out of the running with her Imperial pretensions
increasingly threadbare. In Prussia however there came to
power in 1862 a man who eagerly sought Russian support, a
man as keen to redraw Germany's map as Russia was to
overthrow the Treaty of Paris. For in Bismarck, Prussia found
the leader who would have the strength of purpose to decide
the undeclared contest between Austria and Prussia for the
leadership of Germany. Austria's isolation became more
acute, a fate the Hapsburg Empire had in common with the
Bonaparte Empire. Suspicion between France and Britain
engendered in the Crimea had been confirmed by the circumstances of the unification of Italy. Britain's own isolation and
temporary loss of diplomatic direction under the worn-out
Palmerston left the field to Russia and Prussia.

CHAPTER TWENTY THREE

Empires Rise and Fall 1860-70

France: Liberal Empire

Two Empires in the 'sixties' began to show distinct signs of a loss of self-confidence. Napoleon in 1861 might have expected to feel supremely confident, all Europe looking to him as the great international figure who had defeated Austria. Even at home his reputation apparently stood high. In the public eye Solferino had appeared to be a victory in the true Napoleonic mould, followed by Italian unification without further war. But just as the Empire's position abroad lacked a solid foundation, so at home there seemed to be no real stability.

In part this instability was Napoleon's fault. He always feared an action once he had taken it and never pursued a consistent course. By nature he was an amiable fellow who wanted to be liked with his country united behind him. He wished to appear liberal, and after the French part in the unification of Italy and Rumania, it became necessary to give benefits to her own subjects which he was helping others to acquire. But it is fruitless to expect to see a consistent policy. By nature a man of insufficient will power, a dreamer rather than a politician, he lacked the qualities to see him through a very difficult task. Illness (a stone in his bladder 'the size of a pigeon's egg') crippled him even more. But in part it was the position of Emperor itself which created difficulties. It was similar to that of a liberal headmaster. A dictator in his own establishment, he finds that when, in the best traditions of modern educational practice, he allows the principle of consultation to his pupils he has opened the flood gates of protest rather than the portals of reasonable discussion. To go back to impossible; to go forwards fraught with difficulty. Napoleon was not a headmaster nor was he a firm man, and he wavered between reaction and blind liberality. He became afraid of his authority and used it like a man carrying a hot plate of food, in agony but afraid to drop it and spoil the feast. Moreover, if Napoleon was not a headmaster nor were the French callow youths: they were an old nation adept at political logic, with a tradition of opposition to authority which went back a hundred years.

The election results of 1857 had been disappointing for Napoleon. Although republican representation consisted of only five committed deputies, the weakness of the regime in the towns and cities was more than ever apparent and, while the government was doing better in west France than it had done before, its share of the votes cast in the eastern departments was falling. The Orsini bomb plot provided the excuse for a temporary reaction, but this did not last. From 1860 onwards the regime perceptibly, though with temporary setbacks, liberalised itself.

The reasons for the acceleration of the liberal tendencies — the decline in France's international position, the disaster of the Mexico campaign, economic depression, the growth of opposition allowed by liberalisation itself — these are clear enough. But the causes of the initial relaxation are less obvious, for it is difficult to see what are the motives behind any action of the Emperor. Almost certainly the quarrel with the Pope was something to do with it, and the squabble was not healed. The Emperor did not allow the encyclical *Quanta Cura* to be published in France in 1864, and he encouraged state as opposed to church-controlled education. Such a policy might please anti-clericals but the connection between anti-clericalism and republicanism was too close for this to be useful to Louis-Napoleon. The red scare had largely dissipated itself and no doubt the Emperor hoped to expand his small following among the proletariat. Above all perhaps the people and the deputies were docile.

The legislative body was given (1860) the power to discuss the address from the throne and was allowed greater freedom of discussion. Napoleon, in doing this, stated that the Empire would be an authoritarian regime for a limited time only. As an earnest of his good will he obliged ministers, hitherto excluded, to sit in the legislature and the press was given greater freedom to report debates (1861). Ministers felt happier in the assembly, for they could now officially defend government measures and give leadership; but once the legislature had acquired the right to discuss government measures this right could only be extended.

The result of such relaxation was a more independent electorate which in 1863 returned seventeen republicans and doubled the opposition vote. Napoleon's answer seems to have been to try to win over the working class voters by passing a Combination Act (1864) giving employer and employee equality before the law, and by (1868) permitting the establishment of trade unions, which grew rapidly in number and influence. The policy yielded little; the opposition vote continued to grow.

Whether as cause or result of this liberalisation the government after 1860 seemed to relax its control of elections. In the first years of the Empire very few communes outside major towns would have dared to vote less than unanimously for candidates favoured by the Prefects, but this unanimity declined severely in the sixties. While this was no doubt in part due to the growth of informed public opinion and the inability of the regime to counter the opposition press effectively, it is in part due to a loss of self-confidence in the government itself. It became increasingly vacillating and afraid of popular disapproval; its changes of front caused confusion at election times. The government ceased to give mayors the full backing on which they had always been able to count, though for what reason it is difficult to state. The concession of the right to hold public meetings gave opposition forces the ability to organise opinion on their side and some mayors, bereft of government support, sought arrangements with the opposition, for which they were rarely punished. This indecisiveness on the government's part may simply be part of a planned withdrawal from authoritarianism, but if it was, it was conducted with all the signs of weakness rather than strength and with inconsistencies which require explanation. In 1860, it was decreed that mayors should be appointed before the elections for which they were not to stand. In the next election the decree was reversed.

A major factor contributing to the government's waning popularity was its unsuccessful foreign policy. In 1863, the Polish revolt coincided with a challenge from the left at election time. Napoleon endeavoured to do something for the Poles whom he had failed to help in 1856, but no country would help him, and England's rejection of a suggested congress was brusquely humiliating. Again, when the Schleswig-Holstein crisis arose for a second time France's demands for territorial concessions as the price of aid to Britain prevented any successes being achieved, while the defeat of Austria in 1866 was a disaster for Napoleon who had confidently expected a long war in which he would mediate to his own advantage. He reaped no advantage for himself but he did succeed in getting Venetia from Austria for Italy. This was as nothing compared to the humiliation caused by the rise of Prussia with all that this meant for Napoleon's Rhineland ambitions.

Perhaps in order to counter the poor impression which his diplomacy gave he indulged in foreign adventures of a dubious nature. Colonial expansion in Algeria, China, Indo-China and Senegal were perhaps in nineteenth-century terms acceptable, but his so-called Mexican Adventure (1864–6) produced neither prestige nor profit. The motives for Napoleon's attempt to impose on the anarchic Mexicans a foreign emperor (Maximilian, former Grand Duke of Tuscany) backed by French troops, seems to have been a desire to halt the march of Anglo-Saxon power across the American continent. Unfortunately for Napoleon, and even more so for Maximilian, the adventure won no popular support from the Mexicans, and when the citizens of the United States ended their Civil War they turned the Monroe doctrine in full force on the luckless Emperors. Napoleon's withdrawal and the subsequent death of Maximilian before a revolutionary firing squad brought nothing but hatred and derision, not only from foreigners but also from his own people, and no successes in Algeria, no Suez Canal, could wipe away the shame of this episode.

As the Empire approached its unhappy overthrow its cata-
logue of woes grew larger. Financial scandal in the form of
the Mirès affair and the collapse of *Crédit Mobilier* seriously
harmed government credit. The American Civil War and the
Republican Party's high tariff policy damaged exports and
these did not recover before a new recession set in after
1867. Protectionists blamed Napoleon's free trade policies,
industrialists blamed the increasing incidence of strikes on
him, financiers added their strictures for the loss of *Crédit
Mobilier* and for the unorthodox financial expedients by
which Baron Haussmann had raised the money to rebuild
Paris in so glorious, civilised and ordered a fashion. The disastrous election results of 1869 precipitated the last great
experiment of the Empire — the Liberal Empire, an attempt
to save the Empire by regrouping moderates to defend a
throne which largely retreated from the party-political arena.

The collapse of the Second Empire was by no means a
foregone conclusion. Despite all the failures and all the
opposition it is doubtful whether it would have fallen but for
the disaster of Sédan. By 1870, it had one real achievement
to its credit; it had presided, perhaps unwillingly, over the
birth of a liberal constitutional form of government in which
it was not necessary to overthrow the system in order to
change government personnel. In other words, the Empire
had gone a long way to uniting the moderate majority of the
people of France.

The genesis of the Liberal Empire lies, of course, in the
character of Louis-Napoleon and the decisions taken in 1860.
But it also lies in the regrouping of government supporters in
the legislative body under the impetus of opposition, and the
greater importance given to that body in government. Émile
Ollivier symbolises the Liberal Empire. A moderate-republican
opposition member in 1857, he believed that freedom could
be achieved by reforming the existing regime rather than by
overthrowing it, and, although he preferred a republic, he was
not opposed to the continuation of the Empire. As such he
applauded the changes made in 1860 and broke with the
irreconcilable republicans. His moderation acquired an
increasing following, not only from opponents of the regime,
but also from the moderate reformers among its supporters.

From 1863 to 1865 he had the friendly partial co-operation of the prime minister Morny, and between 1865 and 1869, under the pressure of the issues which the legislative body was called upon to debate with increasing freedom, the government deputies regrouped themselves behind new leaders. Morny's death in 1865 left the government without an effective moderate leader and opinion polarised instead round Ollivier on the left and Jérome-David on the right.

Although Napoleon described the election results of 1869 as 'bad' (the government had fought the election half-heartedly, aware of its unpopularity. The contests had been very free and many government supporters had preferred to fight as 'independents'.), the election was not a triumph for republican or legitimists but for moderates who, like Ollivier, wanted greater liberalism under this regime if at all possible. The strength of moderates in the Ollivier wing of the party and the strength of independent moderates under *Thiers'* banner — the 'Third Party' — obliged Louis Napoleon to change his ministers.

Ollivier became in January 1870 Prime Minister of the Liberal Empire, uniting behind him some of the hundred and sixteen members of the Thiers party and the official candidates, both moderate and right-wing, after Napoleon's announcement of the birth of the Liberal Empire. The Liberal Empire was not perhaps parliamentary government as now conceived. The liberal concessions of 1869, which allowed the legislature to initiate legislation, vote the budget clause by clause and question ministers closely, still did not adequately define Napoleon's own powers. The *Senatus-Consulte* of 1869 laid down that 'the ministers depend only on the Emperor' and preserved the Emperor's powers of war and peace and his position as commander-in-chief. But the people in a plebiscite gave the reform a massive vote of confidence. The regime had received a new lease of life; 'confidence blazed like the dawn', Ollivier claimed, 'The fate of his dynasty is assured' and the Orleanist claimant packed his bags for America. Thus there is no reason to believe that the Bonapartist Second Empire need have ended, as it began, in revolution.

Elsewhere in southern Europe a monarchy was about to be

summarily dismissed. This time however it was no upstart affair, but the Bourbon monarchy of Spain itself. The revolution of 1854 had occurred at a time of famine which exacerbated the already difficult political situation for the constitutionalist victors. The new national militia, based on the old National Guard of France, but without its bourgeois respectability soon lost all discipline and mob rule resulted. As in 1822 moderates sought protection from anarchy in the arms of monarchy and the result was the long and not ineffective rule of one O'Donnell who formed a 'Liberal Union'. This broad-bottomed ministry included all but Carlists and Septembrists, but it held together largely because it attempted no reforms, existing chiefly on slogans and God's good harvests. Apathy was aided by economic development, especially in railways, for in the ten years after 1858 three thousand miles of track were laid, offering rich pickings for the unscrupulous politician. Successful empire-building in Santo Domingo, North Africa and Mexico likewise helped to preserve the calm.

The fall of O'Donnell in 1863, and the death of the ever-ready Narvaez in 1868 left Isabella defenceless except for her lovers and her favourites. Humiliation of Spanish arms in South America precipitated a crisis long staved off, and in 1868 the Bourbon monarchy of Spain temporarily ceased to exist. It would return, for Spain was conservative at heart and moderates felt the need of a monarchy to represent the order for which they so unrewardingly strove.

The year 1868 was also a crisis year in Portugal for Louis I (1861—9) and for the same reasons — the failure to marry representative institutions to a country which did not have the tradition or the will to make them work. The Civil marriage bill of 1868 offended the conservative forces of the peasantry and the church which had never accepted or understood constitutionalism; the re-organisation of local administration threatened the autonomy of the parish as a unit and the sales tax offended all classes, but most particularly the landed classes. Louis I felt unable to give his ministers his backing for he feared palace or army revolt and the country prepared to stagger on to its next crisis. Perhaps had Maria's eldest son, Pedro V survived the typhus which killed him and his two younger brothers in 1861, and had Saldanha been able to continue his work of financial reform and public works, the country might have emerged into the 1870's better equipped to make the Great Experiment of Liberalism succeed.

Austria: Decline and Defeat

The Austrian Empire never recovered from the Crimean war and Italian unification. Her importance under Metternich had been due to blackmail — disguised but nonetheless very real. Austria's strategic position and her control of *Mittel Europa*, coupled with her multi-racial nature made her the automatic leader of a Europe still dynastic and fearful of liberal nationalist tendencies, for Austria's collapse could only, it seemed, lead to war and revolution. The 1848 revoltuions, the Crimean war and Italy together destroyed any hope that Austria could protect *Mittel Europa,* while Russia was transfromed from a power eager to keep the *status quo* to one eager for revision. The years 1859 and 1860 had demonstrated that nationalism need not mean either general war, revolution or French aggrandisement. The 1848 revolutions had shown that Austria and Prussia could be rivals; the economic strength of Prussia and her appeal to German nationalists made Prussia a formidable German power and one which could not wait long before challenging Austria. Thus it was natural that Austria's future should lie in the hands of Russia and Prussia.

Austria's control of her own destiny was visibly faltering. She continued to move falteringly between centralism and provincialism. In 1860, the October 'Diploma' of Count Goluchowski proposed that Imperial laws be passed by consultation between an augmented Reichsrat and Provincial Diets. In 1861, the February 'Patent' of Schmerling reimposed centralisation. This imperial dithering bore little relationship to Austria's needs or any demands of her peoples. Franz-Josef's advisers were either aristocrats who tended to favour provincialism, or bureaucrats who favoured efficient liberal centralism. Neither really considered consulting the people, for this would mean consulting the 'peoples', and of these the Magyars remained the least co-

operative and the most dissatisfied. They resented provincialism, which failed to recognise their specially previleged
position, and centralism which ignored it entirely. Anton von
Schmerling's 'Patent' was as still born as the 'Diploma'. The
convocation of Diets to elect members to go to the
Reichsrat in Vienna was largely ignored in Hungary, which
continued to resist incorporation, especially as the Diets were
weighted in favour of the towns. The only answer the
bankrupt Austrian throne had to this situation was to
threaten a rising of subject peoples.

Such a solution was however not one which recommended
itself to the Hapsburgs: besides, in resisting the Magyars, the
dynasty enjoyed the support of many German moderate
liberals who rightly saw the re-actionary nature of Magyar
resistance; such liberals were averse to any policy of encouraging the minority races. The Magyars themselves were aware
of the temptation to use the subject races against them and
under their leader in the Diet, Déak, attempted, with some
success to meet such a threat with promises of satisfaction
for the demands of all nationalities.

Even the Czech peoples of the Empire were increasingly
troublesome. In part they feared that the dynasty would
come to an arrangement with the Magyars at the expense of
Slovak minorities in Hungary. They also began to resist the
authority of the Reichsrat, in 1863 even going so far as to
withdraw from it. Such a situation obviously could not
continue. The monarchy was bankrupt of ideas and of force;
a solution would obviously have to be imposed by force from
outside.

Prussia: Prelude to Empire

In effect, that solution was imposed by Russia and Prussia.
Although the Prussian regent, and later monarch, William I
was an autocrat, pro-Austrian in sympathy, he could not but
be affected by the growing nationalism in Germany, which
was irrevocably stimulated by the success of Piedmont in
uniting Italy. If 1848 had proved that nationalist liberalism
was incapable of uniting Germany, and if 1860 had shown
that Austria was incapable of preserving control of Italy, it
seemed to follow that Prussian might alone could conquer

Germany for nationalism. Such logic was not yet fully accepted, partly because it was not understood how little Italian nationalism owed to liberalism and how much to armies and navies. Events of 1859 stimulated liberal nationalism and led to the foundation of the *Nationalverein* (1859) a movement for unity on a liberal basis under Prussian leadership. In Prussia itself the Progress party still believed that national unity could be achieved by democratic means. Even so, few nationalists except in catholic states like Bavaria and Württemberg looked any longer to Austria.

History seemed to be moving inexorably in the favour of nationalism of a liberal kind. In the years after Olmütz, the government of Prussia was in general controlled by the Junkers and especially by Baron von Manteuffel. In 1857, however, Prince William had dropped Manteuffel and taken in the liberal Bethmann-Hollweg. But although William was in favour of 'movement' he was essentially an officer and a Junker. The liberal government did not establish any links with the *Nationalverein* and in Count Otto Von Bismarck it found a bitter opponent. Although he had been sent as ambassador to St Petersburg in 1858, he nevertheless maintained close links with home.

Bismarck was no simple Junker; he could see that unless Prussia herself took the initiative in Germany then she would be swallowed up in a liberal nation, and all that it entailed for monarchical and Junker power. He also recognised the weaknesses of the liberals which had been demonstrated in 1848 and after, believing that a show of strength would dissipate their will to resist. He saw that the liberals were weak; they lacked popular support. The peasants remained attached to the old authorities while the workers under Lassalle were striking out in new paths of their own. It was he, moreover, who sensed the anxiety of a bourgeoisie faced with growing proletarian strength, and he who appreciated that, as in the Austrian Empire and in France, they could become the most loyal defenders of bourgeois order.

It was a crisis over military reform which gave Bismarck, the supreme opportunist, his opening. The defeat of Austria by France and Piedmont and Austria's subsequent refusal to relinquish military leadership of the confederacy to Prussia convinced William and his conservative Minister of War, Count von Roon, of the need for extensive military reform. Von Roon aimed to increase the size of the army from 200,000 to 317,000, to extend military service from a two to a three-year period, to found thirty-nine new infantry and ten new cavalry regiments, and to diminish the importance of the *Landwehr*. The *Landwehr* was, in particular, a bone of contention. Dating back to the days of 1813 when the 'nation' rose against Napoleon, it had a sizeable corpus of middle-class officers, thus possessing a mythical and political value of considerable significance. William backed Von Roon's attempts to diminish the importance of this 'civilian' army and the extension of service which the liberals inside and outside the ministry also opposed.

Without doubt Von Roon aimed to drive a wedge between William and the liberals on an issue in which William took a particular interest, and as a friend of Bismarck's it is probable that he hoped to bring his friend into the cabinet.

Liberal opposition was so strong that the reforms could not proceed through the *Landtag*. But the liberals showed their unwillingness to be ruthless by making a 'provisional' grant in 1860, followed by an 'extraordinary' grant in 1861 thus enabling William to continue slowly implementing reforms. Liberal opinion soon sensed the danger and accused the ministry of being too 'obsequious'. In 1861, the Progress party won considerable electoral victories at the expense of the old liberals of the ministry and the conservative parties. The new liberals refused to grant supplies and made even greater gains at new elections.

Deadlock seemed certain but still William hesitated to call for Bismarck. He and many conservatives distrusted him, while Bismarck himself was not prepared to serve as an out-and-out conservative opposed to German nationalism. Only when a last compromise failed did William agree to appoint Bismarck as the new, almost dictatorial, Minister-President.

Bismarck and William based their constitutional arguments on the *Lückentheorie,* a supposed prerogative right of the monarchy when crown and legislature were in dispute. In fact, however, Bismarck did not argue, he challenged. The liberals were challenged to resist his determination to collect the taxes which the liberals would not grant. Bullying and pressure on government officials secured a pliant bureaucracy. Meanwhile his squabble with the *Landtag* continued. In May 1863, he prorogued it and muzzled the press; in November he dissolved it only to be faced with an even more intransigent body. He survived partly by dipping into reserves, and partly by increasing revenue from prerogative sources. Taxes were collected without opposition, for in the last analysis the liberals were not prepared to cause disorder.

The liberals were defeated as much in Schleswig-Holstein and Austria as in Prussia, however, for the results of his foreign policy soon showed that Prussia could unite Germany by 'blood and iron'. Bismarck quickly proved that he was determined to accept only equality with Austria in German affairs. Franz-Josef was persuaded to take advantage of Prussia's internal difficulties to reform the Confederation, calling a meeting of German princes — the *Fürstentag* — to Frankfort (1863). Austria's proposals were designed to perpetuate Hapsburg predominance without conceding anything of substance to liberalism. A chamber of princes under Austria's permanent presidency, and a chamber of delegates elected by state parliaments, were to form the new central confederate body. These proposals were still-born, for Bismarck refused to allow William to attend. Bismarck's counter-proposals insisted on Prussian equality in the confederation and suggested that the Austrian centre of gravity should shift itself to Hungary, a proposal hardly welcome to Franz-Josef. Bismarck moreover made a bid for popular approval by suggesting a state parliament, directly elected by universal male suffrage in place of Austria's second chamber. The first two suggestions were not in essence new and the third was perhaps only half in earnest. Nonetheless Bismarck was aware that universal suffrage could be a conservative force as it had been in 1848 in France and he did not abandon this idea. Moreover Bismarck's position as foreign minister was stronger than that of any of his predecessors and Prussia's foreign policy was his to command. William had surrendered control in return for Bismarck's promise to defeat the Prussian *Landtag*.

> Every success of the Polish nationalist movement . . .is a defeat for Prussia. . . .No peace is possible between us and any revival of Poland.

With these words Bismarck bid for an understanding with Russia, while Russia, searching for a strong conservative ally in central Europe, was only too eager to accept the proffered help. The Polish rising of January 1863 was confined to Russian Poland but drew support from Prussian and Austrian Poland. While Austria tried to ignore the rising for fear of causing further strife within the Empire, and while France tried to summon courage, and Palmerston, to help the Poles, Prussia signed a convention with Russia (February) allowing for military co-operation against the rebels. Temporarily Bismarck was alarmed by the prospect of a French-inspired coalition against him, but Palmerston's ingrained suspicion of Napoleon III prevented any revival of the Crimean coalition. Besides the very mention of Austrian participation alienated Russia even more from her as well as France. The Russo-Prussian entente seemed secure. The entente was now to be fully tested by a new Schleswig-Holstein crisis.

In 1863 the new King of Denmark, Christian IX, signed a new constitution by which Schleswig was permanently incorporated into the state of Denmark while Holstein remained united only by personal union with the Danish Crown. This was undoubtedly a breach of the London agreement of 1852 and was further complicated by the fact that the Duke of Augustenburg now claimed both duchies despite his father's disclaimer in 1852. King Christian was probably hoping to survive by virtue of the confused state of European diplomacy but that disarray was hardly in Denmark's favour. In the earlier crisis Russia had supported France and Great Britain, in 1863 that support was unlikely while Anglo-French relations were at their nadir. Moreover Christian's action alienated German opinion in general and gave great impetus to those forces which sought to impose unity; by providing them with a text-book lesson on how power could unite Germany, though in fact Bismarck never claimed to be acting on behalf of nationalism but rather to defend a freely signed treaty, for Bismarck did not yet wish to alienate

Austria entirely.

Bismarck's actions were designed to achieve the aim of the nationalists without invoking nationalism. Thus despite German support for Duke Frederick of Augustenberg and appeals for the incorporation of both Schleswig and Holstein in the Confederation, Bismarck refused to recognise the Duke's claim, acting with Austria instead to support the Protocol of London (1852). Austria was persuaded by Bismarck that not to act with Prussia was to put the Empire into the hands of the liberals, and it risked losing the leadership of Germany to Prussia. On the other hand to act with Prussia lost Austria any French or English good-will without gaining any real benefits. On the basis of a settlement of the duchy problem by mutual agreement the two powers invaded Schleswig (February 1864) having divested themselves of any other participation, even moral, in their adventure and having thus overtaken and outmanoeuvred the federal forces which had occupied Holstein earlier. Flying in the face of Anglo-French opinion and, more important, of German liberal opinion, which wished a Federal army to invade in favour of Augustenburg, Bismarck acted to defend an internationally accepted treaty. Such defence was mere subterfuge, however, for when the Danes accepted an inevitable truce Bismarck denounced the 1852 Protocol, and the conference, called by Palmerston to settle the affair, broke up when Bismarck supported the Augustenburg claim. This volte-face merely served to cause maximum confusion in the conference, which broke up leaving the fate of the two duchies dependent, as Bismarck had always intended, on Austro-Prussian agreement. This outcome was particularly satisfying to Bismarck since it created the maximum number of opportunities for further progress. Bismarck's achievement appears all the greater when it is realised that William himself favoured the claims of Augustenburg and was fearful throughout of offending Franz-Josef. By June 1864 Denmark had been completely defeated and Augustenburg was again out of the picture, warned off by Bismarck.

At the London Conference, I hitched the Prince (of Augustenburg) to the plough as an ox, to get it moving. Once the plough was in motion I unhitched the ox.

Bismarck wrote;

> Great crises are the very weather which stimulates Prussia's
> growth, if we turn them to our account fearlessly and,
> maybe very recklessly

He did not relax in his efforts to transfer the seat of German
power from Vienna to Berlin.

> . . .if war is waged against Austria it has to bring about not
> only the annexation of the Duchies but a new arrangement
> in the relations of Prussia with the German medium and
> smaller states.

The terms of the alliance against Denmark had spoken of the
future of Schleswig and Holstein in only the very vaguest
terms, and now that the two duchies were in allied hands
Austria felt the need to regularise the position. But Bismarck
was not to be hurried, despite the support from William and
the Crown Prince for the claims of Augustenburg which they
saw as the only alternative to Bismarck's policy and its
tendency towards war with Austria. Opposition from the
liberal *Landtag* to his policies and the possibility of French
involvement in any Austro-Prussian war made stealth a prime
requisite of Bismarck's policy. Even so Bismarck openly
stated at a Prussian Crown Council (1865) his plan to annex
the two duchies and re-organise the confederation. In earnest
of this Kiel was already undergoing conversion into a Prussian
naval base while Von Roon and Von Moltke, Chief of the
Prussian General Staff, prepared the army for the possibility
of a quick war.

Tension rose to such a pitch that, in May 1865, the
Austrian envoy Count Mensdorf met William at Gastein and,
together with Bismarck they 'papered over the cracks' by
assigning Holstein to Austria to administer and Schleswig to
Prussia. Although this temporarily satisfied the nervous and
unhappy William it could not prove the permanent solution
for which Bismarck now prepared.

In October 1865 Bismarck met Napoleon III at Biarritz
hinting at a possible French acquisition of Belgium. To Italy

Prussia could offer hope of territorial acquisitions. Italy still coveted Venetia, which in 1865 Austria had refused to sell, and thus responded with interest to Prussian suggestions of an alliance, especially when Napoleon encouraged this move. The French Emperor mistakenly believed that such an alliance would, in giving Italy Venice, relieve pressure on Rome and he also even more disastrously believed that a long war between Austria and Prussia would allow France to become the arbiter of Europe's future and to acquire considerable territories. Then a secret alliance between Prussia and Italy was signed (January 1866) by which Italy would receive Venetia without Trentino in return for declaring war on Austria after Prussia. The alliance was, however, valid for only three months; Austria had to be goaded into war.

In April, Bismarck repeated his old proposals for a German parliament on the basis of universal male suffrage by direct election. Austria recognised what Bismarck was attempting and knew that she would be at a grave disadvantage in the event of war, for the Austrian army took more than twice as long as the Prussian to mobilise. Austria realised too that Bismarck did not wish to seem to start the war because the King was still very upset at the prospect of attacking the Emperor. Thus the Austrians suggested disarmament, which proposal Bismarck was obliged to accept. But, afraid of Italy's preparations, Austria mobilised against the peninsula and gave Bismarck the opportunity to convince William that Austria was being deceitful. The attempt of Anton von Coblenz to secure a compromise peace was to no avail, and the Franco-Austrian Treaty of June by which Italy gained Venetia only heightened suspicion. Austria finally put herself in the wrong by submitting the question of the future of the duchies to the Federal Diet. Prussia occupied Holstein and withdrew from the Confederation when Bavaria secured the mobilisation of the Federal army. The next day Hanover, Hesse-Cassel and Saxony, who had sided with Austria, were occupied.

The war was almost ludicrously short. Despite the defeat of Italy at Custoza the massive victory of July 3 at Königgrätz (Sadowa) ended the war. Bismarck was certainly satisfied; he had no wish to destroy Austrian power, but merely to shift its centre eastwards. Besides, he knew that a settlement must quickly be reached in order to defeat any French attempts at mediation. The preliminary peace was signed on July 26. At the later Treaty of Prague (August) Prussia acquired Schleswig and Holstein, Hanover, Hesse-Cassel, Nassau and Frankfort. All states north of the river Main joined a new 'North German Confederation' under Prussian leadership, and although the southern states were to form a twin confederation, Prussia secured military alliances with Bavaria, Württemberg and Baden. Italy gained Venetia, despite Custoza and the annihilation of her fleet in August.

Victories and Defeats

Bismarck's aim in defeating Austria had been to show that it was not necessary to unify Germany by nationalist or liberal means, and that it was quite possible for Prussia to survive in a united Germany by the expedient of conquering it. Prussian victory at Königgrätz made Europe safe for conservatives to live in.

On the day of Königgrätz, elections in Prussia greatly increased the number of conservative seats; and when Bismarck introduced in the new chamber a bill indemnifying the government for having ruled without a properly voted budget since 1862 only seven votes were cast against it. The Progress party split, and a new National liberal party began to emerge, prepared to support the government more fully. The liberals of Prussia abdicated as the Empire began to emerge and Bismarck was henceforth to treat them with an amused contempt which was to be enshrined in the Imperial constitution of 1871. The lesson seemed to be that the liberals would forgive anything for security and glory and perhaps that was also the lesson which Louis-Napoleon's regime had taught before the imperial eagles became tarnished. Bismarck and Louis-Napoleon between them were demonstrating that there was nothing to fear in constitutionalism, even perhaps democracy, nothing to fear from liberals who feared the rising urban masses more than the monarch and aristocrat and who had no links at all with the real masses of nineteenth century Europe, the peasantry. Bismarck and the army were to prove in 1866 and 1871 that universal suffrage could be the major conservative force in a Europe still not totally industrialised.

That lesson was to be made fully apparent in the constitution of 1871 but Bismarck's self-confidence was evident in the constitution of the North German Confederation (1867). The President, King William of Prussia had the usual treaty rights and powers as commander-in-chief. A *Bundesrat* was created consisting of representatives of member states voting on instruction from their respective government while the popular weight of the constitution was carried by a single chamber elected on direct manhood suffrage. The twenty two states of the confederation shared forty-three votes in the *Bundesrat,* of which Prussia held seventeen. There was one federal minister, Chancellor Bismarck, who could be dismissed only by the President.

Although a southern confederation was to be created the military alliances with Bavaria, Württemberg and Baden showed clearly where dominant power lay, and however much the catholic south might regret it, Austria now relinquished any claim to leadership in Germany and looked to the east. In 1863, Bismarck had advised Austria to centre herself on Hungary: that necessity Austria could no longer put off. To the Iron Chancellor, Austria's role as a central-European necessity was over but she was still necessary as an ally in the east, capable of resisting Russia, and yet German enough to dominate eastern Europe without at the same time posing a threat to Prussian dominance in Germany. The logic tended towards an acceptance of dualism.

Dualism was the long-demanded Magyar answer to the Hapsburg problem. The centralised autocracy of Bach had long since been modified by his successors, notably Count Goluchowski, the author of the October Diploma, but little progress had been made towards dualism by Schmerling's Patent, or indeed by his successor Count Belcredi who, as a Bohemian, favoured a federation of more than the two equals envisaged by the Magyars. Austria's defeat however gave the Magyar leaders Déak and Count Andrassy their long-awaited chance. They wished to retain the Empire in order to contain the other racial elements but to give the Magyar a superior position. 'The Slavs are not fit to govern', they said, 'they must be ruled'. Franz-Josef was initially hostile to the idea of a Magyar-German partnership and Belcredi tried to raise resistance in the national Diet, but this conservatism was exhausted. Belcredi was challenged by Count von Beust who negotiated the settlement of 1867 with the two Magyar leaders.

The *Ausgleich*, as it was called, established a dual monarchy, giving Hungary constitutional independence within her traditional frontiers. Foreign and military affairs and some matters of finance were to be jointly administered, and commerce and transport were to work according to uniform principles. Opposition in other Diets was quickly silenced. The *Ausgleich* marked not only the disappearance of the old Hapsburg monarchy but also the end of the old expedient of setting off one race against another. Although officially the nationalities under Vienna's direct rule were equal the Magyars were now the dominant race in the whole of the south eastern part of the old Hapsburg patrimony. Hungary turned in on itself; the aristocracy, through the franchise and the bureaucratic machine, perpetuated that pre-eminence the Hapsburgs had long struggled to destroy.

In the space of ten years the Vienna settlement had been almost completely destroyed and with it the hegemony in *Mittel Europa* of Metternich's Empire, for so long recognised as Vienna's most important legacy to Europe. There remained now only the tidying up to be done in western Europe.

Russia: Reform in Isolation

Further to the east another less obviously victorious nation was undergoing considerable change. The effects of the emancipation of the serfs did not simply alter the social and economic status of the serf. The serf had ceased to belong to the gentry; he now belonged to the village community or *mir*, but this alteration was bound to require alterations in local government and legal proceedings; they would have to become far more institutionalised, far less personal than they had been.

Alexander was a conservative and certainly did not consider, as did Hertzen, that emancipation implied civil equality, independent justice, juries, police reform, ministerial responsibility, public control of finance and legislation, free press and free trade. Besides such liberalism required a longer tradition of public debate and awareness than Russia could possibly have acquired. Alexander's reforms were conservative changes imposed by decree.

In 1864, Alexander decreed the establishment of *Zemstva*, councils at district and province level, with representatives elected separately by landowners, townsmen and peasants, the latter representatives being elected indirectly. District *Zemstva* elected a permanent governing board and representatives to the Provincial *Zemstva* who elected their own board. They had the power to raise money through rates and soon effected major educational medical and transport reforms. In 1870 self-government was extended in similar fashion to the towns which before had had limited representation in the largely country based *Zemstva*. These assemblies were a notable success and were immensely popular, but the central government kept control of all police powers and their powers were undoubtedly circumscribed, perhaps not least because people could not understand why the principle of responsible government could not be extended to the central authorities.

Judicial reform in 1864 matched the new administrative changes. Petty sessions were now held by justices of the peace, elected through the *Zemstva*, while criminal cases were tried in courts, where the jury principle, public trials and salaries for judges were all introduced. This was an immense improvement and gave people greater faith in Russian law; nonetheless the central government preserved its right of summary arrest and banishment to Siberia.

In the army Milyutin struggled to abolish brutality, inefficiency and education and to improve the quality of equipment. It was not until 1874 that universal conscription reduced the heavy burden on the peasantry, but perhaps the most striking success of the hard-working Milyutin was to be found in the increasing number of illiterates who were taught to read and write by army education. Such a step forward made the press an increasingly important element in Russian society. Here the government wavered unconvincingly between mildness and repression.

The reforms of Alexander were not confined to the Motherland itself. In Finland, constitutionalism of a very conservative kind was restored after the proclamation of the 'Fundamental Law' of 1867. No modern parliament arose but the old four Estates were better than arbitrary rule. His encouragement of Finnish national sentiment in opposition to pro-Swedish sentiment made Alexander the most popular of Grand Dukes.

In Poland liberality encouraged not gratitude but a desperate attempt to be free, in 1863. The consideration which Alexander gave to agrarian reforms displeased the land-owning classes who led the revolt. The non-participation of the peasantry and the divisions within the revolutionary camp between the moderates under Czartoryski and the radicals under the emancipationist Mieroslavski destroyed what chance ten thousand Poles had against greatly superior Russian forces. It is to Alexander's credit that while he gave up any attempts to pacify liberal forces in Poland and returned to 'Russification' he did not cease to be a reformer in Russia itself.

Although the results lay in the future there were dangers in Alexander's reforms — not just in the expectations aroused for further reforms which a paternalist regime could not accept.

The *mir* was a conservative institution which did almost nothing to encourage any initiative in methods while at the same time tying the peasant more closely to the soil, which in many parts of Russia could not support his numbers. Although there was migration to the cities these were still too few, too conservative and still poorly linked by rail or road. The state, the paternal image of the 'Little Father', remained a potent, often bureaucratic, force in people's lives. It is therefore small wonder that there was no sign of a growing middle class able or willing to create a new industrialised urban world and add a free and responsible element to Russia's rigid and archaic social framework. Small wonder also that Russia found it difficult to develop a mature reforming movement but descended into anarchy.

Alexander was a great reforming Tsar but he was trying to

make existing society more efficient rather than opening up any avenues of social and economic change.

Defeat of France

The defeat of Austria by Bismarck's Prussia had been a severe set-back for the hard pressed Emperor of the French. He had hoped to make territorial gains from the conflict by posing as a mediator — Belgium particularly interested him. Moreover he was being criticised by Roman Catholic opinion within France for a foreign policy which had seemed to leave the Pope defenceless. The defeat of Austria and Prussian hegemony over catholic Germany seemed to the catholics to be further signs of a muddle-headed foreign policy. The revision of the provisions of Vienna seemed to have given France nothing. Napoleon felt the need to regain the initiative and with it prestige and, if possible, territory, either Luxembourg which he tried to buy from the Netherlands, or Belgium.

The most dangerous aspect of Napoleon's position was, without doubt, his lack of allies; Austria-Hungary was too shaken to risk a war of revenge, Russia saw every advantage in friendship with Prussia, which also had an interest in repressing Polish nationalism, and Great Britain totally distrusted the French Emperor especially when his designs on Belgium became known. Thus Napoleon began a duel with Bismarck which he was ill-equipped to fight.

The actual cause of the war stemmed from the chequered fortunes of the Spanish throne. In 1868, Queen Isabella had been ousted by another military coup. The *Cortes* agreed to establish a constitutional monarchy and began to do a little window-shopping among the amply-provided royal families of respectably Germanic and liberal northern Europe. France could hardly fail to be interested as Isabella was pro-French while the likely candidate, Prince Leopold of Hohenzollern-Sigmaringen, though Roman Catholic, was related to the Prussian royal house.

Bismarck worked busily in the background trying to persuade the reluctant Leopold to accept the crown. He even tried to bribe members of the *Cortes*. Bismarck realised that Napoleon might treat the Hohenzollern acceptance of the throne as a *casus belli* but probably hoped that Napoleon would fight shy of war, for certainly the German States would hardly relish fighting to place a Hohenzollern on yet another throne.

After two refusals Leopold accepted the throne of Spain in 1870. This was pleasing neither to King William, who feared war, nor to the new French foreign minister, the anti-Prussian de Gramont. Bismarck moved quickly to procure ratification of the acceptance, but by an error France was given time to protest. De Gramont was clever enough to see that negotiations with King William at Ems was more likely to bring satisfactory results than any negotiation through the office of the devious Chancellor. William, as head of the Hohenzollern family, persuaded Leopold's father, Karl Anton, to withdraw his son's candidature.

Unseemly joy and over-confidence ruined this great French diplomatic triumph. The French ambassador at Ems, Benedetti, was told to extract an undertaking from William that the Hohenzollern candidature would never be renewed. William refused and communicated this to Bismarck in a telegram which was to be published. Bismarck edited the text in such a way as to suggest that after a heated argument William had snubbed Benedetti. Public opinion in France was so incensed that Napoleon, fully aware of the French army's unfittedness, was forced to declare war.

Von Roon and Von Moltke repeated their successes of 1866. The confusion of French mobilisation aided the numerical superiority of the Prussian armies. The Prussian victory of Wörth and two indecisive battles forced Bazaine into the fortress at Metz. Shortly afterwards Marshal MacMahon's army met the German Third Army at Sedan. After three days fighting the French army surrendered on September 1 and among the eighty thousand prisoners was Emperor Napoleon III himself.

On September 4th Paris heard the news. A distraught Empress escaped as a republic was proclaimed. A provisional government of National Defence was formed to carry on the fight. On September 19th Paris was surrounded, to capitulate in January. The tragedy of the Commune was about to begin.

The fall of the French Empire marked the rise of the German Empire, proclaimed at Versailles in 1871. German only in name, it perpetuated Prussian control of Germany foreshadowed in 1848 and 1866. The end of the French Empire was not merely the beginning of the German Empire however, for the final destruction of the Vienna settlement created a period of profound diplomatic unease. Great Britain's withdrawal from active involvement began under the unwilling Palmerston was completed by Gladstone, and even Disraeli played from the new Imperial sidelines. The new Germany could not hope to preserve friendship with both Russia and Austria-Hungary. When these Emperors were to begin again to dispute the future of the Balkans Germany would have to choose between them. The Peace of Versailles was implicit in the declaration of the German Empire in the Hall of Mirrors at Versailles.

In *My Memories of Six Reigns* the late Princess Marie Louise describes a fascinating conversation between the Empress Eugenie of France and the Duchesse de Richelieu, during the course of which the Duchess casually said 'Oui, comme mon mari disait à Louis Quatorze'. It is explained that the lady had been the very young third wife of a very elderly Duc de Richelieu who at the age of ten had been page to the Sun King. Rarely are two ages so apparently distinct and distant in time linked by living persons. But in 1870 there could have been many people then living for whom the years of their youth in the last two decades of the eighteenth century cannot have seemed more remote from their lives than the age of Louis XIV.

A person born in 1780 had been projected into the world of Catherine the Great, Louis XVI and Frederick the Great; he died in the age of Franz Josef, Victoria, Gladstone, President Lincoln and the young Clemenceau. Europe in ninety years underwent a period of quite extraordinary change.

The population of Europe more than doubled; railways and ocean-going steam ships, anaesthetics, the telegraph and gas light were invented or developed. Towns rose where villages once stood and cities rose from the ashes of small towns; a whole new class, the urban proletariat, had been

L

created to alarm and perplex the governing classes. Across the Atlantic a continent stretching from the Arctic to the Antarctic Circles had freed itself from European domination and in Europe itself Italy and Germany had risen as great states from what had been mere geographical expressions. Never had ninety years seen so many revolutions, political, social, economic, diplomatic and artistic, to bewilder the people who lived through them. The readily recognisable landmarks of existence seemed to have disappeared or be about to vanish and in 1870 there was born a man who would create a nation in his own image — Vladimir Ilyich Ulyanov (Lenin).

A man who died in 1870 at the age of ninety must have wondered which of the several distinct personalities he was — child of the *Ancien Régime;* of the French Revolution; of Viennese or Bismarckian Europe? Was he more influenced by the rural, aristocratic world of his youth or the increasingly urban and bourgeois world of his last years?

It seems impossible that in this period of rapid change there could be any theme or connecting link to draw the years together. It may be thought that the title of this book suggests that this theme is to be found in the rise of the bourgeoisie while a great deal of the evidence presented in it might suggest that this rise was by no means smooth, regular or even fully accomplished. In 1870 the monarchies and aristocracies of Europe seemed as strong as ever, except in France, while the peasantry formed the largest class on the continent just as it had in 1780. Already, before the bourgeoisie had achieved hegemony the urban proletariat, which had risen so quickly to prominence, seemed on the point of usurping its position. Nor was the bourgeoisie a homogeneous class with common interests; it had many component parts, professional, industrial and commercial, financial, *rentier*, none of which was itself a single unit. In Russia the middle class, small and dispirited, seemed to be sinking into that attitude of despair and lassitude, which Chekhov so well portrays, without ever having approached the power which the middle classes of England and France wielded. Even in England Bright argued that until 1867 the political power of the middle classes was not consonant with their economic importance. In Prussia the Junkers were to remain a dominant class until the end of the First World War.

But however many exceptions and provisos we introduce, it remains true that the significant trend of the ninety years between 1780 and 1870 was the rise of the bourgeoisie's political, social and economic power, even though we might only be speaking of a section of that wide and ill-defined class. It was the bourgeoisie which had carried through the French Revolution, upheld Napoleon and overthrown the Bourbons a second time. In 1848 despite the failure of the revolutions the monarchs had been forced to take notice of the existence of the middle classes and give them a limited share in government. Although the German and Italian nations had been created by 'blood and iron' they would not have been created without the demand from the bourgeoisie which also benefited most from the creation of the new states. It was this class which had carried through the industrialisation of Europe, albeit with considerable government help. The romantic artists turned to this new audience for patronage; journalists expected it to buy the newspapers and magazines which came out in ever-increasing numbers to feed the growing demand created by developing education systems.

In doing all these things the middle classes had initiated a process which could not be stopped. In giving the impetus to the spread of education, literature and newspapers it disseminated those ideas and concepts which it had seemed to make its own in 1789. *Freedom, liberty, equality* and *fraternity* are abstract but powerful ideas which cannot and could not be made the property of one class. In 1792 they had already been appropriated by the *sansculottes* who gave them their own meaning. The success of revolutions and revolutionary armies, the spread of the Industrial revolution, the growth of towns, all made sure that the ideas first proclaimed by the bourgeoisie would be carried to all classes and nations to create a powerful force for changes not always to the liking of the bourgeoisie itself. In the numbers, economic power and philosophy of the working classes which the bourgeoisie, with the aid of demographic changes, had created dwelt a powerful challenge to the proud self-

confident middle classes. Perhaps this was what lay behind
Marx's belief in the inevitability of revolution, for he saw
clearly that the logic of the rise of the bourgeoisie implied its
destruction by forces which it had itself created and
nurtured.

So Marx envisaged the future. It remained to be seen
whether this particular development was inevitable or
whether the bourgeoisie would survive in even more lively
fashion than had the aristocracy. Perhaps, as Bright believed,
the middle classes would only come into their own when full
democracy was achieved and perhaps the proletariat would
prove as conservative as Bismarck suspected. Revolution,
social democracy or dictatorship — all seemed equally
possible as the nineteenth century entered its seventh decade.

It had usually been believed by the confident protagonists
of nationalism that wars were the product of despotism and
that peace would result when each nationality lived within its
own boundaries. In 1870 this confidence was being dissipated. It was seen that nationalism could ally itself with
authoritarianism as well as liberalism and that monarchs
could be enthusiastic nationalists. As the French Revolution
might have foretold, nationalism as displayed by Germans,
Italians and Frenchmen could be aggressive, proud and irrit-
able, manifesting itself not in international brotherhood but
in the building of navies and armies. When Germany and
France went to war in 1870 it was certain that whoever won
there would be some national humiliation to be revenged,
some national feeling of inferiority to be combatted, some
sense of disappointment to be assuaged. Now that national,
and not merely dynastic, pride was in question, peace treaties
would cease to be arrangements between gentlemen and
become arguments between largely ill-informed and preju-
diced peoples. Never again would a treaty so level-headed,
workable, uncomplicated and long lasting as that agreed at
Vienna be possible.

The forces unleashed through the agency of the middle
classes were, it is clear, powerful and perhaps uncontrollable.
But it was not just in the rise of democracy and the results of
nationalism that changes could be seen. The very organisation
of government itself was changing. Vast, unplanned and

frequently unhealthy cities led to disease, disorder and crime on a scale which no civilised society could long tolerate. The result was that as the nineteenth century entered its second fifty years governments found it necessary to involve themselves more closely in the lives of their peoples and slowly abandon the increasingly untenable tenets of laisser-faire. Bismarck borrowed ideas from Lassalle while Napoleon was known at St Simon on horseback not merely because of his ideas but because of his practical work in rebuilding Paris, encouraging education and permitting trade unions. Governments gave aid to industry, finance, and railways, permitted the growth of unions and developed education; all this was on a scale of involvement undreamed of by eighteenth century mercantilists and heretical to most of the middle classes brought up on laisser-faire orthodoxy.

Similarly the very techniques of government had to develop. Ever since the revolution France had begun to elaborate a trained bureaucracy. Now with the need for expert knowledge of all kinds, financial, medical, administrative and technical, to meet the demands created by the population explosion and industrial revolution government had to become increasingly professional, drawing its personnel from among a growing pool of well-educated people.

Thus increasingly complex demands developed and changed the rôle of government which came to assume a greater interest in the lives of the individual. In 1870 this process had only just begun, but already both Napoleon and Bismarck had appreciated the change. Bismarck was turning over in his mind a National Insurance Scheme to protect the workers and it was Louis-Napoleon who argued that governments now had to rule with the consent of the masses whose interests had to be served. In place of the individual's concern for his own welfare there was growing the collective concern of the state for all its members.

The developments which had followed the rise of importance of the middle classes went further than the deputies of the Estates-General in 1789 could ever have envisaged. In 1870 Europe was on the threshold of war, collectivism, socialism and Imperialism, all of which held dangers but in whose development the bourgeoisie had been prime movers. The pace of change had quickened in the nineteenth century. In 1780 the lives of the people had hardly changed in two hundred years; in 1870 it was as though a millennium had passed in ninety and there was no sign that that pace of change was about to decelerate. Whether the bourgeoisie was to survive another century depended on its ability to adapt to change as readily as it had in the previous ninety years.

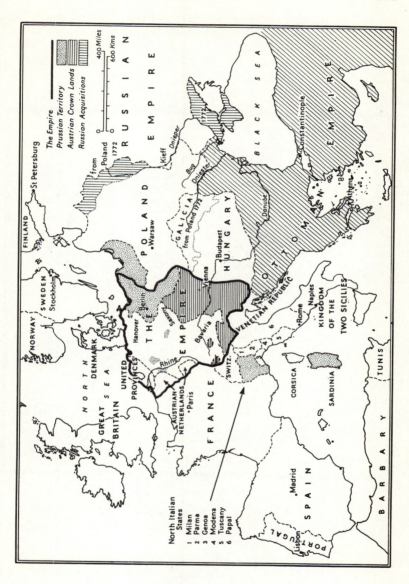

Europe in 1780

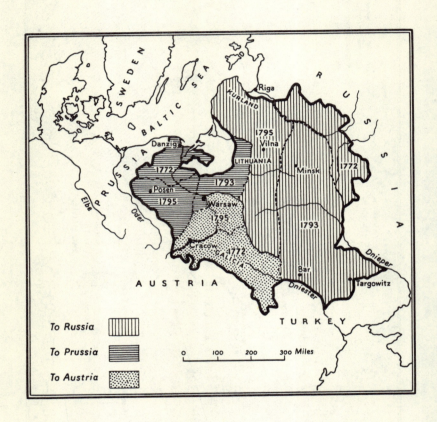

Partitions of Poland

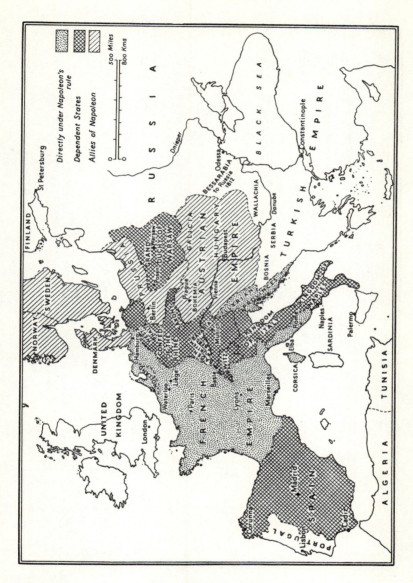

Europe in 1810

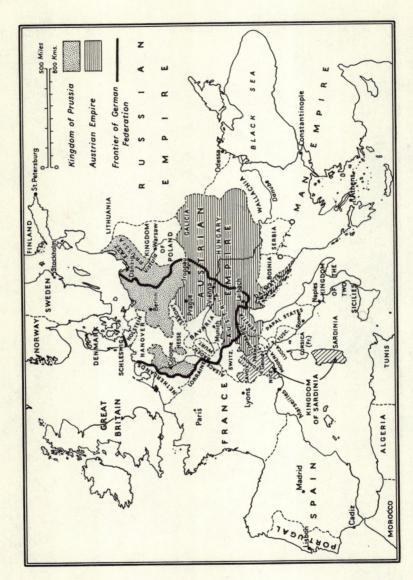

Europe in 1815

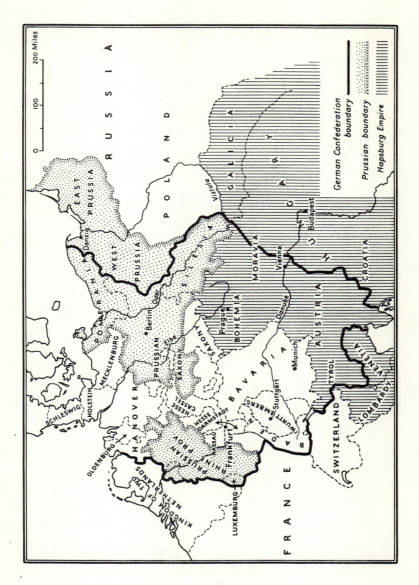

Germany in 1815

Italy in 1859

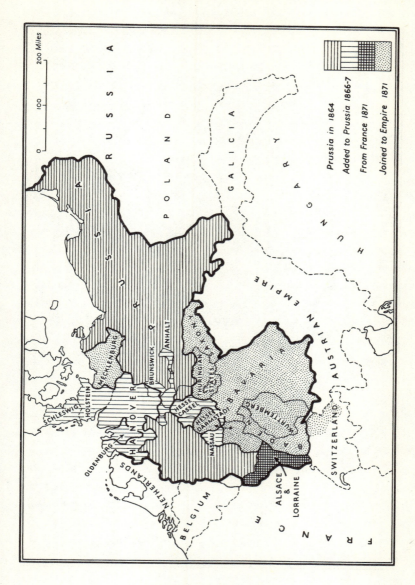

Germany, 1864-71

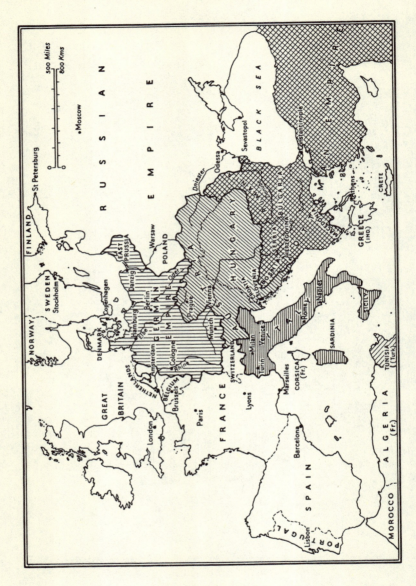

Europe in 1871

The Historiography of the French Revolution

The revolution is without doubt one of the most difficult periods in European history and because of its importance and the passions it arouses, it has certainly had more than its fair share of re-interpretations, each containing a kernel of truth and spotlighting new and useful avenues for exploration. Increasingly it had become clear that to imagine one revolution lasting ten years is bound to lead to confusion. There seems to have been more than one revolution, each naturally precipitated by the original revolution and affecting others, but not concerned with the same ends. Each revolution peasant, bourgeois, *sansculotte* and aristocratic, political, social and economic, has had its protagonist.

Naturally enough the individual historian's place in time and his political opinions dictate to a large extent the view he takes of the revolution. Accordingly the restoration liberal will praise the early work of the revolution in destroying the privilege of individuals and corporations, in terminating guilds, tolls, corporations and in creating a nation, but will gloss over, or disown, the excesses of the republic. Conservatives of the same period see the whole epoch as wholly bad and the result of conspiracy.

With the secure establishment of the Third Republic, republicanism and democracy became respectable, so Aulard was able to view the Robespierre years with a less jaundiced eye. Madelin, on the other hand, a Bonapartist sympathiser, stressed again how the revolution began in an attempt to impose order on administrative and social anarchy, and collapsed into total anarchy from which Napoleon, in securing the aims of the men of 89, rescued it. Lord Acton similarly judges the revolution from the standpoint of order rather than democracy which, as a late nineteenth century Whig historian in the Macaulay tradition, he distrusts.

The twentieth century having absorbed what is acceptable in the sociological history of Marx, has attempted to go beyond the leaders to the revolutionary grass roots. Hence the twentieth century has high-lighted class divisions and divisions within classes, the many different needs of the revolutionary masses and has made interpretation of the revolution more complicated. Jaurès dissected the Third Estate and Mathiez tried to discover the social and economic pressures on revolutionary politicians which led them to differ, and high-lighted the differences between the bourgeois and sansculotte revolutionary demands. Such work stimulated study of price and wage movements in which Labrousse led the way. The greatest of the twentieth century historians of the revolution is, however Lefebvre, whose work showed the complexities and divisions of peasant society and the total separateness of the peasant revolution from that of Paris in 1789.

The historian is always affected by his environment and revolutionary France holds a peculiar fascination for ideologists of the 'permanent revolution' as well as for those who see in such Trotskyism, and in the revolution itself, the seeds of a new and terrible totalitarianism.

The Revolutionary Calendar

The new calendar initiated by the Jacobins in 1794 was an attempt to rationalise the dates and seasons and rid the passage of time of superstition.

The new year began on September 22nd and was, as before, divided into twelve months but each of these months had only thirty days. The five or six extra days were holidays left over at the end of the year (the following September). The months were grouped into seasons and attempted to give an indication of the nature of the month: thus Germinal was the spring month of germination.

Autumn:	*vendémiaire, brumaire, frimaire*	(late September – late December.)
Winter:	*nivôse, pluviôse, ventôse*	(late December – late March)
Spring:	*germinal, floréal, prairial*	(late March – late June)
Summer:	*messidor, thermidor, fructidor*	(late June – late September)

Each week, of which there were three in each month, consisted of ten days (the décade) and it will be easily seen how difficult it was for the church to fit into such a scheme.

The revolutionary calendar dates from September 1792, but it was abandoned in Year XII.

Brief Lives

Andrassy, Gyula (1823—90)

Although he was a radical in his youth he came to assume a more moderate but typically Magyar stance in the history of Austro-Hungarian relations. A member of the Diet of 1847 he supported Kossuth, though not entirely trusting him, and he fought the Hapsburgs in 1848. He later spent some time in exile and prison, becoming a supporter of Déak(q.v.). Later as Prime Minister of Hungary, he presided over the settlement of the *Ausgleich*, achieving for the Magyars a position of equality with the Germans in the Empire. He resisted the Czech nationalist movement and supported German supremacy in the Empire and Europe generally, His career effectively sums up the peculiar position of the Magyar nationalist; he was forced to be an enemy to the Empire upon whose continued existence depended the supremacy of the Magyar in Hungary itself, hence his opposition to Czech nationalism and Hapsburg centralism, both of which he defeated.

Babeuf, Francois Noël (1766—97)

He began his career as a *commissaire à terrier* and thus was made aware of peasant grievances and in 1789 drew up a cahier for them. Going to Paris in 1794 he published *Le Tribun du Peuple* which manifested its disgust in the Thermidorean reaction by attacking the regime on behalf of the *sansculottes*. Up to this point it was his genuine sympathy with the poor which guided his actions but in prison he mixed with former terrorists and emerged as something of a communist, hoping to achieve Utopia through the never-implemented constitution of 1793.

Deteriorating economic conditions gave his *Société des Égaux* ready hearers and after Bonaparte had closed their meeting place in the Pantheon club the members, led by Babeuf, planned a *sansculotte* revolt with the aid of disaffected soldiers of the Grenelle camp. The Directory's infiltration of the movement scotched the rising planned for 22 Floreal, Year IV. Babeuf used his trial magnificently for revolutionary propaganda and this, with his reputation for Roman virtue helped establish a revolutionary myth. So although he was executed, one of his accomplices, Buonarrotti, survived to link Babeuf with the socialism of Louis Philippe's reign through the Blanquistes of which Buonarroti was a member. From Babeuf stems a major element of the socialist tradition which gave much to Marx, and perhaps even more to the protagonist of permanent revolution.

Barras, Viscomte Paul de (1755–1829)
Barras emerges from the history books as an aristocratic version of the Good Soldier Schweik or the Vicar of Bray. Although an aristocrat he sat in the Convention and voted for the King's execution. A leading terrorist the Vicomte achieved infamy for his repression of counter-revolution when Toulon was vacated by the British fleet. The only Director who survived throughout the Directory, he held military command of Paris on three occasions. It was Barras who arrested Robespierre, who helped Bonaparte administer the 'whiff of grapeshot' in 1795, and who held sway as virtual dictator in the crisis of 1797. Although he was largely responsible for the marriage of his former mistress, Josephine de Beauharnais, to Bonaparte he was nevertheless discarded by Bonaparte in 1800. The Vicomte was too practised an intriguer ever to be able to give it up and, more of a turncoat but less of a contortionist than Fouché, was exiled in 1813. He illustrates the type of career revolutionary who could survive most turns of the wheel of fortune and who must have existed in large numbers, more especially in the

provinces. Perhaps not an estimable character but a politician who helped maintain necessary continuity between crises.

Blanc, Louis (1811—82)

Blanc saw competition as the source of all social evil and demanded common property and the equalisation of wages — 'to each according to his needs, from each according to his abilities'. He was thus in the main stream of those thinkers who deplored the inhumanity which came in the wake of rapid industrialisation and believed that it was possible to return to a mythical pre-industrial 'golden age'. In developing the idea of social workshops, a cross between a trade union and a co-operative, Blanc evidently owed much to the experiments of Robert Owen. One of the writers of the extremist paper *La Réforme* he was a prominent exponent of the revolutionary banquet and in 1848 was a member of the provisional government which appeared ready to meet so many of the workers' demands. The new National Assembly shunned his ideas and he was not re-elected to the government. His 'Luxembourg Commission' for the re-organisation of industrial relations was ignored and the actual 'national workshops' were a travesty of his ideas. Forced to flee after the June days he did not return to France until 1870.

Blanqui, Louis Auguste (1805—81)

Soon disillusioned with the bourgeois, ossified monarchy of Louis Philippe this son of a member of the Convention founded *La Société des Saisons* with Barbès. This revolutionary organisation attempted a futile uprising in the distress year of 1839. Released from prison in time for the revolution he was soon leader of the *Société Républicaine Centrale*. Although a Jacobin he did not support the futile attack on the Assembly but still landed in gaol where he used his time in developing his theories. He felt the need, made more obvious by the events of 1848, for a dictatorship of the proletariat exercised from Paris but was not a member of the 1871 Commune. By the end of Louis-Napoleon's reign he had become a gradualist, urging revolution still but coupled with a slow transformation from capitalism to socialism.

Always a Carbonarist and owing much to the Babeuf tradition he nonetheless sums up in his own career the progress of revolutionary socialism towards social democracy.

Brissot, Jacques Pierre (1754–93)

Like many other French revolutionaries he saw service in America and began his revolutionary schooling there and at the board of the Duke of Orleans. He was elected to the First Municipality of Paris after the fall of the Bastille. After Varennes he became a member of the Jacobin club and was noted for his interest in foreign policy and his eagerness for war on Austria. After his election to the Legislative Assembly he became a member of the Diplomatic committee where he put forward the theory that only through war could the revolution achieve unity and purity. His speeches in the Assembly did much to bring about war. He also became leader of a groups of deputies in the Assembly and Jacobin club who became known as Brissotins or Girondins. This group quarrelled violently with other Jacobins in the club and all its members were expelled. The Jacobins were opposed to war and saw it as counter-revolutionary or merely for the narrow party benefit of the Girondins. Paris refused to elect him to the Convention but he secured a seat elsewhere. He suffered with the other Girondins for his connection with Dumouriez and was executed. Not a republican he used the monarchy as a useful political tool and so helped destroy it.

Carnot, Lazare Nicolas Marguerite (1753–1827)

'The Organiser of Victory' first attracted the attention of the military authorities of the *Ancien Régime* as a fine engineer. Although he early developed an interest in politics, military considerations were always paramount with him, a fact usually forgotten by many with whom he collaborated. On the left in the Constituent Assembly, he was also a deputy *en mission* to the army and in the Convention voted for the King's execution, largely because he saw the monarchy as a divisive force. He became a member of the Committee of Public Safety where he was in charge of military affairs. Beset by *Hébertists* in the war ministry he nevertheless succeeded in appointing generals who were competent, not merely politically acceptable, and in securing discipline when the very idea of officers was unpopular in some quarters. With Robespierre's help, after the Flanders campaign of 1794 he liquidated his enemies. Soon afterwards he too became an object of Robespierre's obsessive suspicions and was not unaware of the plans for Thermidor. Nonetheless only his twenty-seven victories in seventeen months saved him from attack. He proved incapable, however, of dealing with either the royalism or terrorism of post-Thermidor politics and after the failure of the Fructidor coup d'état, in which he was implicated, he fled.

He was a supreme organiser at a time when political extremism often outweighed common sense and needs out-weighed supplies.

Czartoryski, Prince Adam Jerzy (1770—1861)

A member of a great patriotic princely family in Poland of which Stanislas Poniatowski was also a scion he early developed a paternalist liberal philosophy which endeared him in 1795 to the Grand Duke Alexander of Russia, where the prince had been taken as a hostage and where he attempted to recover confiscated lands. Called on by Alexander as Emperor to help him reform Russia, besides his work in foreign affairs and internal re-organisation, he worked for the restoration of Poland under the Russian Crown. Later he was Polish representative at the Vienna Congress.

At the disastrous fatalism of the Emperor developed in the face of the enormity of his task and the influence of Metternich Czartoryski lost faith in Alexander. He withdrew from public life until 1830 when he headed an insurrection against the despotic rule of Nicholas I. He spent the rest of his life in exile working to undermine Russian influence in his native land.

Déak, Ferencz (1803—76)

A moderate, pragmatic Magyar who strove to achieve an equal position for Hungary with Austria in the Empire by constitutional means. Thus, though he supported Kossuth's aims he was never happy with his methods. It was Déak's 1847 programme, presented to the Diet of that year which was the basis of the 1848 (March) agreement with the Hapsburg court and of the *Ausgleich*. Despite his experiences as a member of Batthyany's government in 1848 and his subsequent arrest he remained a loyal subject of the Empire which he saw as the best protection against Pan-Slav nationalism.

Décazes, Élie Duc (1780–1860)

A judge of appeal under Napoleon he remained faithful to Louis XVIII during the Hundred Days. Succeeding Fouché as Minister of Police he alienated the Ultras by his opposition to the White terror and by his success in persuading Louis to dismiss the *Chambre Introuvable*. He became acknowledged leader of the amorphous moderate 'constitutionalist' party in whose favour he manipulated the 1816 elections. Minister of the Interior in 1818, Prime Minister in 1819, he was accused by the ultras of being responsible for the situation which led to the murder of the Duc de Berry and by the left of accepting too willingly the new electoral law of that year. His constitutionalist support was whittled away from both sides and he was forced to resign. He is typical of the class upon which Napoleon based his support and upon which the Bourbons depended after 1815 — the upper bourgeoisie. His career also shows the difficulties faced by any government which tried to base its existence on so narrow a franchise when faced by so many enemies.

Desmoulins, Camille (1760–94)

A great pamphleteer and emotive speaker, his impromptu speeches to the strollers in the gardens of the Palais Royal after Necker's dismissal helped create the atmosphere which led to the fall of the Bastille. His pamphlets *La France Libre* and *Discours de la Lanterne aux Parisiens* won him a reputation and close association with Danton in the Cordeliers club. He opposed war in 1792 and as a member of the Convention attacked the Girondins for trying to use war for narrow party ends but was not in favour of their execution. Although a regicide he soon became known as an *indulgent* for his opposition to enrage demands and dechristianisation. He was arrested and executed along with Danton (1794). A pleasant and not inaccurate portrait of him is given in Büchner's play *Danton's Death*. He appears as the archetypal poetic revolutionary betrayed by his own idealism. The antithesis of Barras.

Dumouriez, Char les François Du Périer (1739—1823)
Dumouriez achieved high rank in the army of the *Ancien Regime* and although he joined the Jacobin club his revolutionary feelings were akin to those of Lafayette and Mirabeau. For him war was a way to restore royal power. As Minister for Foreign Affairs in 1792 he was largely responsible for war which, as Minister of War, he found France losing. He replaced Lafayette as commander and with Kellermann won the battles of Valmy and Jémappes, on both occasions apparently deliberately allowing the enemy to escape. Shortly after the King's execution he was defeated at Neerwinden in 1793, while invading Holland, and agreed with the Austrian commander, Mack, to evacuate Belgium and march on Paris. When his plans became known he was outlawed and fled to the Austrians. He was never allowed to return to France: Louis XVIII seemed capable of forgiving the terrorists of the revolution but not the moderates.

Fouché, Joseph Duc d'Otrante (1759—1820)
An arch-terrorist and brilliant survivor, Fouché joined his local Jacobin club at Arras in 1791 to be elected to the Convention where, after siding with the Girondins in supporting the war, he moved towards the Jacobins on voting for the King's execution. During the short period when he was an almost autonomous *représentative en mission* in Lyons he acquired the sinister reputation which his albino appearance accentuated. Mass shootings, guillotinings, dechristianisation and destruction were his remedy for reaction. Recalled to Paris when Robespierre began tightening the reins of centralisation and rooting out *Hébertists,* Fouché, fearing for his life intrigued against Robespierre. He disapproved of the Thermidorean reaction and went into hiding until the pendulum began to swing back to the left. The Directory made use of his peculiar talents in Italy and Holland, preferring him at a distance. He supported Brumaire but resisted Napoleon's life consulate. Minister of Police in 1804 and Interior in 1809 his regard for Napoleon, always

guarded, declined as he saw the growth of megalomania and the return of royalism. Sometimes but not always he protected Jacobins especially when he knew that royalists, not they, were guilty of crimes imputed to them, but perhaps only in order to have victims always available to satisfy his master. Disgraced in 1809, he nevertheless returned as Minister of Police during the Hundred Days and again under Louis XVIII. Royalist reaction drove him into exile in 1816. A man not without consistency, he was apparently without feeling.

Fourier, François Marie Charles (1772—1837)
Like Blanc he aimed to take the destructive competitiveness out of life. He aimed to do this through phalanxes, free co-operative associations of producers. Each phalanx would contain four hundred families living in common dwellings (*Phalanstères*), engaged mainly in agriculture. Each individual would be rewarded, more or less, according to the productivity of the whole phalanx. Fourier's plan is interesting for the vision it gave of social welfare with its schools, libraries, health and insurance services. It is typical of its period in its rejection of the less pleasant aspects of industrialisation.

Garibaldi, Giuseppe (1807—82)
At an early age he met and was influenced by Mazzini whose Young Italy movement he joined. He never shook of the conspiratorial and idealistic approach of his first mentor. Condemned to death for his part in a revolutionary plot in Piedment in 1834 he spent fourteen years in South America. In 1848 Charles Albert was too worried by the activities of the left in Piedmont to accept the sword of the young republican who, with a small band of followers, went instead to the aid of Milan and then Rome. It was his leadership above all which inspired the ramshackle Roman republic to beat off French and Neapolitian troops. When the city fell he conducted a brilliant retreat with his red shirts and escaped to America leaving behind the inspiring legend of the Roman republic.

Returning to Caprera in 1854, Garibaldi, convinced against his will that only through the power of Piedmont could Italy

M

be re-united, was soon giving unofficial aid to the dubious Cavour, who was less an Italian than a Piedmontese patriot. After Villafranca he had to be persuaded not to invade Rome and was made furious by the cession to France of Nice and Savoy, his birthplace. Despite the ill-feeling between him and Cavour, his greatest exploit, the red shirt capture of Naples and Sicily was made for the benefit of the House of Savoy. Refusing rewards for himself Garibaldi went into a disgruntled retirement. His wish to seize Rome and Venice was frustrated and he loathed Italy's loss of moral fervour. *Realpolitik*, conservatism, big-power pretensions and corruption, all of which seemed to be the result of the Risorgimento disgusted him.

Guizot, Fr Pierre Guillaume (1787—1874)

The Protestant son of an executed federalist he was, besides being a distinguished historian the foremost French champion of constitutional conservative monarchy. In 1816 he resigned as secretary-general of the Ministry of Justice to devote himself to the writing of history. In 1830 he was elected a deputy and wrote the declaration of sixty-three of his fellow deputies against the July ordinances.

Under the July monarchy he would not co-operate with Laffitte whose association with Paris radicals he distrusted and he soon became recognised as the most formidable members of the *parti de résistance*. As Minister of Education he was responsible for the only progressive legislation of the Orleanist period in creating a primary school system: as ambassador to London from 1840 and Minister for Foreign Affairs under Soult he worked to further the entente with Britain which he saw as a source of stability in France itself. From 1846 he was the chief conservative force in government, upholding the *juste milieu* with the aid of patronage and strengthening the government against revolution. Unfortunately *juste milieu* came to mean complete immovability, a refusal to widen the franchise coupled with the advice to passive citizens to make themselves rich enough to vote 'by work and savings'. He became Prime Minister in 1847 but even his resignation at the height of the crisis of 1848 could not save the Orleanist monarchy.

Hébert, Jacques René (1757—94)
He was the most famous of many users of the pen-name 'Le Père Duchesne.' An early 'drop-out' from the bourgeois world of his youth, he learnt of the lives of the poor and became their ribald spokesman and propagandist in the revolution in his Père Duchesne pamphlets. He was a representative of his section in the August 1792 Commune and was one of the first to insist on the full implementation of the Terror — the execution of the King and the Girondins, revolutionary government, class legislation and dechristianisation. His extremism and his leadership of the sansculottes were unwelcome to Danton and Robespierre, but probably his actual committed following was smaller than suspected, for the *sansculottes* failed to respond to the insurrectionary call as a result of which he was executed. His death marks the true beginning of the reaction.

Herzen, Alex Ivanovich (1812—70)
A radical Russian author much influenced by the Decembrist revolt he read widely and thought a great deal during an enforced exile. His émigré newspaper *The Bell* was smuggled into Russia and widely read until his connections with Bakunin anarchism and his support for the 1863 rising in Poland were unearthed. Ascribing the failure of revolution in Europe to the decline in moral values occasioned by bourgeois acquisitiveness he hoped to create in Russia a loose-knit republic of agrarian communes, hence his interest in anarchism.

Hugo, Victor Marie (1803—85)
Drawn into Romantic circles soon after his first book of poems was published in 1822 he established his reputation with his verse drama *Cromwell* (1826) and *Odes et ballades* and *Les Orientales*. At the same time he developed the radical leanings of many of his contemporaries in the world of the arts who were in revolt against the authority of the *haute bourgeoisie's* classical artistic and political hegemony. His play *Hernani* (1830) was something of a *cause célèbre* not only for its idealisation of the passionate romantic hero at odds with society but also for the novelty of the rhythm and

sound of its verse. It became a testament of a younger generation's revolt.

Hugo's output was prodigious. Plays like *Notre Dame de Paris, Ruy Blas, Le Rhin* and four major collections of poems followed quickly, accompanied by political writings which complemented the political content of much of his literary output. At first a supporter of Louis-Napoleon he soon saw through Saint-Simon on horseback and in exile devoted himself to anti-Imperian satire — *Napoleon le petit, Histoire d'un crime,* and his poems *Les Châtiments.* His production of new works did not diminish even after 1870 and was probably the most prodigious of any contemporary writer.

Kosciuszko, Tadewsz Andrzej Bonaventura (1746—1817) A patriotic Pole of lesser gentry stock, he was noted by King Stanislas Poniatowski who sent him abroad to learn from the more advanced west. Like Lafayette he received both military and political education in the American War of Independence. He fought for Poland in 1791 and in 1793 was invited to take command of the Polish army. Lacking weapons he relied on numbers but after defeating a Russian army at Racawice he retreated to Warsaw where he was unwillingly obliged to make peace with radical elements before the defence of the city could begin. He was taken prisoner by the Russians who later allowed him to go to America. He refused to support Napoleon's plans for the recreation of Poland, rightly distrusting the Emperor. At Vienna Alexander of Russia preferred the advice of Czartoryski.

Kossuth, Lajos (1802—94) Of gentry stock but landless, he was an advanced radical and nationalist who saw all Hungary's ills as stemming from Vienna. He became a popular hero and martyr after his imprisonment in 1836 and became leader of the Reform party in the Diet of 1847, seizing the opportunity offered by 1848 with both hands. In Batthyany's government as Minister of Finance he refused to supply troops for the Hapsburgs in Italy, thus precipitating the final crisis, which his own reckless disregard for the ethnic minorities of

Hungary allowed the Hapsburgs to turn to their own advantage. As military dictator he inspired his people but bungled military affairs. He fled to Turkey and thence to America but neither there nor in Britain did he elicit aid for his cause.

Lafayette, Marie Joseph Paul Yves Gilbert Du Motier Marquis de (1757—1834)

After distinguished service in the American War of Independence and as a result of it he became associated with French reform movements, demanding as a member of the 1787 Assembly of Notables not an Estates General but a National Assembly. He had Thomas Jefferson's help in writing a *Declaration of the Rights of Man* which had such influence on the eventual official version. He was made commander of the bourgeois militia of Paris after Bastille day and thus became the leading figure in the National Guard. Through his friends he influenced the Assembly of which he was perforce an absentee member but did not, though a moderate constitutionalist, secure a working alliance with Mirabeau and thus was unable to stop the dangerous slide to the left. Attacked from both left and right he retired until called upon to command the army at Metz which he organised well. Unfortunately he was caught unprepared by the declaration of war and suffered defeats. His position, like that of the King, fast declined and Lafayette was unable to carry out his plan to lead an army on Paris to restore the royal cause. He fled to Austria, returning to France in 1799. He disapproved of Napoleon and during the Restoration actively aided underground liberal movements. In the 1830 revolution he took command of the National Guard and finding little support for a republic he gave his support to Louis Philippe though he turned against him again in 1832.

Laffitte, Jacques (1767—1844)

A wealthy banker who made himself useful to both Napoleon and Louis XVIII, he was a 'liberal' who opposed censorship and the electoral law of 1819. His position was essentially that of a member of the *haute bourgeoisie* who wanted stability but feared the *Ancien Régime* tendencies of the

restoration government. He was not an irreconcilable therefore, and approved of the sound financial policies of Villèle
and Martignac. He opposed the policies of Charles X, though
he was offered the premiership during the revolution. He
played a leading part in the successful attempts to avoid a
republic in 1830 and became Prime Minister in November.
Louis Philippe did not trust him because he was associated
with the *parti de mouvement* and with a forward foreign
policy, particularly in Belgium and was delighted when
Laffitte was attacked from both sides of the political fence
for his policies during the distress riots. He resigned in March
1831 and joined the opposition.

Lamartine, Alphonse de (1790–1869)

Rather than as a politician he is remembered for being one of
the earliest romantic poets of France, with a Wordsworthian
response to nature. He abandoned poetry in 1839 concentrating on the political career begun in 1833. Naturally a
conservative he failed to convince his fellows of the need to
prevent socialism's victory by bringing about reform. As a
result he quixotically joined the radicals trying to guide them
in the paths of righteousness. His *Histoire des Girondins* was
one factor which secured him the leadership of the
provisional government of 1848 but the conservative
assembly would not follow his lead and in June he was
thrown out of office. Forgotten and discarded he polled only
twenty thousand votes in the presidential election and
returned to writing.

Lassalle, Ferdinand (1825–64)

He is significant as a socialist advocate of constitutional
progress towards democracy. Although in 1848 he was on the
extreme left he did not associate with Marx and Engels and
when the revolution collapsed their exile left him as the most
obvious leader of German socialism. In 1849 he organised
resistance to the collection of taxes which the Prussian
National Assembly had refused to sanction. The uniqueness
of Lassalle is not in his ideas, which were not unusual, but in
the way that he kept more extreme opinions strictly to
himself, aiming to bring about his social revolution and the

abolition of property by constitutional means. He advocated universal suffrage and state intervention in economic affairs to break the 'iron law of wages' of the market economy. His ideas were not widely accepted – the General German Workers' Association only achieved a few thousand members but some of his ideas influenced Bismarck whose policies, Lassalle ironically believed, would lead to the overthrow of the Prussian government. In 1864 he died as the result of a duel.

Marat, Jean Paul (1743–93)

A political journalist driven to extremism by events rather than by inclination, Jean Paul Marat began by asserting in *L'Ami du Peuple* (1789) that the revolution could be carried through with the aid of Louis and the National Assembly. Returning from involuntary exile in 1790, denouncing all moderation, he urged the sansculottes to organise, His conspicuous success led other journalists to emulate him, thus increasing the radical temper of Paris. Despite this and his advocacy of popular dictatorship he failed to secure election to the Legislative Assembly and fled to England for a second time, returning to oppose war with Austria and to urge insurrection.

He approved the September massacres but probably did more than any other man to control them; in fact his language was always more violent than his actions and he was not a democrat, preferring dictatorship to popular government, and it was in this vein that he attacked the Girondins and favoured the apparatus of Terror. It is thus ironic that he should have become a democrats' martyr after his murder by Charlotte Corday. David's painting of him lying dead in his bath is the Jacobin *Pietà*, and part of the mystique of revolution.

Mazzini, Guiseppe (1805–72)

From his youthful beginnings as a member of the Carbonari to the end of his life he was a conspirator, even when conspiracy had proved its pathetic ineffectiveness. Nonetheless he was an inspiration to Italian nationalism. In exile in 1831 he founded *Young Italy* but his attempts to foment insurrection in Piedmont twice failed and his existence soon became a furtive flitting from place to place, writing short-lived journals and plotting, always plotting. If the blood of the martyrs helps to create a cause then Italian nationalism owes much to Mazzini's failures. After 1848 unification became the province of *realpolitik* and Mazzini's work was over, though he refused to accept the truth. Italy's new mood had little place for his radical, republican and democratic ideas. On his own part he said of Italy in 1860, 'all I find before me is a corpse'.

Moltke, Helmuth Karl Bernhard, Graf von (1800–91)
Convinced from an early age that only the army could unify Germany, he was the natural ally of Bismarck whose foreign policy he so brilliantly served. Unlike his contemporaries of the Austrian general staff he saw the importance of railways, not just because they were a way of moving trops quickly but because they dictated a new sort of warfare on wider fronts, with larger armies and with a new relationship between commanders and staff officers who would have to be given far greater initiative than formerly.

Morny, Charles Auguste Louis Joseph, Duc de (1811–65)
The illegitimate son of Louis Bonaparte's estranged wife Hortense (Beauharnais) he only emerged from obscurity on the elevation of his half-brother to the Presidency of France in 1848. He was given a major part in organising the *coup d'état* in 1851 and though he was not a successful minister, as president of the *Corps Législatif* he found a secure niche. He saw that the regime suffered from the weakness of the *Corps* and put pressure on the Emperor to liberalise the regime and allow greater discussion in the legislature. Perhaps most important of all he introduced Louis-Napoleon to Ollivier. His death removed a man who could have done much to secure the success of the Liberal Empire.

Necker, Jacques (1732–1804)
Much, and mistakenly, fêted in his life-time as a financier, economic wizard and statesman, Jacques Necker made his

name attacking Turgot, and was made Director of the Treasury in 1776 and Director General of Finances in 1777. He covered up the disastrous deficit caused by the war with Britain by his *Compte Rendu au roi* which pretended to show a profit and which made it impossible for either De Brienne or Calonne to make Frenchmen realise the gravity of the financial situation. He was dismissed in a court intrigue, but recalled after the fall of Calonne. Moreover, although in the early days of the Estates General his role was immensely difficult, many of the problems were of his own making and he cut an uninspiring figure. It was Necker's dismissal that provided the signal for the fall of the Bastille. His recall brought no relief to King or country and he retired to Switzerland in 1790 (Sept). Like the *parlements* he enjoyed a popular liberal reputation; it is curious and sad that his own reputation should have outlived that of the parlements. His daughter was Madame de Staël.

Ney, Michel, Duc d'Elchingen, Prince de la Moskowa (1769–1815)

Ney rose to high rank in the revolutionary wars and was a fine trainer of troops. Although contributing considerably to the victory of Ulm and at his greatest in the retreat from Moscow he was a rash general and impulsive as he showed in Spain in refusing to serve under Massena. He tended to be moved by the emotion of the moment; one of the first to demand Napoleon's abdication; eager in his protestations of loyalty to Louis XVIII; as eager in joining Napoleon in the Hundred Days; rash at Waterloo. Louis XVIII was horrified when Ney did not make good his escape from France at the second restoration and was unable to prevent his trial and execution. His dignified death gave a martyr to the anti-Bourbon cause as Louis realised it would. It also poisoned relations between the people of France and the Allies and helped to maintain the Bonapartist mystique in the French army.

Ollivier, Émile Olivier (1825–1913)

At first a romantic socialist, Ollivier moved towards a moderate republican position and was elected to the legislature of the Second Empire in 1857. Unlike his more extreme republican contemporaries he was not in favour of violent revolution and was prepared to work with the regime and persuade it to adopt a more liberal tone. He worked with Morny, welcoming the concessions of 1860 and those that followed. He was the premier of the liberal Empire's short reign which began in January 1870. If the Empire had survived it is probable that Ollivier would have confirmed the tendency of the Empire towards a true parliamentary system in which the regime would have been able to survive changes in public opinion.

Polignac, Duc Jules de, Prince of the Holy See (1780—1847) The most ultra of the ultras, he was made a Prince of the Holy See in 1820 for refusing to take the constitutional oath of 1815 as in violation of the Pope's rights. Such ultramontanism and royalism made him Charles X's favourite, Foreign Minister (1829) and Prime Minister (July 1830). In the early months of the July monarchy the left demanded his execution but he was later released.

Proudhon, Pierre Joseph (1809—65) Proudhon's great dictum was that 'property is theft'. He disliked the tendency of competitive capitalism to concentrate economic power in few hands, but he did not advocate the abolition of private property, only its widest possible disposal among owner proprietors who could form associations. Credit should be supplied, not by Rothschild, but by a Peoples' Bank which would give credit at very low interest. By making the credit available in return for wage notes, Proudhon hoped to separate money from gold and silver and in effect make labour and what it produced ready money, so making goods retail at the price they cost to produce. The scheme is not far removed from Marx's theory of labour value but Marx attacked Proudhon for not seeing that monopoly capitalism was a necessary stage on the road to revolution, and for not realising that finance and industrial capitalism are not distinct but two sides of one coin. Perhaps now he has more appeal to the petty bourgeoisie than to true socialists.

Sand, George (1804—76)

George Sand is unfortunately better known now for her love affairs, than for her romantic novels. The greatest influences on her early life were her love of nature and the mysticism she imbibed while being educated at a Paris convent. After her unhappy marriage, and several love affairs, she began to write novels, making a particular success with the semi-autobiographical *Indiana* (1832). In *Valentine* (1832) and *Lelia* (1833) she developed one of the main themes of her works, the protest against the subjection of wife to husband; she wrote 'a union in which there is neither liberty nor reciprocity is an offence against the sanctity of nature'.

Besides Chopin she formed liaisons with Prosper Mérimée and Alfred de Musset among others, but was not by nature promiscuous: 'I have always believed. . .in fidelity'.

Her interest in the freedom of women led her naturally to an interest in the plight of the exploited and the idea of a classless society: *Le Compagnon du tour de France* (1841); *Le Meuner d'Augeboult* (1845) and *Le peche de M. Antoine* (1847). After this her themes became more rustic, reflecting her early love of the countryside, and although she wrote many appeals on behalf of the revolution of 1848 this marked a declining interest in revolution.

Although after her death interest in her work waned she is important as an example of the involvement of romantic artists with the real world, even if on a rather theoretical and idealised plain.

Schiller, Johann Christoph Fredrich (1759—1805)

. . .'we should be ashamed to have it said that the material world formed us, instead of being formed by us.' A heroic figure, like many of the characters in his works, Schiller was chiefly concerned with the problems of power and its misuse. His first play *The Robbers* is a protest against convention and corruption and it is a literary equivalent to Rousseau's *Social Contract*. The play was a sensation but he was forced to flee from the wrath of the Duke of Württemberg and for some time lived in poverty. *Kabale und Liebe,* his second play was also a great success and soon after *Don Carlos* (1787) he struck up his famous friendship with Goethe, through whom he became professor of history at Jena.

Histories of the Netherlands revolt and the Thirty Years War helped him to write *Wallenstein*, perhaps his greatest work (1800). During and after this period essays and poems show Schiller under the influence of Kant and trying to discover the function of literature in society. Unfortunately ill-health dogged his last years; he died at the height of his powers, having recently written *Maria Stuart* (1805) and *Wilhelm Tell* (1804).

Surprisingly modern in outlook Schiller shows the plight of the artist in a world whose landmarks are collapsing and he is concerned with the role of the artist in the world of the new individualism, and the danger to human personality and individuality under regimes ruled by convention or naked power. His knowledge of history enabled him to see clearly the problems facing the artist who wishes to be not merely an ornament but an influence for good in society. (For further reading: *Wallenstein* − translated by   Coleridge;   F. W. Maitland, *Schiller and the Changing Past,* 1957).

Schubert, Franz Peter (1797−1828)
Schubert had the initial advantage of belonging to a musical family and later became a scholar of the Imperial court chapel choir in Vienna. Soon after his voice broke in 1813 he was composing string quartets, Masses and an opera. But it was his settings of poetry which were to win him lasting fame as the creator of German *Lieder*. of which Brahms and Schumann were to be other leading exponents. In 1815 came 'Erlkönig', perhaps his most famous work of this kind, a brilliant example of his ability to create in music the details described by the poet.

Lieder did not use up all of his creative energies; between 1813 and 1818 he wrote six symphonies, four Masses and ten piano sonatas. Only his teaching duties and his popularity as performer and accompanist damned the flow of his genius; in 1819 there came the 'Trout quartet', in 1820 the 'Rosamunde' overture and in 1822 the 'Unfinished' Symphony, one of many works which Schubert could never find the time to complete. From 1822 his health declined but he was still able in 1827 to complete his setting of Muller's poems, known as 'Die Winterreise'.

A great composer, certainly, but one difficult to place. Perhaps it is best to see him as a bridge between classicism which his music most resembles in form, and romanticism which it resembles in subjects and emotion. (Read Blom: *Schubert: a Documentary Biography*).

Siéyès, *Emmanuel Joseph* (1748–1836)
Siéyès was a major importance in the French Revolution though perhaps more for his failures than his successes. Chancellor of the Diocese of Chartres in 1788, the Abbé Siéyès was author of the pamphlet *Qu'est ce que le Tiers État,* which was of fundamental importance in rallying revolutionary opinion and formulating bourgeois ideas during the elections for the Estates General.

Throughout his life he wished to see power in the hands of the enlightened bourgeoisie; thus although in many ways a radical, (he fought against the King's veto) he was opposed to universal suffrage and any attacks on property, such as the abolition of tithes. Although he helped organise the *département* system, he faded out of sight during the extremist years of the revolution though he voted for Louis XVI's execution, probably out of fear rather than conviction. After Robespierre's fall he became more active; the Directory disappointed him. Though elected, he refused to serve as a Director in 1798 but accepted in 1799 chiefly in order to destroy the system.

For Siéyès the Directory failed to supply the stability needed by France and threatened to place power, by default, in the hands of demagogues or royalists. To avoid this, and to place power in the hands of 'notable' bourgeois, he and his fellow *Idéologues* planned a *coup d'état.* He realised the need to come to an arrangement with Bonaparte and the army but underestimated Napoleon seriously. Siéyès' constitutional safeguards of 1799 were swept aside by Bonaparte and the 'balanced' system collapsed.

After some initial opposition Siéyès accepted a *fait accompli* and retired to his estates. Banished in 1815 he returned to France in 1830.

Bibliography

All Books listed below are readily available in good public libraries. *P* before the name of the publisher indicates that a paperback edition is also available.

BIBLIOGRAPHIES

W. N. Medlicott, *Modern European History 1789–1945* (Historical Association).

A. Bullock and A. J. P. Taylor, *Select Lists of Books on European History 1815–1914* (Oxford 1954).

GENERAL HISTORIES

D. Thomson, *Europe Since Napoleon* P (Longmans 2nd Ed. 1962).

A. J. P. Taylor, *The Struggle for Mastery in Europe* (Oxford 1954).

M. Beloff, *Age of Absolutism* P (Hutchinson 1966).

L. C. B. Seaman, *From Vienna to Versailles* P (Oxford 1954).

THE LANGER SERIES (HARPER-ROWE)

Leo Gershoy, *From Despotism to Revolution 1763–1789* (1944).

Crane Brinton, *Decade of Revolution 1789–99* (1946).

Geoffrey Bruun, *Europe and the French Imperium 1799–1814* (1938).

Fred. B. Artz, *Reaction and Revolution 1814–1832* (1935).

Robt. C. Binkley, *Realism and Nationalism 1852—1871* (1935).
New Cambridge Modern History Vols. VIII, IX & X.
Albert Sorel, *Europe and the French Revolution* P (Fontana 1969).

ECONOMIC HISTORY

W. O. Henderson, *The Industrialisation of Europe 1780—1914* P (Thames and Hudson 1969).
W. O. Henderson, *The Industrial Revolution on the Continent 1800—1914* (Cass 1962).
J. H. Clapham *Economic Development of France and Germany 1815—1914* (Cambridge 1935).
Tom Kemp *Industrialisation in Nineteenth Century Europe* P (Longmans 1969).

RELIGIOUS AND IDEOLOGICAL HISTORY

A. R. Vidler *The Church in an Age of Revolution* P (Pelican 1962).
N. Hampson *The Enlightenment* P (Pelican 1968).
J. J. Rousseau *Social Contract.*
Edmund Burke *Reflections on the French Revolution*
K. Marx *Communist Manifesto.*
J. Plamenatz *Man and Society Vol. II* P (Longmans 1963).
J. Plamenatz *German Marxism and Russian Communism* P (Torch 1962).
G. Woodcock *Anarchism* P (Pelican 1962).
K. R. Popper *Open Society and its Enemies Vol. II* P (Routledge & Kegan Paul 1945).

DIPLOMATIC HISTORY

M. S. Anderson *The Eastern Question* P (Papermac 1966).
A. Sorel *Europe and the French Revolution* P (Fontana 1969).
H. Nicolson *Congress of Vienna* P (Oxford 1945).
W. E. Mosse *The European Powers and the German Question* (Octagon 1968).
A. J. P. Taylor *Struggle for Mastery in Europe* (Oxford 1954)
Cambridge History of British Foreign Policy.

FRANCE

General

Alfred Cobban *History of Modern France* (3 Vols.) P (Pelican 1957).

Gordon Wright *France in Modern Times* (Murray 1967).

J. P. T. Bury *France 1814—1940* (Methuen 1954).

John Lough *France in the Eighteenth Century* (Longmans 1960).

Aspects

Sanche de Gramont *Epitaph for Kings* (Hamish Hamilton 1968).

De Tocqueville Patterson *The Ancien Regime in France* P (Blackwell 1956).

G. Lefebvre *The Coming of the French Revolution* P (Vintage 1957).

N. Hampson *Social History of the French Revolution* P (Routledge & Kegan Paul 1963).

A. Goodwin *The French Revolution* P (Hutchinson 1966).

G. Lefebvre *The French Revolution* (2 Vols.) (Routledge & Kegan Paul 1961).

C. Brinton *The Jacobins* (Russell 1930).

H. J. Sydenham *The Girondins* (Oxford 1961).

J. H. Thompson *Robespierre and the French Revolution* (E.U.P. 1952).

G. Lefebvre *The Thermidoreans* (Routledge & Kegan Paul 1964). *The Directory* (Routledge & Kegan Paul 1964).

G. Rudé *The Crowd in the French Revolution* P (Oxford 1967).

J. Kaplow (Ed) *New Perspectives on the French Revolution* (Wiley 1965).

Lord Elton *The Revolutionary Tradition in France (1789—1871)* (Arnold 1923).

J. M. Thompson *Napoleon* (Oxford 1952).

G. Lefebvre *Napoleon Vol. I: Brumaire to Tilsit Vol. II: Tilsit to Waterloo* (Routledge & Kegan Paul 1969/70).

J. Robiquet *Daily Life in France under Napoleon* (Allen & Unwin 1962).

Pieter Geyl *Napoleon: For and Against:* P (Yale U.P. 1949).

Duff Cooper *Talleyrand* P (Cape).

F. B. Artz *Bourbon Restoration* (Russell 1931).

D. O. Evans *Social Romanticism in France 1830—48* (1951).

T. E. B. Howarth *Citizen King: Life of Louis Philippe* (Eyre and Spottiswoode 1961).

J. P. T. Bury *Louis Napoleon and the Second Empire* (E.U.P. 1964).

F. A. Simpson *Louis Napoleon and the Recovery of France 1849—56* (Longmans 1932).

T. Zeldin *The Political System of Louis Napoleon* (Macmillan 1958).

T. Zeldin *Emile Ollivier and the Liberal Empire of Napoleon III* (Oxford 1963).

AUSTRIA

General

A. J. P. Taylor *The Hapsburg Monarchy 1809—1918* P (Hamish Hamilton 1948).

O. Jaszi *The Dissolution of the Hapsburg Monarchy* P (Chicago U.P. 1961).

C. A. Macartney *The Hapsburg Monarchy 1709—1918*.

Topics

S. K. Padover *The Revolutionary Emperor: Joseph II* (Archon 1967 2nd Ed.).

G. de Bertier de Sauvigny *Metternich and His Times* (Humanities Press 1962).

Algernon Cecil *Metternich*.

GERMANY

General

R. Flenley *Modern German History* (Dutton).

W. H. Bruford *Germany in the Eighteenth Century* (Cambridge 1935).

E. J. Passant *Germany 1815—1914* (Cambridge 1962).

A. J. P. Taylor *Course of German History* P (Hamish Hamilton 1945).

Topics

G. A. Craig *Politics of the Prussian Army 1640—1945* (Oxford 1955).

G. Ritter *Frederick the Great* (Eyre & Spottiswoode 1968).

W. O. Henderson *Economic Policy of Frederick the Great* (Cass 1963).

T. S. Hamerow *Restoration, Revolution, Reaction: Economics & Politics 1815–71* (Princeton U.P. 1958).

E. Y. Eyck *Bismarck & the German Empire* P (Allen & Unwin 1958 2nd Ed.).

A. J. P. Taylor *Bismarck: Man & the Statesman* P (Hamish Hamilton 1955).

RUSSIA

General

B. Pares *History of Russia* P (Cape 1953).

A. G. Mazour *Rise & Fall of the Romanovs* P (Anvil 1960).

Topics

Gladys Scott-Thomson *Catherine The Great and Expansion of Russia* (E.U.P. 1962).

P. Dukes *Catherine the Great & the Russian Nobility* (Cambridge 1967).

L. Kochan *Life in Russia under Catherine the Great* (Batsford Putnam 1968).

T. Riha (ed.) *Readings in Russian Civilisation Vol. II* P (Chicago U.P. 1964).

J. Blum *Lord and Peasant in Russia* P (Princeton U.P. 1961).

W. E. Mosse *Alexander II & the Modernisation of Russia* (E.U.P. 1958).

ITALY

General

A. J. Whyte *Evolution of Modern Italy 1715–1920* (Blackwell 1944).

Topics

E. E. Y. Hales *Mazzini and the Secret Societies.*

G. M. Trevelyan *Garibaldi and the Thousand* P (Longmans 1969).

D. Mack-Smith *Cavour & Garibaldi in 1860* P (Kraus).

E. E. Y. Hales *Napoleon & the Pope* (Dufour 1965).

E. E. Y. Hales *Revolution & Papacy* P (Univ. of Notre Dame 1966).

Derek Beales *England & Italy 1859–60* (Nelson 1961).

Agatha Ramm *The Risorgimento* (Historical Association).

THE REST OF EUROPE

H. V. Livermore *History of Spain* P (Minerva 1968).
H. V. Livermore *New History of Portugal* (Oxford 1966).
Raymond Carr *Spain 1808—1939* (Cambridge 1966).
W. F. Reddaway *Cambridge History of Poland 1697—1935* (Cambridge 1969).
R. F. Leslie *The Polish Question* (Historical Association).
B. J. Houle *The Scandinavian Countries 1720—1865*.

SPECIAL TOPICS & PROBLEMS

The Heath Series: Problems in European Civilisation P.
1 *Economic Origins of the French Revolution: Poverty or Prosperity?*
2 *Metternich, The 'Coachman of Europe': Statesman or Evil Genius?*
3 *Romanticism: Definition, Explanation and Evaluation.*
4 *1848: A Turning Point?*
5 *Napoleon III — Buffoon, Modern Dictator or Sphinx?*
6 *Otto Von Bismarck — A Historical Assessment*

Problems & Perspectives in History — P. ed. Kearney.
 Enlightened Despotism: Stuart Andrews.
 The Romantic Movement: A. K. Thorlby.

Anatomy of Revolution: Crane Brinton (Vin. Roudan 1957).

HISTORICAL ASSOCIATION PAMPHLETS

Interpretations of the French Revolution: Rude.
Historians and the Causes of the French Revolution: Cobban.
Liberalism in the Nineteenth Century Europe: Collins.
Enlightened Despotism: F. Hartung.
The Polish Question: Leslie.

1848
1848: A Turning Point (Heath Series).
1848: Revolution of the Intellectuals L. B. Namier: (Oxford).

Index

INDEX   355

Laffitte, Jacques, 187, 335
Laibach, Congress of, 161
Lamartine, Alphonse de, 211, 218f, 336
Landrat, 39
Landsturm, 139
Landwehr, 156, 294
Lassalle, Ferdinand, 251, 336
Le Brun, P.H.H.M., 95
Le Chapelier Laws, 88
Leipzig, Battle of, 136, 139
Legislative Assembly (France), 88
Legislative Assembly (Russia), 42
Leopold II of Austria, 36, 108f
   As Grand Duke of Tuscany, 8, 10,
      25, 51, 65, 142
   France, 92
   Poland, 92
Leopold I of Belgium, 172
Liberum Veto (see under Veto)
Liebknecht, Wilhelm, 252
Ligurian Republic, 116, 119
Lille Peace Negotiations, 114
Limberg, 199
Lisbon, 160
Liste communale, etc., 124
Lithuania, 12, 30
Lodi, Battle of, 113
Lombardy, 113, 150, 261
London Conference 1830, 199
London Protocol 1852, 297
Louis I (King of Portugal), 290
Louis XIV (France), 59
Louis XV, 104, 110, 126
Louis XVI, 8, 58, 65,
   Character, 82, 83, 93
   And Fall of Monarchy, 80ff, 93f, 151
   And Paris, 86
   And Austrian Committee, 86
   Trial and Execution, 94
Louis XVII, 153
Louis XVIII, 135, 148, 149, 153ff, 160,
   167f
Louis Napoleon, (see under Napoleon
   III)
Louis Philippe, King of the French, 122,
   168, 170f, 185f, 199f
   Fall of, 217f
Luneville, Treaty of, 116
Luxembourg, 199
Lyons, 97, 103, 176, 187, 188

Maastricht, 199
Magdeburg, 40

Magenta, 279
Magyars, 53 (see Hungary)
Malta, 115, 130
Mantua, 113f
Manzoni, 210
Marat, Jean Paul, 96, 337
Marengo, 116
Maria, Queen of Portugal, 164, 201,
   235f
Maria Theresa, 47, 69, 265
Marie Antoinette, 30, 82, 86, 98, 109,
   134
Marie Louise, Empress, 134
Mars, Champ de, 90
Marseillaise, 102
Marseilles, 97, 176
Martignac, Vicomte de, 169
Marx, Karl, 208f, 215, 232, 250f,
   309f (see also Socialism)
Masonic Societies, 9, 52, 65, 117
Maximilian, Archduke of Austria,
   Emperor of Mexico, 261, 287
Maximum, 98, 100
Mazzini, Joseph, 193, 230, 337
Mehemet Ali, 165, 198ff, 202f
Melzi, d'Eril, Count, 142
Mendizabal, Juan Álvarez, 234
Mensdorf, Count, 298
Menshikov, Alexander, 273
Mercantilism, 17, 39
Mercier de la Rivière, 74
Mesta, 56
Métayers, 15
Metternich, Prince, 134, 143, 149, 151,
   155f, 158f, 160, 165, 171,
   190, 192, 198, 201, 223,
   260, 269
   And Congresses, 147ff, 159ff
Mexico, 285, 287
Middle Class, 17ff, 143f
   In France, 17, 58ff, 82f, 163, 167f,
      170, 174f, 176, 218, 254
   Germany, 1, 17, 137f, 194, 246f
   Prussia, 17, 137f
   Poland, 17
   Russia, 1, 17
   Hapsburg Empire, 17, 54
   Belgium, 172
   Netherlands, 17, 18, 172
   Spain, 17
   Italy, 17
   Portugal, 17
Miguel, Don, 164, 201